COUNTRY BRANCH LINE

An Intimate Portrait of the Watlington Branch

VOLUME TWO

THE STATIONS

PAUL KARAU & CHRIS TURNER

ISBN 1 874103 46 1

Title page: Aston Rowant station on 23rd September 1951. *R. C. Riley*

Above: A postcard view showing Station Road, Princes Risborough. *Author's collection*

Contents page: 57XX class 0–6–0PT No. 9722 with the Watlington branch train in the west bay at Princes Risborough on 23rd July 1955. *H. C. Casserley*

Designed by Paul Karau
Printed by Amadeus Press Ltd, Huddersfield

Published by
WILD SWAN PUBLICATIONS LTD.
1-3 Hagbourne Road, Didcot, Oxon, OX11 8DP

CONTENTS

IN the portraits of the other stations in this volume we have attempted to present cameos detailing changes in day-to-day life, staff changes, traffic, etc., since the 1920s. However, as the main story in Volume 1 revolves around Watlington itself, much of this ground has already been covered. This account of the terminus, therefore, largely concentrates on the daily routine there in 1939, based on the recollections of the two porters, Frank Saunders and George Howlett, who worked on opposite shifts.

When Frank was on the early shift, 7.15 a.m. to 3.0 p.m. (or 3.15), he arrived on his bicycle, and, entering the deserted station through the side gate, began by unlocking the station building and the shutters protecting the office window. He would then return to the station entrance to unlock and open the yard gate.

In winter months the late-turn porter laid the fire in the office at night after the 6.50 p.m. train, when he also locked the room. Frank therefore only needed to put a match to the fire before going over to unlock the goods shed office and light the one in there too. He left his bike at the goods shed but, if it was raining and he needed to put it inside (on the deck), he walked through the shed to unlock the large sliding door which opened onto the forecourt. All three main doors were secured internally by long pins dropped through hasps.

When he returned to the station building, the office was beginning to warm up and he gave it a quick clean and dust over. There were usually a few parcels outside the office door ready for the first train. These had been brought in the previous night after 6.0 p.m.

The entrance gates and forecourt approach in 1951. Access to the platform was via the gateway near the bicycle shed. It was used by everyone although there was another gateway at the opposite end of the building. This picture shows some of the concrete fence posts put in a few years earlier to replace rotting wooden ones. If the old palings were retained, they were certainly re-mounted on new arris rails. There is some doubt as to whether the main entrance had previously been fitted with double gates, but it is doubtful whether we will now discover any photographic evidence. Watlington was equipped with two 4-wheeled trolleys of the type shown and two 2-wheeled luggage trolleys with a rigid blade. *R. H. G. Simpson*

WATLINGTON STATION

8m 66c

For many years the corrugated iron carriage shed which survived from the independent W&PR Railway, housed the standby four-wheel coach used to strengthen certain trains. In recalling the 1920s, driver Harry Humphreys said the auto-trailer "wasn't kept in there at all, it was kept in the yard." "We used to put anything in there, horse-boxes or anything spare", because they were "out of the way" but "handy to get hold of". They were "not allowed to keep anything like that hanging about". In subsequent years, at least 70ft auto-trailers were housed here overnight and even cleaned from the wooden catwalks inside, the farthest of which appears to have been shortened, presumably from damage or deterioration. By May 1939, reserve coal was mistakenly stacked so close to the carriage shed siding that it was no longer possible to get the branch trailer past. Instead, it was kept in the spare road and for some considerable time the siding was only used for loco coal wagons and, in the late 'forties, the strengthening coach. The two pairs of steps and planks seen lying around in various photos were used to form platform-height staging for cleaning the opposite side of the auto-trailer on Sunday mornings. They did not use detergents, just buckets of water drawn from a tap housed in a recess in the platform face. When the porters were cleaning the platform side, they filled the buckets from a tap outside the gents.

It is possible that Wilkinson of Lucas and Wilkinson, Westminster, the line's engineers, was responsible for the design of the W&PRR station buildings. This seems likely because an uncannily similar pavilion design subsequently appeared at Caister on Sea and Great Ormesby on the Midland & Great Northern Railway in Norfolk, the contractors for which were Wilkinson and Jarvis, also of Westminster.

The little station building at Watlington is seen here early one Sunday afternoon in May 1949. John Ahern, who took this picture, succinctly described it as "a natty little structure in the very best mid-Victorian Gothic style". The central door had led into the main booking hall, from which doors led into the station master's office, on the right, and the ladies waiting room on the left. For the convenience of plumbing, the ladies WC was traditionally situated adjacent to the gents, which, isolated by an internal wall, was entered by a separate door in the northern end of the building and illuminated by the top half of the left-hand window. As originally constructed, the hall was completely open to the platform on the other side, the solid floor being covered with Staffordshire blue brick pavers with a diamond pattern grip, in continuation of the platform surface in front of the building.

In 1900 this hall was enclosed with timber panelling to provide "waiting room accommodation", £51 being authorised by the Traffic Committee on 4th April that year for the same work to be carried out at all three stations. The resulting waiting room was certainly not in the usual tradition with a welcoming fire and mirror or publicity pictures above. Instead, the two fireplaces were tucked away in the ladies waiting room and station master's office. The only seat was a wooden bench against the wall dividing off the lavatories, the inside of the forecourt wall bearing strong brackets for the rows of fire buckets, three each side of the doorway. No one we have interviewed could remember the forecourt door being used because it was blocked by a parcels weighing machine which stood behind it. With the cramped nature of the building, the 'waiting room' was in practice more of a utility room; frequently littered with piles of parcels, the soft broom used to sweep out the office, and a number of bicycles, including Reg Pocock's 'brown railway bike'. Other than when it was raining, few people waited inside, and they tended to stand. The piles of parcels often overflowed onto the bench seat but then the auto-trailer was usually in the platform when there were any passengers around, and that was far more welcoming.

The ladies waiting room overlooked the platform and was provided with a tiled floor, a bench seat under the window and a small fireplace. The fire was "only lit on bad days" and a coal bucket left by the hearth. Maureen Miller, who travelled to one of the factories in Risborough in the early 1950s, said "The fire was just like being in your own front room".

On entering the waiting room from the platform, there was a small ticket window just inside, on the left, and further along the same wall, almost in the far corner, the door into the office, which was invariably flanked by piles of parcels. Inside it was very cosy with heavy brown cork lino on the wooden floor and a fireplace between the door and the ticket window. The fireplace had a cast-iron surround and a stone or slate mantlepiece all painted black. The concrete hearth where the coal bucket stood was surrounded by a low cast-iron fender, whilst the fire itself was protected by a wire safety cage. The switches for the electric lights were above the left of the fireplace, just behind the door. There were cupboards along the rest of the wall to the right of the fireplace below the ticket bench with a clock also to the left of the ticket window, a dating machine to the right and a wall-mounted ticket rack which stretched into the corner.

Although there were narrow shelves below the cill, it was possible to stand at the window overlooking the platform, unlike the opposite end of the room where the forecourt window was obstructed by a desk used by the porters. The clerk sat at a long row of cupboards against the southernmost wall, with his back to the ticket window. There was no knee hole and the shelves against the wall at the back of the worktop left a surface just wide enough to take the accounting books. The station master's desk to the right also faced the wall.

The shutters on the office window were locked each night (see the handmarks!) to deter any thieves, but anyone mildly determined could have climbed over the fence and broken in through the office window overlooking the platform, but there was less crime in those days.

The concrete-framed, corrugated asbestos-clad bicycle shed was put up towards the end of the war to cater for the increased number of workers using the train to reach the aircraft factories in Risborough. Bicycles had previously been left against the south end of the building or, as mentioned, inside the waiting room. The work, costing £54 17s 4d, was completed on 18th August 1944 and paid for by the Ministry of War Transport. This starkly functional structure must have been a welcome addition by all, but it certainly marred the lovingly tended station garden on which it was erected. Lengthman Charlie Adby looked after the garden for Mr. Pocock. *J. H. Ahern*

and labelled and registered by the late-turn man. Only if Cecil Tappin brought up a parcel in his taxi was there any booking to do. The taxi was an old Humber, but Tappins also ran a little Austin and a Ford.

The next job was to sweep out the trailer which was stabled in the carriage shed overnight. The vehicles provided for the Watlington branch were electrically lit, so there was no problem working inside the dark shed. The trailer was entered via steps and a wooden catwalk running along the inside of the corrugated iron side sheets and the sweepings were brushed straight out of the central doorway for the permanent way men to clear up now and then. George Howlett, who went to Watlington on 1st May 1939 to replace Joe Nicholson, remembers that by then the trailer was kept in the 'spare road' overnight because the reserve coal stacked alongside the carriage shed siding was too close to the rails and fouled the steps of the trailer!

In the meantime, the clerk or the station master arrived, the two of them alternating on shifts of 8.0 a.m.–5.30 p.m. and 10.0 a.m.–8.30 p.m. When Ken Cox was on 'earlies', he had an hour's break and went home to lunch, whereas on the later shift he had two one-hour breaks.

Unless he was particularly busy, Frank would go out onto the platform to meet the branch goods when it arrived back at Watlington around 8.20. He uncoupled the train, then operated the ground frame to allow the engine to run round to the other

The modest station platform, barely long enough to accommodate two coaches, is shown here on 13th June 1947. The timber-built extension at the far end was erected c.1924 to ease the loading of milk traffic in the mornings, but by the time Frank Saunders worked at the station in 1937, it was no longer used. It did, however, continue to provide a fine vantage point for peering over the fields to look for any intending passengers hurrying to catch the train. Driver Harry Humphreys said "We never used to leave anybody behind". The electric fittings mounted on the cast-iron posts of the old oil lamps were installed in 1936 when electricity first reached the site. They were equipped with 60-watt bulbs which were changed by standing on the short length of sleeper left against the base of the column. In 1940, an application form to the Wessex Electricity Co., 62 High Street, Wallingford, listed lamps totalling 435 watts and motor 1hp. If the platform became slippery during frosty weather, the porters used to sprinkle it with sand taken from the sandboxes inside the cab of the engine or from one of three fire buckets hung along the north wall by the door to the gents. The other two buckets there were filled with water. *J. H. Russell*

end. The wagons were then usually drawn back clear of the loop entry points and propelled onto the carriage shed siding to collect the trailer which was put into the platform for the guard to load and for any passengers to board.

Occasionally this routine had been interrupted when the return working of the goods had conveyed a horse-box for Peter Schwier which had to be unloaded on the platform first.

The short run-round loop at Watlington held just eight wagons and a brake van, so on mornings when this number was exceeded, the train was usually brought to a stand well short of the yard entry points and divided so that it could be run round in two parts. Of course, this was time-consuming so if there was a way of avoiding extra moves, then all concerned were only too pleased to take it — and there was more than one unofficial way round it.

In Frank's time, extra wagons "if they were not important" were sometimes left at Risborough, especially if they were vacuum-fitted and could be brought down on the back of the trailer on the next trip. Alternatively, one wagon beyond the capacity of the loop could be left "on the back of the engine" while it was running round, as the headshunt was just long enough to accommodate a pannier and one wagon. The staff referred to this as 'one on the engine'. Such a vehicle would be propelled up to the throat of the station and gravitated into the back siding while the engine fetched the rest of the train. Another unofficial method unknown to Frank is described in Volume 1, page 135.

While the train was being put away into the yard, the guard took the leather bag containing paperwork for the goods and handed it into the office. Frank might have already opened the large doors closing off the rail entrances to the goods shed, but if he had not, then as soon as he had set the road for the yard, he left the ground frame smartly and opened the doors ready to accept the two station trucks. These were usually conveyed on the front of the train and propelled into the goods shed for unloading. There was no time for any other shunting, so the rest of the train was propelled into the back road and left there until later.

George Howlett recalls that by his time station trucks were simply left with the rest of the train in the back siding (not necessarily even together in the train) and unloaded there. This change seems to have come about because, by mid-1939, the goods shed siding was already occupied by traffic for the construction of the nearby Military Ordnance depot, and perhaps even Chalgrove airfield, but more of this later. If any of the items in the station trucks had to be unloaded using the crane, they had to wait until later in the day when they could be put in the goods shed during a yard shunt. Although time was very tight first thing in the morning, George usually managed to open the truck and make a start on sorting the contents ready for Tappins, the delivery agent. If Cecil Tappin was on the agency work, he was rather impatient to get on his way with the horse and cart, although he had to wait while George made out the necessary paperwork after despatching the 8.40.

However, to return to Frank's recollections, he was usually on duty with Mr. Pocock, whilst Joe Nicholson was usually on with the clerk. Reg Pocock cycled in and when he was on the early shift, arrived around 8.20, or soon after the arrival of the early goods, comfortably in time to book the tickets for the first train.

In the usual ritual, Frank operated the ground frame while the engine ran round, then, as soon as he had set the points for the yard, the guard took over the frame so that Frank could nip over to the yard and carry out the shunting. As soon as he had finished with the ground frame, the guard went back up on the platform and collected his stock of tickets from the office and loaded them into the rack in his compartment ready for sale at the halts.

Both he and Frank would then load the parcels into the guard's van, together with the cash box containing the previous day's takings from Watlington and Aston Rowant, which had been held overnight in the office safe.

The staff were busy with their routines, but in truth it was tame compared with the hectic scene of the 1920s described in Volume 1. There were usually about five or six passengers for London, a few schoolchildren for High Wycombe or Risborough, and various workers for Chinnor, but mainly Risborough.

There were sometimes more passengers on Monday mornings when a few people were returning from weekend visits to their families, often having arrived on Friday night. Occasionally during the summer, there were also school camps, which sometimes required an extra vehicle, a Siphon for instance, for luggage.

Most passengers would get to the station on time but occasionally someone would telephone and ask them to hold the train because a friend or relation was on their way by car to catch it. One or two passengers sometimes drove to the station and left their cars there for the day, parked either by the now redundant milk platform, or by the station building. Bicycles, including Mr. Pocock's, were left in the waiting room, or 'parcels office' as it was often referred to by the staff, but if there was not enough room, Mr. Pocock's was put outside again. Although equipped with a couple of bench seats in one corner, the official waiting room was actually a sort of entrance hall with a small ticket window and doors leading into the station office and ladies waiting room and lavatory. There was a weighing machine blocking the doorway from the forecourt, and a pile of parcels outside the office door, so the bicycles just added to the clutter. With no fireplace, it was hardly the traditionally cosy waiting room normally associated with railway stations at that time. The ladies waiting room was not used much, but, on really cold mornings, the early-turn porter lit the fire in there. Coal was collected from the pen behind the platform and carried to the station in a large bucket.

Frank remembers that if the engine was blowing off noisily, it was held out at the water tank and only run into the platform and coupled onto the trailer at the last minute, otherwise people could not hear one another speak! Around departure time the guard picked up any internal mail for Paddington and checked with Reg that it was alright to leave. Tom Bowler would say "Alright to go then, Sir?" Reg Pocock by this time had put his station master's hat on and stood in the doorway onto the platform, where, "looking every inch a proper station master" in his smart official uniform, he pulled a pocket watch out of his waistcoat to check the time. Then in a deep voice, he said "Yes, right away, Tom". If there was anyone around, Tom waved his green flag for the driver but otherwise he would just put his arm up to driver Harry Humphreys.

After the train had left, the station was quiet and Frank went over to the goods shed to unlock the station trucks, using the keys from the pouch handed to him earlier by the guard. The two station trucks were usually together, but, if separated by a single wagon, there was still room for them in the goods shed. They were usually vans but sometimes sheeted wagons with a 'high bar', one from Paddington and one from Oxford, loaded so that everything for delivery around the town was just inside the doorway of each vehicle. This was a great help in stacking it all on the edge of the loading bay ready for the agent to collect. Everything was logged, and as soon as this was done, Frank took the paperwork into the lean-to office on the end of the goods shed to make out the delivery sheets.

While he was doing this, Francis Tappin arrived in one of his motor vans and started to load up. Francis only delivered within a mile radius of the town, so other goods for outlying districts had to be collected by the addressees.

When the agent had left, the rest of the goods were unloaded, checked and recorded, and stacked in the goods shed to await collection. Anything valuable was locked in the security cage. When all this was done, Frank

Reg Pocock at Watlington in the late 1930s when Frank Saunders served there as a porter. "That's how he used to stand . . . he always wore a stiff collar."
Cty. Gwen Clarke & Rita Watts

went back into the lean-to office and prepared the letters or cards sent to all the addressees of the 'non-carted' goods to advise them of their arrival. These letters, which went out in the afternoon post, also advised that items had to be collected within 48 hours to avoid demurrage charges.

Alf Higgs, who wore a pink patch over a blind eye, ran a bus from Chalgrove, which arrived about 9.30 a.m. after dropping off schoolchildren in the town. He collected any parcels for Cuxham and Chalgrove and, after loading them into the bus, "spent ages talking to Reg Pocock" while he waited for the arrival of any more parcels on the 10.30. Unofficially, he gave any passengers off the train a lift into the town, then called at the White Hart "for a quick half" before returning to Chalgrove.

Alf, who had been the Chalgrove carrier since late Victorian times, had previously run a Model T Ford bus from Chalgrove Primary School at 8.30 a.m. to Watlington Secondary School before calling at the station. By the late 1920s he had bought a Chevrolet which was "a dirty grey colour with no name on the side".

The fact that Alf was leader of the Chalgrove Silver Band which collected for charities including Watlington Hospital, perhaps sheds light on some of the conversation

The 3.0 p.m. to Risborough leaving the station on 13th June 1947. One of the permanent way men can be seen by the coal stage. Frank Saunders remembers they "swept the yard and kept it all tidy". The replacement concrete fence posts were put up by the Watlington PW men during the 1940s, the staff scrounging the old timber ones "for pig pens or firewood". *P. J. Garland*

This view, taken in May 1949, shows an area of mysteries. It is not clear whether any part of the seldom-used cattle pen illustrated here survived from the one which appears behind the palings in the 1919 photograph on page 68 of Vol. 1. According to earlier plans, the near face of the platform on which it stood, had paralleled the passenger platform, so the blue brick facing and angled fencing of this side of the pen at least must have been a subsequent addition, built to parallel the realigned sidings serving the end loading dock. The end loading dock itself, with its solid concrete facings, was probably built at the same time, perhaps when the wagon turntable featured on earlier plans was removed. We have no date for these alterations, which must have taken place between 1919 and 1934. As Reg Pocock details the milk platform in his memoirs but makes no mention of the cattle pen, it is tempting to suggest the work was carried out before he came to the branch in 1922. Incidentally, the sleeper-built enclosure on the left housed coal for the station fires, a small door in the left-hand end providing access. The short sleeper-built fence or wall leading off the side of the dock was a remnant of Weedon Brothers' coal pens which had been situated along this end of the goods shed siding. They feature in the picture on page 23. Photographs of the yard have been extremely difficult to find, especially this area, so Weedon's coal office, which stood on the other side of the surviving wall of the coal pens, has proved even more elusive. It backed up against the side of the end loading ramp, the roof of the building appearing in the background of the picture on page 94 of Volume 1. Les Tappin recalls that this building was timber-built, with plain gabled ends, a sash window in the middle of the back, and was painted green. A door in the left-hand end of the front elevation led into a small store used for sacks whilst another centrally-placed sash window also illuminated the office. The least predictable feature of this simple, approximately 8ft x 12ft shed, was the right-hand door which was recessed, creating a sort of small porchway. Inside was a reception corridor with a pay hatch, and, at the far end, a half door leading into the office proper. The building was removed around the Second War after Weedons had sold out to Tappins c.1939. It was taken down by Tappins and re-erected in their yard in the town, where it remained for many years before being scrapped. Even there it still escaped the camera!

J. H. Ahern

with Reg Pocock. Alf was sometimes known as 'the Colonel' after his favourite tune!

When the station trucks had been emptied, Frank walked along any other wagons in the goods shed road, recording their numbers and collecting labels and invoices tucked behind clips on the solebars. He would then do the same with the rest of the wagons which had arrived that morning and been left on the north end of the back road. These were all 'through loads' like fertilizer, corn and domestic coal.

The labels were all recorded in the wagon book and the invoices checked, then the daily rolling stock return was made out for sending to Paddington on the 11.30 a.m. Books were maintained of all the wagons received and despatched. If only they had survived!

On average, before the arrival of the branch goods each morning, the back road was about half full in Frank's time, so there was ample room to stable the train brought in from Risborough. However, during the height of the summer, seasonal traffic might leave the back road two-thirds or more full, in which case the incoming train might be left on the spare road.

Inwards parcels traffic was brought into Watlington on the 10.6 from Risborough, which arrived at 10.32. Frank met each train and was responsible for coupling and

No. 2112 lurking in the shadows with the 11.30 a.m. to Risborough on 10th September 1949. *E. S. Russell*

uncoupling throughout his shift. Not many people used the service, but it conveyed a whole variety of goods travelling as passenger-rated items, including boxes of wet fish, shirts and other clothes for Brown Brothers, bulk parcels and cartons for Searleys, the gents outfitters on the corner of the Couching Street/Hill Road crossroads. Bernard Griffin, working for his father's shoe shop in 1927, recalls shoes from Lilley & Skinner Wholesalers arriving on Tuesdays and Saturdays and being delivered by Dick Smith. Frank Saunders also recalls cartons of shoes arriving for Griffins in his time.

The fish (from Grimsby) was collected by Messum and Dover, whose van would invariably be waiting in the station forecourt.

In the spring there were pheasants' eggs for Englands of Christmas Common, the poults from which would be despatched in the summer.

The porter and the clerk worked together to book all the parcels in, but sometimes, Frank recalls, they also had to unload cattle wagons and guide the animals across the platform into the pen. In addition to occasional cattle received for Watlington farmers, animals en route elsewhere were also sent to Watlington when Risborough was congested. In this case, the cattle wagons were sent down with the 10.6 a.m. for the animals to be fed and watered before continuing their journey. Afterwards, they were reloaded through the opposite side of the pen, using the spare road where the wagons were left awaiting collection.

Francis Tappin would call again for any parcels off the 10.06 which might need delivering, at the same time dropping off any goods he had collected during his first round. He was also advised of any wagon load traffic he might have to deliver on the railway's behalf. Some large houses, like Watlington Park, the home of Lord Esher, for instance, bought coal by the wagon load.

After the parcels had been unloaded, the trailer was backed out of the platform, run round and taken into the back siding to collect the goods brake van which was required to work the Chinnor goods from Risborough at 12.20. The loco then stopped by the water column where the trailer and brake van were uncoupled and allowed to run into the platform by gravity so that the guard's van could be loaded with parcels, etc, and passengers could board while the engine either took water or coal before working the 11.30 passenger to Risborough.

Inevitably with such a routine, things sometimes went wrong, and George Howlett remembers one unnerving occasion when, after the vehicles had begun to roll towards the platform, he climbed on the steps of the trailer in order to apply the brake, only to find the door locked! He shouted to the guard who luckily acted quickly and jumped onto the goods brake, screwing its brake handle on as quickly as possible and narrowly escaping a nasty collision with the buffer stop.

George remembers that he did not get chance for a sandwich on the early shift until after the departure of the 11.30 a.m. although he might have managed a cup of tea while doing the paperwork for the wagon load traffic. The porters always took their official 12.30 break in the goods office. Mr. Pocock would never have allowed them to take their break in the station office.

The late-turn porter's duty was from 1.0 p.m.–9.0 p.m. providing a two-hour overlap

The goods shed was a fairly conventional design constructed of timber on a base of brick and flint, and equipped with the usual 1-ton fixed hand crane which remained the only one on site as traffic never justified a yard crane. The rail entrances were secured with a large single sliding door on the northern elevation and a hinged one alongside the office extension, whilst another sliding door was fitted to the forecourt entrance. Internally, a central bay intruded into the solid loading platform or 'deck' so that carts and lorries could be backed inside for loading. The old crane No. FM141, which had pivoted on a vertical axis between bearings in the deck and roof trussing, was replaced during the war with a 1-ton overhead 'runway' with hand-operated pulling block, as mentioned in Volume 1, page 127. The runway, a horizontal steel joist, was supported on steel joist legs, one each side of the cart dock just inside the doorway and the other, because of the limited clearance, against the outside of the east wall of the building presenting a curious appearance. When Frank first went to Watlington in 1937, Watlington was issued with a fairly conventional ladder which was stowed upright inside the shed, adjacent to the lock-up. When this ladder got broken, they ordered a longer one (probably the one featured here) which had to be kept along the inside wall of the shed, between the cart bay and the office. The empty fish boxes stacked outside because of the smell, were left to accumulate until they justified a wagon load. In Frank's time, they were kept inside on the deck against the south wall. As mentioned in Volume 1, the steps leading up to the office had been repaired after damage by an army lorry on 5th June 1944. This photograph was taken in May 1949. *J. H. Ahern*

before the early man finished at 3.0 p.m. This was arranged so the two men could work together on the heavier tasks including shunting the yard after the branch engine returned with the 1.55 p.m. from Risborough.

When he was on the late shift, Frank had a cooked meal at his lodgings around midday before cycling to the station. When he arrived, sometime between 12.45 and 1.0 p.m., he parked his bike in the goods shed, then walked over to the station to sign on duty in the attendance book, which hung on a nail on the right-hand wall of the station master's office. Everyone used this book except the engine crews who signed on in their own cabin which, by this time, was a grounded horse-box body.

Reg Pocock usually went to lunch around 1.0 p.m. — if he came back, he returned at 2.0 p.m., otherwise he might cycle out to visit traders to sort out claims, etc.

George Howlett would be in the goods office finishing his lunch break when Frank arrived. Before making a start, they discussed the work they had to do together, such as unloading heavy items left in the station truck or perhaps sheeting wagons. The only regular traffic which required sheeting was hay and straw collected from local farms, within a 5 or 6 mile radius, by Dunlops of Reading. They were coal merchants and haulage contractors whose lorries for the area were sent out from Reading for this seasonal traffic, arriving at Watlington about 9.30 to 10.0 a.m. They were drawn up right alongside the appropriate wagon which the driver then loaded himself. Frank says that hay and straw, often destined for Wales, was, if possible, conveyed in LMS opens which are remembered for their greater capacity than GWR types. The bales were usually stacked about four high above the sides, with two, or exceptionally three, wagons being loaded at any one time. If it was raining, the early-turn porter threw sheets over the loads, but they were not lashed down until the late-turn man arrived. Otherwise they waited until both men were on duty and the wagon could be pinch-barred along the siding to check that the load would clear the loading gauge before sheeting, one man operating the gauge while the other watched for clearance.

Sheets were kept in the lock-up cage inside the goods shed or even outside, and had to be declared on the daily rolling stock returns. They were heavy canvases which were taken to the wagons on an 18in lip sack barrow. Using a ladder kept hung inside the goods shed for the purpose, one of the porters would climb to the top of the load with a sheet on his shoulder while the other one held the base of the ladder. Because of the bulk of the ungainly load, two sheets were used, overlapped and tied together, then lashed down at the sides and ends.

Hay was lashed diagonally from buffer to buffer and straw across the wagon from side to side. It was hard work with lots of effort required to keep the ropes taut while securing them. Two LMS opens took about an hour to sheet but it was a satisfying task and Frank and George took pride in the fact that no complaints were ever received about loose sheets or shifted loads as a result of poor loading.

As most of the smaller items despatched from Watlington could comfortably be accommodated in the brake end of the branch trailer, the return working of the station truck was not a daily event. Some of the more awkward items, like locally made garden seats from Ives or hurdles from Coles, for instance, accumulated until they justified at least a part load. Frank recalls the seats being sent to the Midlands.

Heavy items left in the station truck until the two men were together might include the occasional crate which had to be manhandled out of the van and lifted onto a

A rare glimpse inside the goods shed, showing the weigh office which projected inside. There had also been a security cage on the north end of the 'deck' to the right of the weigh office. In Frank's time, this was still used for valuables but also held all manner of items including rope, slings, scotches, ladders, skids and wagon sheets.

This crop from a 1948 picture used in Volume 1 has been included to show something of the back siding. The two-storey barn alongside it belonged to 'Chiltern House' next to the station. Porter Cyril Saunders recalls that it belonged to Brigadier General More. "He was there as long as I can remember; he was a widower." (He is certainly listed at the address in 1931.) The shallow windows beneath the eaves of the barn were protected by the projecting boards (bearing enamel advertisements) perhaps in consequence of damage caused when loading wagons. Coal was regularly unloaded here by various merchants.
W. A. Camwell

waiting lorry using the goods shed's 1-ton rope crane, the vertical part of which pivoted between housings in the loading platform and roof timbers. It was not always possible to use the crane in the shed, and if heavy items needed to be unloaded in the yard, most likely on the back road, they used 'skids'. These were steel plates, one end of which hooked inside the wagon door flap while the other rested on the back of the lorry onto which the load was being transferred. This operation could be quite a struggle at times but the two porters were nearly always assisted by the lorry drivers. Ropes, slings, levers, scotches, two types of skids, and sheets were all kept in the lock-up.

The early-turn man made out the wagon labels during the morning, then, when they were together, the two porters walked down each side of the wagons putting the labels in the clips on both sides along with the occasional invoice which may have been prepared by the clerk. Any heavy doors of empty wagons were also closed while both men were there. Another of the jobs tackled when the porters were together at lunchtime was filling and trimming the lamps. The most important one which they kept an eye on was the red lamp on the buffer stop at the end of the running line. The vessel for the fixed distant had to be taken to the signal and exchanged for the depleted one. It was a 7-day lamp, changed every six days to be on the safe side. As Watlington had electric lighting by this time, the only others were the hand lamps.

One of the porters went over to the station to meet the 1.55 from Princes Risborough which arrived at 2.21 with, at best, only one or two passengers and perhaps a few parcels. The train crew changed over at this time and the late-turn men were usually waiting on the platform when it arrived. When the train had been backed into the loop, the same porter uncoupled the engine which ran round to the other end of the trailer and collected the goods brake brought back from Risborough. This was put in the end of the spare road 'on the stops' alongside the cattle pens behind the platform, any wagons on that siding being drawn out first to allow this. The up goods was then formed 'on top of the brake'. By this time of the day, all outgoing vehicles had been labelled, and 'up road' traffic (for London direction) was marshalled at the rear of the train against the brake, and 'down road' at the front or Risborough end. This helped simplify movements when the train reached Risborough where the 'down road' traffic was placed in the down sidings at the south end and the 'up road' traffic was propelled over to the up sidings on the opposite side of the main line.

The yard was tidied with help from the guard, or, if he was not around, the fireman. If Harry Humphreys was the driver, he always did the shunting but Geoff Pearson would go off for a drink and leave the fireman to do it all on his own.

The late-turn guard began his shift by manning the ground frame while the porters did all the shunting. Prior to sorting the yard, the traders were warned and all the wagon doors were shut and lorries moved clear. Invariably, most of the wagons in the yard were moved in the process of collecting empties. For instance, coal merchants Tappins and Stanmores both unloaded their supplies from wagons in the back road, and, if one of their empties was trapped at the south end of the others, the whole lot had to be drawn out to retrieve it, then replaced again afterwards. The coal wagons were either stabled at the far end of the siding or to the north of the goods shed, where the yard was wider so that lorries could back up to the wagons without blocking access.

Some coal arrived in 'Charlbury Colliery', 'Baddesley' and 'Wolverhampton Coal Co.' wagons, but which colliery supplied which merchant is not recalled,

Activity in the yard was unpredictable; if they were waiting for supplies, coal merchants would sometimes be there early in the morning as soon as the goods train arrived, whilst at other times, if they were out on deliveries, they would not be seen until the afternoon. Although propping wagon doors was against GWR regulations, this convenient, if precarious, practice nevertheless continued at Watlington and no doubt numerous other places throughout the system. The technique involved holding a suitable length of timber, perhaps an old sleeper, vertically in front of a wagon side door while the pins securing the door were drifted out using an old hammer, shovel or similar implement. As the second pin was removed

A later view of the goods shed, taken in the mid-1950s, and showing the weighbridge and a closer view of the small window illuminating the weigh office. The 20-ton machine No. 7951, with an 18ft x 8ft plate, dated from 1931, the previous cart machine being one of a large number which the GWR had to replace in order to comply with the Board of Trade Weights and Measures Regulations, 1907.
A. Attewell

A companion view, showing the opposite end of the goods shed and the external support for the overhead runway crane. This picture also reveals further work on the brick steps serving the office. The two 6ft x 4ft corrugated iron huts in the foreground had originally stood at the opposite end of the platform. They were moved to allow the construction of the milk platform c.1924. The nearer of the two was used to store cotton waste and soft brooms for cleaning the auto-trailer – the cotton waste being used on the windows without any soap or detergent. The stiff broom for the platform was also kept there together with a variety of wood blocks – sleeper offcuts. In postwar years, the hut had sometimes even been used for the overnight storage of fish deliveries. The other hut was used as a lamp shed, a barrel of paraffin being mounted alongside. *A. Attewell*

from the hasp, the weight of the coal inside ensured the heavy door would fly open instantaneously, crashing onto the prop which prevented it from opening beyond a horizontal position, while coal cascaded down either side of it onto the ground. With the prop in place, the door made a convenient platform on which to stand while shovelling it directly into the merchant's lorry waiting alongside or backed up to it. More commonly, however, it was shovelled into bags (stacked vertically on the back of

the lorry) ready for delivery or transfer to the merchant's yard. Bulk deliveries for Ducat Hamersley, the Shirburn Estate or Lord Esher's place at Watlington Park on Watlington Hill, were carted by Tappins, often in one of the tipping lorries they used for the delivery of gravel collected from the pit at South Weston. Local coal deliveries were made with a horse and cart or one of their other lorries.

Frank remembers that when Weedons wagons arrived, the manager, Mr. Simmons, who at 6ft 3in was "a big man", put a boiler-suit on and "helped shovel them out". Their deliveries were made by horse and cart, which presumably restricted their range, although sometimes a lorry from one of their other depots is said to have been sent to help.

Weedon Brothers had coal pens at the end of the 'shed road' and an adjacent office, and obviously preferred to have their wagons left alongside their wharfage. However, as there was no time to shunt in the mornings when the goods first arrived, they frequently had to unload their vehicles wherever they found them and transfer stock coal over to the pens as required, often using wickerwork 'skips'

Another of the photographs taken by Jim Russell on 13th June 1947 when he and Pat Garland, who features on the left, thankfully visited Watlington with their cameras. This view shows the trailer and the goods brake left on the running line while the engine went on shed to pump water after working back from Risborough with the 1.55 p.m. The trailer was in all-over wartime brown livery.

J. H. Russell

The north end of the goods shed and another glimpse of the back road. The sliding door on this end of the building dated from about 1950, the one just discernible on page 33 being smashed in a shunting accident. *A. Attewell*

with handles. Their own 8-ton wagons, referred to by the porters as 'tubs' because of their size, usually arrived two at a time, each loaded with different grades of coal. They were often left on the north side of the goods shed. Sometimes the two might last them a week and occasionally a larger wagon of coke arrived from the Birmingham Coke Co., often in an LMS vehicle fitted with coke rails.

The yard shunt frequently included putting a wagon of loco coal over onto the carriage shed siding and collecting an empty, or, more occasionally, a wagon of ash for despatch in the up goods. Sometimes, when there were a lot of wagons, the outgoing vehicles were beyond the capacity of the spare road and a second portion was assembled in the back road. In George Howlett's time, after the train had been formed in the spare road, it was drawn out and put on the northern end of the back road ready to go the following morning, leaving the spare road clear for the overnight stabling of the trailer.

The engine took water before recoupling onto the trailer in the platform and departing with the 3.0 p.m., which again was very lightly loaded. If he had not already gone out on the 11.30 and arrived back on the next one, Mr. Pocock often used this train for his twice-weekly visits to Aston Rowant to check the books. He took his bike if the need arose to make an official visit from there and would return with the station cash.

When the train had gone, Frank would sweep the platform, tidy the waiting room and the office, to help the morning man, then do any paperwork like recording wagon labels in the wagon book and filing them. He might also help the clerk.

When on the early shift, George Howlett worked until 4.0 p.m. (he recalls working 7.0 a.m.–4.0 p.m. with an hour's break) but, even if he had run out of work, Mr. Pocock would never let him go home to Chinnor on the 3.0 p.m. train, so he had to cycle. Even so, when asked about Mr. Pocock during one of our interviews, George described him as "firm, but fair", "he always wanted a job done well".

When George was on the late shift, he arrived on the 1.55 with his bike. The late turn was much quieter, mainly because there was less activity in the yard which officially closed at 5.0 p.m. Frank had a tea break in the goods office around 3.45. This time of the afternoon was a good opportunity to catch up with any paperwork and prepare any remaining postcard advice notes for goods awaiting collection, 'non-carted traffic', and reminders to coal merchants of any demurrage about to fall due on trucks not released.

Weedons' card was put through the letterbox of their office; Tappins' might be given to Cecil Tappin if he came to the station on taxi work, or, if not, then handed to him the next morning. Details of other postcards were entered into the stamp book where the cards were left for Mr. Pocock to deal with the next day. He or the clerk would arrange to post them, usually in the postbox in the wall outside the station.

The schoolchildren returned on the 3.55 p.m. from Risborough, which brought some activity to the station with the arrival of the odd car, or a few parcels to meet the train when it arrived at 4.22. Just 11 minutes later, it was off again to collect workers from High Wycombe, Risborough and Chinnor and some businessmen from London who travelled on the 4.35 p.m. from Paddington which connected with the 5.45 p.m. branch train. The 5.45 usually had a few parcels on board and sometimes included a Siphon van for watercress traffic.

Before the train returned at 6.11, Frank had a 20-minute meal break, around 5.0 p.m., in the goods shed office where water for the tea was boiled in a GWR cast-iron kettle heated over the fire. He often cooked a meal over the fire or made toast or took sandwiches.

Depending on the season, he might then help weigh and label watercress, which was the principal traffic in the evening. It was usually sent out on Thursdays and Fridays for the weekend market. The watercress came from several growers, but the greatest proportion was despatched by Smiths of Ewelme.

Edward Smith and his son Gerald took baskets of cress to the station on a 10ft long trailer designed to allow the water to drain through. It was towed behind their Austin car, and on arrival backed up to the gateway alongside the station building, where the cress was unloaded onto the two four-wheeled platform trolleys. From here the porter took it round to the platform and weighed a sample of one in ten of the baskets on the scales in the waiting room. In Frank's time they were smaller baskets weighing 28lb, each of which was labelled with a brush and glue pot. The labels were detached from a long roll hanging from the wall by the scales, then the baskets were reloaded onto the trolleys ready for the train when it arrived. Finally, an invoice was prepared and placed on top of the consignment, indicating the number of 'skips', to avoid confusion with other loads. Frank says all this was hectic and usually done on the platform, unless it was raining badly.

While all the baskets were being weighed, young Gerald Smith usually bought something from one of the sweet machines dispensing Frys mint cream, Nestlé's chocolate and PK chewing gum.

When the train arrived, Frank uncoupled the engine, then worked the ground frame so that it could run round, taking coal and water on the way.

Edward and Gerald would help the porter and the guard load the baskets into the Siphon. They were generally destined for Birmingham, Wolverhampton or Manchester.

This snapshot of Reg Pocock, Tom Tunnicliffe and Esme Jarmaine provides the only record of Weedon Brothers' none too substantial coal pens alongside the end of the goods shed siding. The presence of both Tom and Esme makes it likely that this picture was taken in 1944. Therefore, if Weedon Brothers sold out to Tappins in 1939, the pens evidently continued in use by the new owners.

Looking north from the station platform one Sunday in May 1949 with 2112 on shed. *J. H. Ahern*

"Everyone used the signal box . . . it was always open – only the frame was locked." The single-line staff, which incorporated the key to the frame, was carried on the engine all the time. "It was hung on the sandbox handle" in the cab. Before being removed c.1928, the signalling at Watlington had comprised a fixed distant, a down home, an up starting signal and revolving ground lamps at some of the turnouts. Apart from the lever frame, the building was quite empty, although the guard's bicycle was often put inside if the weather looked doubtful.
Collection P. J. Garland

Frank remembers one end of the van was for Covent Garden traffic (often from Moffat of Brightwell Baldwin) via Paddington and the other end for Wolverhampton. The baskets were stacked into the van, usually no more than two high, and roped over to hold them steady, although the wedge shape created by the lids, which were traditionally not quite closed due to overhanging bundles of cress, helped this.

When the crew were ready, they took the engine back towards the platform and stood off the train. If Frank was still busy loading cress, the fireman would couple up, otherwise Frank did it. He put the handbrake on hard in the trailer, watched the engine onto the coach while he put rubber gloves on, then went 'inside' (between the engine and trailer) and called out for the driver to 'ease up' so that he could put the screw link coupling onto the hook of the drawbar. After connecting the vacuum pipes and putting the tail lamp on the rear, he took the handbrake off so the train could be propelled back into the platform. The fireman changed the engine headlamp.

When the passengers had boarded the trailer, the train left at 6.50 with the Siphon in tow. At Risborough, the smaller part of the load, usually the delivery to Covent Garden,

The timber-built coaling stage was authorised by the GWR in January 1884. It was 28ft long, 10ft wide, with heights to the floor and top of the sides of 5ft and 9ft 4in and is said to have held about 20 tons. In the 1890s the area beneath was used as a firewood store and appears to have been fitted with a door. However, by the time this picture was taken in May 1949, it had begun to look ramshackle. Fireman Tony Benham remembers the stage was higher than the floor of a coal wagon so it was not possible to drop the door open. Instead, coal was shovelled out of the top, which was very difficult until enough had been dug out (bottomed) so that it could be shovelled off the floor. A 10-ton wagonload might last about a week. Following the improved electric pumps for raising water from the well in 1947, there was no longer any need for the engine to be connected to the steam elevator pumps at the end of the shed siding, so it was possible to stable the loco coal wagon behind the bunker while the engine was over the inspection pit. This enabled the bunker to be coaled direct from the wagon to save work. The coal wagons were generally left in the carriage shed siding during the day, so they had to be drawn out and run round while the coach was left clear by the water column. Alternatively, the wagon was drawn out of the shed and left alongside the coal stage while the engine moved clear, then pinch-barred into the siding. Coaling direct into the bunker did not mean the end of all double movement because a stock of coal was maintained at Watlington in case the supply was interrupted. This stock was kept at either end of the stage and replenished on Sunday mornings. The firemen shared the work which began by opening the wagon door to allow the coal to cascade out. It then had to be neatly stacked with "small stuff", backfilling walls built of larger lumps. The firemen were allowed four hours each (8 hours for a 20-ton wagon) to unload coal on about ten Sundays each year. *J. H. Ahern*

No. 9789 pumping water after returning from Risborough with the 1.55 on 13th June 1947. In addition to the two ground hydrants on the west side of the pit, 1919 correspondence refers to a standpipe on the other side which "was put in to enable an engine to take water at the same time as it was standing for pumping". According to lengthman Charlie Adby, who started at Watlington in 1929, the grounded horse-box body, beyond the engine, replaced the old stores in the early 1930s. It may have been provided in lieu of the corrugated iron pump house which, accidently demolished on 11th August 1935, probably doubled as an oil store. The engine crews had previously shared the platelayers hut as a mess, but the horse-box was divided to provide a cabin at the south end and an oil store at the north. The cabin was entered through the near end of the east side, along which were drivers' lockers with bench tops to sit or lay on. Just inside the door, on the south wall, was a switch block for the electric light (and perhaps some connection with the pumps?), then a table, and in the corner, facing south, a checker's desk with a sloping top and a telephone. In the corner, diagonally opposite to the door, was a stove, the chimney of which can just be made out in this and the edge of the picture on page 29, whilst the wall partitioning off the stores was equipped with coat pegs. The store beyond was entered from another door at the opposite end of the eastern side and contained a bench, oil drums, firelighters, cotton waste and jacks. The large oil drums inside were topped up with the 5-gallon cans brought down on the fresh engine each week

from Slough. Illuminated by a single 60-watt bulb, the engine crews made tea in there and spent their breaks on the benches. The lavatory at the station was not locked overnight, but the WC cubicle (which had a large brass lock) was, so a spare key hung inside the cabin. The horse-box body was accidentally destroyed by fire in 1951 when some overalls drying over the stove caught light. Fireman Colin Bowler said he turned up to work one night to find Mr. Portsmouth (the Slough shed foreman) and the late-turn fireman, among other onlookers, staring at the charred remains.

J. H. Russell

MODERN WATER PUMPS

Pumping water using steam from the engine was both time-consuming and demanding on crews. It was therefore a considerable relief when in 1936 new electric pumps were authorised at various locations including Watlington. The old steam-driven pump was replaced with a Beresford-Garvens submersible pump and motor with automatic control from a float switch. James Beresford & Son Ltd were based in Cato Street, Birmingham. The ladder and timber cover to the well were also renewed at the same time, the work costing £128 (of which £43 was for the pump) being completed on 28th January 1937, a few days ahead of the electric lighting at the station.

The crews must have been delighted to have had a self-governing supply of water constantly on hand and no doubt the hassle experienced with the old system soon became merely the topic of conversation with junior men who were probably told that they didn't know how lucky they were. As driver Harry Humphreys said, "When they electrified the pump we always had a tank of water", that is until January 1944 when the pump failed and a steam injector had to be rigged up instead. This change of equipment also brought about a deterioration in the quality of the water, as explained in an internal letter of 8th May 1944:

> 'About 4 months ago the electrically operated pumps failed . . . a steam injector has since been employed to lift the water from the well to the storage tank . . . noted whilst sampling that the stored water was warm and that the inspection door of the tank was wide open, this latter apparently to assist cooling . . . Whilst the bacterial count @ 20°–22°C and the number of coliform bacilli are satisfactorily low, the number of bacteria capable of growth at blood heat is extremely high and is indicative of the multiplication of undesirable organisms, and possibly of dangerous types, in the warm stored water. The arrangement whereby the tank remains partially uncovered considerably increases the latter risk since contamination of the water by airborne excremented matter can readily occur . . . until such time as the electric pump has been reinstalled and I have tested the water, all water required for drinking and culinary purposes should be boiled.'

The electrically operated pump (P1189) was repaired and put into use again on 28th October 1944 but it was supplemented with a new one (P1490) from Beresfords on 27th April 1945. The average daily consumption of water at Watlington at this time was 'in the region of 5,000 gallons', the two pumps yielding 380 and 460 gallons per hour respectively. At the beginning of April 1947, one of the pumps was removed from the well for attention, and in June £24 15s 0d was authorised for Beresfords to overhaul the pumping plant. By the end of the year, concern about dirt entering the well through a missing portion of brick coping to the well, removed to allow the steam elevator pipes to pass through, prompted the comment 'As duplicate electric motors for the pump have now been installed, it is unlikely that these pipes will again be used and you may consider removing them'.

This was not quite the end of the matter as an emergency injector system was again in use on 18th September 1953 when both electric pumps had failed, and on 6th October 1953 arrangements were being made 'to re-install one of the repaired submersible pumps'.

Although the electric pump was there when fireman Tony Benham went to Watlington in March 1947, he remembers using the steam injectors for about a year or so. In order to connect the engine to the equipment, the engine had to be tight up to the end of the siding 'nudging the sleepers'. It was a tricky task to get the system running with 40lb from the steam-heating connection to lift water from the well to ground level and boiler pressure from the whistle valve to drive it up to the tank. Tony used to hang a shovel on the whistle chain to keep the valve open when pumping. Once the system was running, 'it was fine and would pump all night', but if it didn't work 'it could take ages and ages to get going – even all night'. If it could not be made to work at all, water was taken at Risborough in the morning and a fresh attempt was made the next day.

WATER QUALITY

The quality of the water for drinking purposes had long been the cause of concern. Although the water from the well was not officially recognised as drinking water, according to November 1919 paperwork, 'Traffic and Permanent Way men do drink the water chiefly from the hydrant near the engine pit'.

> 'There are no mains belonging to a local Authority in the neighbourhood from which a drinking supply could be obtained, and it seems to me [C. Crump] the only thing to do is to continue using this water, but to issue a proper notice that it should be boiled before use. As a further precaution, I will give instructions for the tank to be thoroughly cleaned out every six months.'

To stem waste from the hydrants 'for filling their tea cans etc.', a tap was subsequently authorised (November 1922) to be fixed on the pillar tank and labelled 'not drinking water'.

As early as 1904 the laboratory tests on the water proved it 'quite fit for drinking purposes' but many factors could conspire to make it otherwise, not least surface water percolating into the well, 'foreign matter' dropping through the necessary openings (for the pump) in the loose boards covering the well, and even the conical cover of the new pillar tank originally shed rainwater into the tank rather than down the outside of it. Samples examined in October 1919 and December 1934 'were polluted with matter of faecal origin to a dangerous degree', yet on most other occasions it was fine.

Further correspondence dated 3rd January 1920 reveals: 'The pump gear stands on top of the well and is exposed to the weather. The fact that the well is covered with a timber top does not prevent foreign matter being dropped through the necessary openings that the pump requires for working'. This implies that the corrugated iron pump house at the end of the loco siding, featured on page 88 of Vol. 1, was not provided until after this date and that the pump gear had been left in the open since the engine shed was destroyed by fire in 1906. However, as mentioned in the text, the pump house and pumps were wrecked by the branch engine in 1935, so this was a relatively shortlived arrangement.

In October 1938 it was recommended that the interior of the well was lined with cement rendering to a depth of 10ft and that a brick plinth and steel cover be provided, and the following June £35 was authorised for the pillar tank to be sealed with a 1/8in thick iron closer plate welded around the base of the conical top (and other openings).

The 1938 steel well cover is just discernible in front of the smaller electrical control cabinet in this mid-1950s photograph of the end of the loco siding. The concrete block backing the makeshift sleeper wheel stops is said to have been the base of one of the old signals. It had lain alongside the track by the neck of the yard, as seen on page 33. The sleepers were placed across the track to prevent the loco coal wagon rolling off the end. *J. H. Russell*

As detailed in Volume 1, chapter 3, the pillar tank was taken from Taunton and re-erected at Watlington in August 1919. This picture, taken on 13th June 1947, also provides another glimpse of the ill-fated permanent way hut and the grounded horse-box body which served as an enginemen's mess. Tony Benham recalls that the fire devil was lit and kept going whenever there was any sign of a hard frost which would freeze the valves or make the leather bag rigid and unusable. *J. H. Russell*

Another of John Ahern's beautiful compositions, looking north-east from the end of the goods yard in May 1949, some nine months after the permanent way hut had been destroyed by fire and only the brick chimney stack remained. The pre-cast concrete coal bin for the fire devil under the pillar tank was evidently added since the previous picture had been taken. The railbuilt loading gauge replaced the wooden one featured on page 51 of Volume 1 whilst the allotment in the bank alongside it was kept by one-time sub-ganger Tommy Johnson, who in the 1920s and early 30s took his son Laurie with him to the station in the evenings to help. Laurie enjoyed watching the trains and later, in 1937, joined the railway as a porter. *J. H. Ahern*

Looking south-west towards the buffer stops from the station throat on 13th June 1947. The three sidings which served the yard were known as (from left to right) spare road, shed road and back road. The 'safety points' incorporated in the second point were authorised in November 1893 (for £34) to protect the running line from any unauthorised movement or stray wagons. The station and yard were on a barely perceptible down grade towards the buffer stops, advantage of which was often taken when shunting, or even running round a goods train, as detailed elsewhere. The sleeper-built platelayers or gangers hut on the left was shared with the Locomotive Department who also signed on there before the provision of the grounded horse-box which was used as an enginemen's mess. Locomotive Department paperwork was carried out at a desk in the PW hut. They "all got on well". Fireman Tom Saunders recalled that the loco crews also left their bicycles against the PW hut or put them inside if it was raining. The hut had many warm associations for the members of the PW gang who enjoyed hearty breakfasts in there, all gathered around the fire like a family. *J. H. Russell*

was barrowed over the crossing to the London train, whilst the van was collected from the bay by the engine of a northbound train for conveyance as a through vehicle, sometimes filled with other traffic from Risborough. If the volume of cress did not justify a Siphon from Watlington, it was carried in the luggage compartment of the trailer.

Normally, Mr. Pocock or Eric Nash, the clerk, 'booked up' after the 6.50 departure and left about 7.0 p.m., although if Mr. Pocock was working late, he would stay until Frank finished and cycle down the road with him.

Frank was on his own after the 6.50, so he might sit at the desk in the station office and enter traffic into the book. At this time, shop owners, after closing, often brought a few parcels for despatch the next morning.

Occasionally, Control might ring and request a wagon, which he labelled straight away and recorded in the wagon book.

It would be difficult to find a much better or more heartwarming example of the cooperation and teamwork, which so often existed at Watlington throughout Reg Pocock's reign, than Frank Saunders using the time at his disposal, before the arrival of the last train, to help the nightman unload the loco coal wagon onto the stage. He could have just spent this slack time sitting idly in the goods shed office, from where he could see anyone approaching the station. Only when there was absolutely nothing to do did he pass the time reading any newspapers left on the train or a library book.

The branch train returned from Risborough at 8.0 p.m., often conveying local tradesmen who had been to town buying for their businesses. Frank Hyde also travelled back from Aston Rowant on this one. When it arrived, any parcels conveyed in the guard's van were put in the office and the engine was run onto the other end of the trailer, which was then put into the carriage shed, or, by George Howlett's time, into the spare road.

On rare occasions, the branch engine would run out to Chinnor, with the guard and late-turn porter travelling in the brake van, to clear cement traffic from the works ready for the morning goods, and put empty vans into the works for loading. The Chinnor staff had gone home by this time. The engine and van returned as soon as this task was over, which was usually about 10.0 p.m. Frank Saunders remembers making about an hour's overtime, but this only happened on a couple of occasions during his time there.

By 1937 Frank says the evening goods was no longer normally run, so, after putting the trailer away, the engine was taken on shed.

Normally, Frank had collected his bike and locked the goods shed before the last train arrived. He also changed the date on the ticket machine ready for the morning. After passengers had gone, he closed the shutters on the office window, turned off all

When this picture was taken on John Ahern's visit one Sunday afternoon in May 1949, the auto-trailer had already been cleaned by porters Dick Smith and Tom Tunnicliffe. Doubtless by this time all evidence of the water splashed over the platform and track had long since evaporated in the warm sun. *John Ahern*

the lights and locked the station building, then the yard gates. Mr. Pocock and each of the porters had a set of keys.

Even though he was prepared for a prompt departure, Frank was usually beaten to the gate by Geoff Pearson who was soon away on his bike for a pint at the White Hart, leaving his fireman to do the disposal and wait for the night man to arrive. Jimmy Nelms, who had some paperwork to do before he could leave, was not far behind him. He walked back to the town with distinctive, short, quick steps and a little tuck box in his hand.

On Sunday mornings, the porters took it in turns to earn a couple of hours overtime for cleaning the auto-trailer, which they would find left in the loop. Frank used to get there about 9.0 a.m. and began by gravitating the trailer into the platform, then sweeping it out and dusting. There was no soap or detergent of any kind for washing the outside, just a long-handled broom and water drawn from a tap by the gents. To make life easier, the four fire buckets, which hung on the south end of the building, were also used to provide a reasonable quantity of water as it was only by soaking the dirt that it was possible to shift it. Most of the grime resulted from smoke drifting from the chimney of the engine as it rattled along the branch.

It was hard work washing the outside even when stood on the platform, but the opposite side had to be reached by means of a plank supported on folding trestles kept alongside the carriage shed. This was a precarious job which inevitably meant the other side failed to receive the same attention. However, by concentrating on the windows, this would go unnoticed because, apart from Lewknor and Kingston Halts, the trailer was only normally seen from one side!

GOODS AND PARCELS TRAFFIC

In the absence of accounts books and ledgers, it is difficult to be precise about the traffic handled, especially at this distance in time, and, in any case, by its very nature it was subject to fluctuation and variation. However, after much research, we think that the notes appending each station description provide a reasonable picture from the 1920s onwards. They have been compiled over many years, by piecing together fragments of evidence and interviews with former staff, traders, farmers, passengers and other local people. We would love to hear from anyone who can supplement our findings.

GOODS TRAFFIC

Mr. Pocock regarded goods traffic as being at its height in 1924 when the chief goods forwarded were hay, straw, agricultural produce, livestock and timber.

Hay had been stored alongside the station during the Great War and sent out by rail for the horses at the front. Local farmers were apparently being compelled to contribute as part of the war effort. Peter Schwier was told that timber cut down from land to the north of the station was also despatched in large quantities during the Great War and afterwards the Board of Trade timber supply department were evidently sending away a sufficient quantity to justify an agreement between them and the GWR to station a 30cwt portable crane in the yard at Watlington from January 1920 to August 1921. We are not clear whether timber traffic completely ceased after the removal of the crane or not, but in 1929 a large walnut butt grown at Cuxham was brought to the station for conveyance to London Docks for export. It required a special wagon and the requisition of a travelling crane, probably from Reading, to load it.

Mr. Pocock recalled that Watlington sawmills (occupying the old brewery) despatched quantities of round timber and manufactured wooden utensils (see Ives page 37 for details).

Hurdles, made by two brothers, Albert and 'Midge' Coles, in a lean-to at the Anchor public house, Cuxham Road, were delivered to the station by Tappins and sent out as full load traffic, as were five-bar sheep gates, another Coles speciality.

Other outgoing traffic included wheat and barley. Percy Peyman remembered that during the 1920s corn was stored at the farms in ricks and threshed in the winter, then put into 2¼cwt sacks ("plus 4lb for sack"). These were brought to the station and packed into vans outside the goods shed, where the farm carts were backed up to each vehicle. This went on over a period, each farm taking up to 2–3 days to despatch. Traditionally, this was a special time when the horses and their harnesses were all spruced up specially and farmers gave their workers 2-gallon stone jars of ale to drink on the cart.

Sugar beet grown in the area tends to be associated with the Second World War, but Percy Peyman also recalled sugar beet being loaded at the station each autumn during the mid-1920s, apparently on its way to a factory in Eynsham.

The local corn and seed merchants, J. Donaldson & Sons (Oxon) Ltd., brought steady business to the railway. Donaldson, who came from Monkland, near Glasgow, moved to White House Farm, Brightwell Baldwin, in 1891 and later set up the corn and seed business at premises in Couching Street. Donaldsons also owned Hambleden Mill on the Thames. In earlier years they received grain by rail and sulphate of ammonia, which came in hessian (and later paper) sacks from the South Eastern Gas Co. at Greenwich. Tappins delivered to the farms for them and took supplies from the station to Donaldsons' premises between 7.30 and 8.0 a.m. as one of their first jobs of the day. Donaldsons also received sugar beet pulp from Kidderminster and the Eastern Counties and they were also agents for the West of England Sack Co., local farmers hiring sacks for the storage of corn through the winter.

In the 1940s, stock or 'pig' potatoes used for animal feed, were loaded by local farmers and sprayed with a blue powder dye in the wagon — usually after the staff had helped themselves to one or two! There could be five or six wagons a day when these were in season. Incidentally, the staff at Watlington were often given a bag of potatoes as a gesture of thanks from local farmers.

Livestock traffic seems to have been very meagre at Watlington with less than fifty wagons a year forwarded or received. Statistics show 1931 as an exceptional year with a recorded 153 wagons of livestock, but this is sharply contrasted by 1934 when there were just fifteen. Mr. Pocock recalled several wagon loads of sheep from Scotland and lambs from Kent, and Cyril Hopkins remembers bullocks arriving for breeding. Nevertheless, even after the war, members of staff and traders we've spoken to have their own memories of pigs, sheep, horses and cattle.

Tony Benham recalls two or three loads of cattle arriving by rail after the war and being unloaded through the pens for farmer Roadnight, whilst Ian Donaldson remembers his father receiving about two truck loads of cattle each year in the 1950s. These apparently came from Ireland for fattening and were driven along the road to their farm in Brightwell Baldwin via Pyrton Lane and Cuxham. Farmers Frank Nixey of Cuxham and Jimmy Smith of Pyrton Field Farm (near the station) are remembered as sending cattle out by rail, as was farmer Jim Tappin of Chestnut Farm, who drove his animals along the road to the station, where they were apparently loaded on the passenger platform.

Cyril Saunders remembers six rams for Roadnights arriving without notice in the early 1950s. They did not know where to put them while they contacted the farm, and ended up shutting them in the bicycle shed! Altogether Cyril remembers "three lots of rams in horse-boxes" for Roadnights and another time a couple of boars. As the pens were rotten by this time, the vehicles were left in the goods shed for the farmer to unload.

Predictably, the main incoming traffic was coal, coke, fertilizer, cattle feedstuffs and, during the 1930s, wagons of roadstone must have been a regular sight. The fertilizer was principally bagged sulphate of ammonia, nitrate, chalk and basic slag, which arrived in several box vans at a time. Most of the local farmers received supplies but Roadnights was the main customer. For many years cattle cake was received in bags and in the 1920s at least there were also locust beans for cattle. Cyril Hopkins also remembers peat from Ireland.

Scotch seed potatoes had been sent to Watlington by rail from various parts of Scotland, but by the late 1940s they came down by road.

SMALLS AND PARCELS

General merchandise, largely for the shops in the town, arrived each day in the station truck which brought regular consignments of groceries, clothing, tobacco, etc., as mentioned on page 8.

Tobacco for Worleys, tobacconist and confectioner, came from Wills in Bristol. Worleys had a small van and often collected from the station. Wet fish for Messum & Dover (detailed separately) travelled in the guard's compartment of the branch trailer, usually accompanied by bags of ice.

Maybe as often as a couple of times a day, at least in the 1920s, baskets of pigeons arrived from the Midlands for release.

George Howlett remembers locally killed rabbits being sent out. These were hung on sticks, with bags covering their heads. He also recalls Smiths of Lewknor dealing with honey from Ewelme.

By 1951 the old brewery was occupied by the Venables mail order department, which advertised in all the daily papers and brought appreciable parcels traffic to Watlington station, as detailed separately.

MESSUM & DOVER

The partnership between Tim Messum and Bert Dover began c.1918 after Tim returned from service in the Royal Marines. The family came from Tottenham and his brother worked at Billingsgate Fish Market, but after the war his parents moved to Watlington. Bert was the brother of Arthur Dover, the local carrier.

Their premises in the High Street, just to the west of The Pineapple, was formerly occupied by a butcher. Messum & Dover were 'Fish, Poultry and Game Dealers', buying fish from Billingsgate and pheasants, partridges and hares, from the Earl of Macclesfield, farmer Roadnight and Milton Harris Whittaker of Britwell House. From the mid 1930s they also fried fish and chips on selected nights. In the early postwar years these were Tuesdays and Thursdays, 4.0 to 8.0 p.m. and Saturdays from 11.0 a.m. to 2.0 p.m. and 4.0 to 8.0 p.m. "There simply wasn't the demand at other times."

When Tim's stepson Tom Snow was demobbed from the RAF in 1945, he bought out Bert Dover who retired, the business subsequently being known as 'T. Messum & Son'. They also bought a 10cwt Ford van, to replace 'a similar one', and had it painted dark green with gold-leaf lettering 'T. Messum & Son, Fish, Poultry and Game Dealers, Watlington 31'. The van was equipped with scales, and a water tank and gas heater for washing hands.

Tim ran the shop and Tom drove the van, but on Mondays when there were no fish deliveries ("there were no catches on Sunday"), the shop was closed until 12 noon while they collected poultry and game. Sometimes there was such a glut from weekend shoots that the surplus game was packed in hampers and sent by train to Smithfield or Billingsgate.

During the rest of the week, Tim started at 7.0 a.m. preparing the fish in the cold store whilst Tom set out at 8.0 a.m. on his rounds. "We had our regular clientele." Typically, this involved deliveries in the Pyrton, Shirburn and Lewknor areas, Tom returning via the station to collect supplies of fish brought down on the 10.22 a.m. Later on, he went out to Kingston Blount and even as far as Turville Heath, usually returning about an hour before the shop closed at 6.0 p.m. While Tom was out on his rounds, the town was covered by delivery boys on bicycles.

In the postwar years, fish came from Billingsgate and Grimsby, then Grimsby and Fleetwood, fish from the north being transhipped at Banbury and Risborough. Regular supplies were principally cod, haddock and plaice, but they also received Dover sole, halibut, herring and salmon. Latterly, regular suppliers were Norton Brothers of Grimsby, and Jack Elphick of Fleetwood whose names appeared on the fish boxes.

Typically, Messum & Son would receive deliveries of five or six boxes, each containing 6 stone (124lb) of fish. The lids were secured with steel straps, nailed and bolted each end, and at Watlington they were unloaded from the guard's van and stacked on the platform by the fire buckets ready for Tom who would back his van up to tbe gateway.

Tim retired in 1957 at the age of 76, leaving Tom to run the business, but when passenger services were withdrawn from the branch that year, fish supplies had to be collected from Oxford station, which was not so convenient, so Tom finished with fish and kept the shop as an off-licence instead.

WATERCRESS

Cress growers around Watlington at various times included Charlie Coles, whose produce was taken to the station by Arthur Dover; Harpers from Ewelme who, in the 1920s, sent a few baskets at midday, but up to twelve baskets in the evening which travelled to Risborough in the guard's compartment; Clement Ives of Watlington who at one time before and during the war had beds near the Bull public house and in a stream between Chalgrove and Cuxham and at Brightwell Baldwin; Moffatts, who had beds opposite the Lord Nelson at Brightwell Baldwin (also at Upperton), took cress to the station with a horse and cart; and Les Goodchild of Bledlow, although it is not clear whether he used the railway. However, George Smith of Ewelme was undoubtedly the main grower in the area.

Smith's cress beds in Ewelme had been dug in the late 1880s by George Smith. His son Edward inherited the business and for a short time, prior to the late 1930s, he was joined by his brother Bert. Edward's son Gerald remembers the working day ran from 7.0 am. to 5.0 p.m. and at the height of the season four agricultural workers were employed picking.

When Edward died in 1939, the business passed to his wife. Subsequently, she rented beds at Lewknor alongside the village streets, and Kingspool, Ewelme.

Most of the beds were basically on an earth mix and produced brown cress, whereas the combination of clear water and pebbles at South Weston was used to grow the superior French green cress. The peak season for cress was from January to May (peaking at Easter), after which the beds were cleaned out ready for another shorter season from September until the end of November.

Ron Gilbey, who worked for Smiths (but "not full time") in the 1940s and 50s, recalls cress grew best during the months with an 'R' in them, so much so that cress grown through other months was cut and discarded. It grew in three cycles of about 2–3 weeks apart and was harvested from the first and second. On the third, the roots were destroyed and discarded into the bottom of the bed to enable the seeds to rejuvenate the beds after they had been cleaned out. After being cut on the second and third cycle, the stems were patted down (with a basket lid attached to a long pole) to even-up the growth.

'Block holes' (like sluice gates) in the transverse wooden boards separating the beds, normally allowed water to pass over the cress but, for cleaning out, these holes were plugged to stem the flow.

Cress was cut, never picked, and laid at the sides of the bed to allow the flowing part of the stream to keep it moist. This was vital. Strung bundles were arranged in alternating directions and tightly packed into 28lb hampers, protruding around the top, the partly closed lids (allowing maximum air circulation) being held in position with leather straps. The partly wedged-open lids also made for better stability when stacking the baskets on top of each other. Before the war, each basket bore an indentification plate inscribed 'GSSW' which stood for George Smith, South Weston.

The Watlington branch was useful because of the direct connections with the Midlands, via Banbury, as most of the cress went to Birmingham and Wolverhampton which were reached in three hours ready for the next day's market. If cress did not reach the customer within 24 hours it was useless. Reg Pocock recalled "Watercress is despatched in large quantities to Birmingham, Wolverhampton and Manchester, a through truck load being despatched to Birmingham on certain days of the week."

In the 1940s and early 50s, Ron Gilbey remembers cress being taken to the station in a Packard van, sometimes with a trailer, presumably the one towed earlier behind Edward Smith's Austin as described on page 23 (in the 1930s Smiths used a Humber and an Austin). Edward had apparently bought the Packard secondhand before the war and found the 'dicky seat' useful for holding extra baskets of cress. The Packard was later replaced with a Morris Isis van.

In postwar years, Ron remembers that Tom Tunnicliffe, dubbed 'the station master', was very fussy about the placing of the baskets, which, by this time, were sent out in the guard's compartment of the trailer. "They had to be stacked just so." Tom also ran water into the open ends of the baskets prior to despatch, and was tipped for his trouble.

Empty hampers which, incidentally, despite bearing the grower's initials, were actually owned by the market wholesalers, were returned roped together in tens and usually stacked somewhere on the station awaiting collection.

CLEMENT IVES, THE OLD BREWERY — W. T. HARRIS AND VENABLES

Among a number of other business interests, Clement Ives had taken over the furniture business of W. T. Harris which had once been based in Wycombe. They also had a factory in Gypsy Hill, South London. Millie Lawrence's recollections point to 1946 as the year when Ives established his furniture factory at the old brewery in Couching Street. Mrs. Ives says her husband kept the name W. T. Harris and sold domestic furniture, wooden packing cases and garden furniture. In the early postwar years he also had a small furniture shop in Watlington High Street, near the memorial cross.

Ives collected old seat fillings and leather offcuts from Morris Motors in Cowley and Roots in Coventry, and stored them in sacks at the Watlington premises until they amounted to a wagon load. Then they were taken to the station and loaded into an open wagon, sheeted, and sent to the Gypsy Hill factory which specialised in soft furnishings.

Before Ives set up his furniture factory, the old brewery was apparently occupied by the Watlington saw mills. This was recalled by Reg Pocock, who made no mention of the premises' use as a youth hostel afterwards.

'I understand that some time ago there was a small brewery at Watlington, which was closed down during the First World War, but I have not come across any records of traffic from the industry being dealt with in any appreciable quantities. During my period of office the old brewery premises were occupied by the Watlington Sawmills Coy, who despatched quantities of round timber as well as manufactured wooden utensils, chiefly for the feeding of cattle, pigs, etc. After this firm closed down, another type of manufactured goods appeared on the market, namely semi-rustic garden furniture, such as chairs, seats, tables, etc, and this was, for a time, passing in regular quantities and I believe the original designer of this unique commodity was a local tradesman. He now lives in retirement at Watlington.

'The old brewery premises are now occupied by Messrs. Venables Mail Order Dept (est. 1886) who specialise in fireside adjustable chairs, upholstery, leathercloth, rugs, slippers, etc. This brings quite an appreciable amount of parcels traffic to the station and as the firm extensively advertise in all the daily papers it is likely to increase as time goes on. This is obviously a very enterprising and go-ahead concern and its location in the town gives it an air of industrial development and progress.'

Reg Pocock wrote this in 1951. The Venables mail order company was another of Ives' businesses. He took over Venables' furniture shop at St. Clement's, Oxford, and despatched rugs, carpets, small items of furniture, etc, continuing in business at Watlington until about 1954.

As mentioned previously, Clement also grew watercress at various sites around Watlington near 'Two Ways' and in streams between Chalgrove and Cuxham and at Brightwell Baldwin. In the 1950s some went to the station and, as often as he could, he would take cress to market in Coventry on the occasions when he collected upholstery offcuts.

Clement Ives moved to Watlington in 1935 and lived in a housed called 'Two Ways' (previously called 'The Folly') along the Cuxham Road. He bought a blacksmith's forge, which was situated opposite the house, and after the war used the building as an office. His son Tony developed a scrap business there (on the site now occupied by the fire station) and later at How Hill. This is discussed in Vol. 1, page 207. In the early 1960s, Tony built a bungalow near 'Two Ways' and subsequently demolished the house.

Adelaide Smith, Gerald's mother, and Percy Strickland cutting cress at Ewelme about 1950. Percy worked for the Smith family for many years. The bridge on which the wheelbarrow is seen was known as Nellie Bridge and the ash tree in the background was used to shade the cress until it was carted away. In later years the tree was replaced by a shed which was used to keep the cress cool.

CARTAGE AND COAL

ARTHUR DOVER, CARRIER

Born in Watlington in 1883, Arthur Dover started out as a stable lad, then a horse driver at the Hare & Hounds. After serving in the Great War, he bought a horse and cart and started his own carrier service operating from 47 High Street. Later on, he bought a lorry which he ran mainly to Oxford, Thame, Wallingford and Henley. He issued cards printed with a large letter 'D' which his customers displayed in their window when they wanted him to call. Although he did not have a regular connection with the railway, he appeared at Watlington station from time to time on miscellaneous deliveries which included, for instance, water cress from Charlie Coles.

Arthur worked right up until he died in 1958, his son-in-law Wolseley Keen carrying on the business until the early 1960s.

F. A. TAPPIN & SONS, CARTAGE CONTRACTOR AND COAL MERCHANT

Francis Abraham Tappin set up his cartage business sometime between 1907 and 1911. Based in Brook Street, his adverts offered 'brakes, wagonettes, broughams, traps, etc. at reasonable prices'. In the mid-1920s, Francis expanded into the coal trade and became a farmer at White House Farm, Brook Street, where he also kept his stock of coal.

By this time he was joined by his four sons, Eric, Cecil, Aubrey and Ernest, and the business became known as F. A. Tappin & Sons. He also had employees for deliveries or bagging coal at the farm, although, whenever possible, coal was bagged direct from the wagon at the station.

In 1926 he took over the GWR cartage agency. Agreements show this was previously held by Jim Jones of Brook Street (from 1st January 1909), then Arabella Jones (from 22nd April 1925), then F. A. Tappin from 10th March 1926.

Francis also had cars for hire work and met trains by arrangement, Cecil often driving them in the afternoon after returning from his coal rounds.

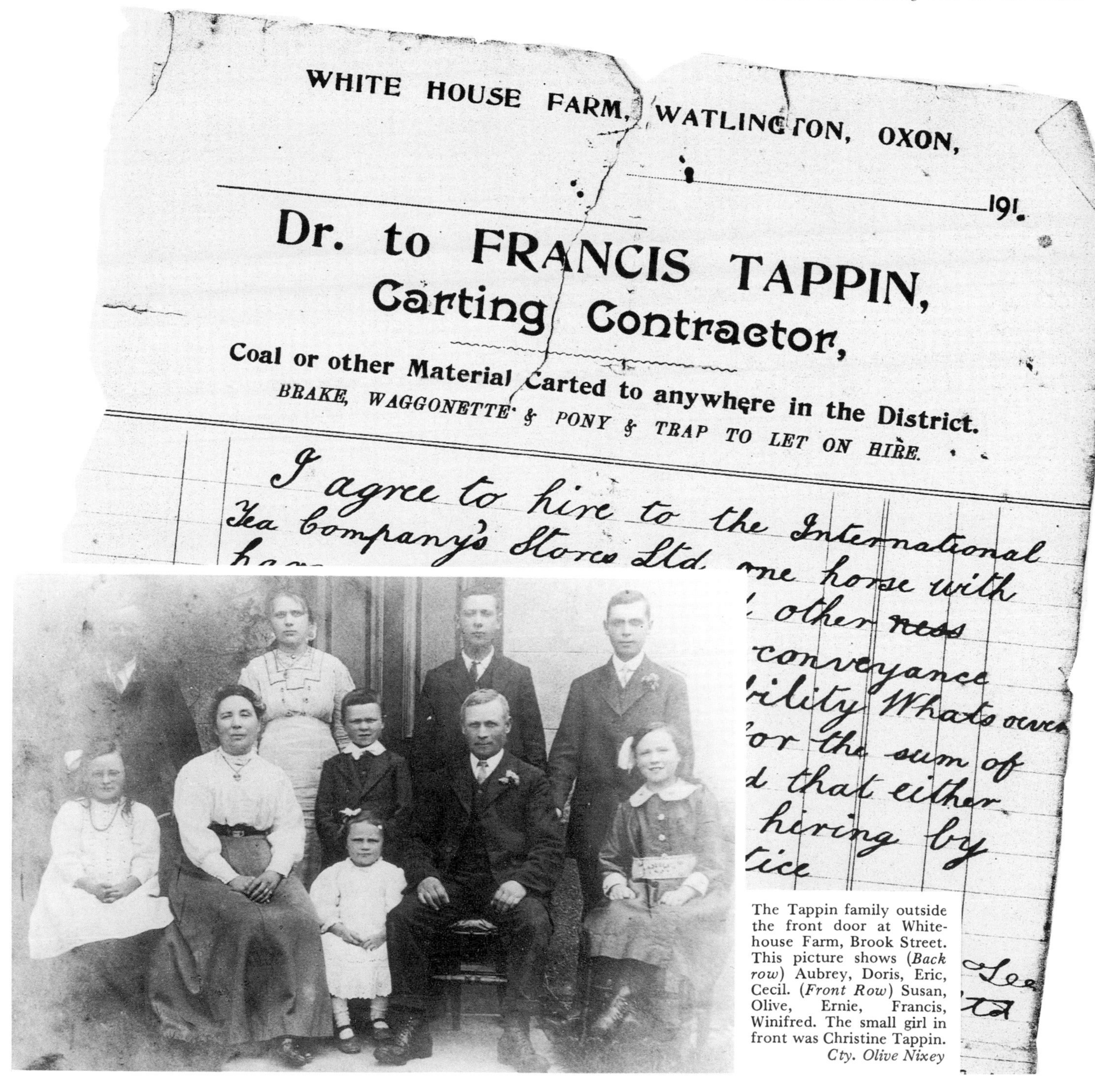

WHITE HOUSE FARM, WATLINGTON, OXON,

191

Dr. to FRANCIS TAPPIN,
Carting Contractor,
Coal or other Material Carted to anywhere in the District.
BRAKE, WAGGONETTE & PONY & TRAP TO LET ON HIRE.

I agree to hire to the International Tea Company's Stores Ltd. one horse with ... other ness ... conveyance ... ility Whats ... or the sum of ... d that either ... hiring by ... tice

The Tappin family outside the front door at Whitehouse Farm, Brook Street. This picture shows (*Back row*) Aubrey, Doris, Eric, Cecil. (*Front Row*) Susan, Olive, Ernie, Francis, Winifred. The small girl in front was Christine Tappin. *Cty. Olive Nixey*

Francis bought well-kept ex-chauffeur-driven cars from local well-to-do people including an Austin York and a large Humber which, he used to joke, "could hold a cricket team". Trindall's and Willoughby's garages and House Brothers also ran taxis and hire cars.

During the 1930s granite chippings were taken by horse and cart to council roadworks at Stadhampton. Tappins also carted corn to the station for the farmers and delivered cattle cake out to the farms.

Before the war, Tappins had seven or eight horses kept at White House Farm, tended by Francis Tappin, who spent his last years looking after them. The horses had been used on general delivery and contract work such as road surfacing for the council. Through the war years, they were gradually replaced with vans and lorries.

For six months a lorry was dedicated to taking coal from Watlington station to Chalgrove while the aerodrome was under construction. The coal was used by the contractors for cooking and heating there. Initially, a 4-ton Dodge was used for the run and later a 5-ton Bedford, Albert Sheppard and Ernie Tappin handling the work between them. Ernie remembers up to 30 wagons at a time in the yard at Watlington with coal for Chalgrove, and special goods trains being run in the afternoon.

At one time, the Earl of Macclesfield was a good customer of Tappins, taking a wagon load of anthracite at a time for the boilers at Shirburn Castle. The Earl also used Stanmores. Ernie Tappin remembers that the delivery was arduous because, owing to the narrow bridge, the bags had to be carried 125 yards to the castle to reach a chute into the cellar. The Earl appreciated their efforts and tipped the three men involved 2/6d each.

As the official GWR cartage agents at Watlington, Tappins collected and delivered for a distance of about one mile from the station. The majority of consignments were paid home, and if this entailed a distance outside the mile radius, a charge was made to the railway. Payment for any items charged to the station only, but which subsequently needed to be delivered, was negotiated between Tappins and the customer.

Ernie Tappin with a Morris Commercial at Whitehouse Farm. *Cty. Olive Nixey*

Les Tappin (son of Cecil and grandson of Francis) began with the company in 1939 and recalls starting his day by taking a horse and cart to the station at about 8.30 a.m. to collect 'smalls' items for the town which had arrived on the early morning goods. He says they were unloaded from the back road rather than in the goods shed, which he thinks was rarely used by that time. In fact he remembers the goods shed road and 'front road' usually accommodated any wagon overflows or exceptional traffic such as coal for Chalgrove airfield.

The necessary documentation was prepared in the goods shed office before he left on his rounds about 9.0 a.m. He could not leave earlier because the porter was occupied on the platform with the first two trains.

While Les was carrying out his deliveries around the town, any shops with something for collection would put an official GWR agents card in the window so that he would know to call. By this time, Tappins also handled the delivery of passenger-rated traffic (mainly parcels). His father Cecil collected any of this, which included perishables, off the train which arrived around 10.45 and when taking them into the town, he usually passed Les on his way back.

He returned to the station about 11.0 and unloaded whatever items he had collected into railway wagons. After completing the paperwork and exchanging delivery notes, he was free to assist his colleagues in the yard unloading coal or other full load traffic such as fertilizer or cattle cake.

Thursdays varied in that following his delivery and collection round, Les returned to the town with a special run for Richards stores, which, owned by South Oxfordshire Supply Stores, received a van load of provisions sent up from Budgets of Bristol, wholesale grocery suppliers. After the outbreak of war, the Budget van ceased to run, and provisions arrived as part of a composite load. By the time rationing was over, most food supplies were carried by road.

Left. Les Nixey and Aubrey Tappin at Whitehouse Farm. The baby is thought to have been Ken Nixey. *Right:* Les and Kenneth Nixey. Les married Olive Tappin, and Ken drove for Tappins. The lorry appears to have been an ex-army vehicle of Canadian origin. *Cty. Olive Nixey*

This picture, taken alongside the back siding at Watlington station in the 1950s, shows Albert Shepherd inside the wagon, Ernie Tappin on the back of the 4/5 ton Commer lorry, Ray Tappin, Maurice Selwood and John Beechie. ***Cty. Messrs. Tappin & Sons***

TAPPINS' COAL BUSINESS

By the 1940s, Tappins were the principal coal merchants in Watlington. They did not have their own wagons but dealt with coal factors, their supplies arriving in wagons from Stevco of Oxford, Toomers of Reading, and Howland & Bush of Thame. The majority of their coal came from Coventry Colliery and Griff of Warwickshire, whilst anthracite came from South Wales and coke from Reading and Oxford gasworks. Tappins received two or three wagons a day and sometimes there were up to eight wagons in the yard at any one time.

Wagons were generally unloaded fairly promptly, but as demurrage was charged at three shillings a day after 48 hours, the station staff would often tell the powers that be that any overdue wagon was 'out of reach'.

Deliveries were made by lorry to places like Cuxham, Lewknor, Stokenchurch, Nettlebed, Stadhampton, Chalgrove, Russells Water, North End and Christmas Common. Francis started with a l-ton Ford, soon followed by a 4 or 5-ton left-hand drive German Anson, which apparently caused quite a stir as it was the largest lorry in Watlington. After that they had a variety of vehicles; all painted in green with cream lettering.

Tappins took over Fred Hoar's coal business in Cuxham, and around the beginning of the Second World War they also took over from Weedons. However, they did not transfer any of the administration to Weedons' office on the edge of the station forecourt, but used the building as a sack store. Eventually, it was moved 'on skids' to Tappins' depot in the town.

Tappins also took over Stanmore Brothers' business from Percy Bush and continued to receive coal at Watlington station right up until it was closed in 1961. Even after that, they continued to receive supplies by rail at Chinnor until 1964.

WEEDON BROTHERS

The Weedon Brothers were Frank Keep Weedon of Winterbrook, Wallingford, and George Gray Weedon of Whiteknights Road, Reading, but the original company, F. H. & G. Weedon, had been established since at least 1865 with a superphosphate (artificial fertilizer) works at Goring and a brick kiln at Woodcote. The coal business may have been a later venture. Based at Goring, they also had coal depots at Wallingford, Watlington, Wheatley, Tiddington, Wantage, Upton, Compton, Hampstead Norris and Benson. Weedons are listed as trading from Shirburn Street in Watlington in the mid 1870s but they are not shown at the station until 1907 when they were also in Church Street. By the 1920s they were at Gorwell. The company had its own railway wagons, which were painted grey with white lettering shaded black, but by the late 1930s they had become outdated, other coal supplies arriving in larger more modern ones. Consequently, they were irreverently referred to by some of the railway staff as 'tubs'.

Weedons seem to have been the only company to have leased wharfage at the station, where they also occupied a small wooden office on the edge of the forecourt. Even so, most of their supplies were stored at their own premises (and stables) in Gorwell, next door to a house called 'Chestnuts'. The manager of the Watlington depot was a Mr. Simmonds, who apparently had a white moustache and lived at the Gorwell premises. He also played the flute in the Watlington silver band. Their delivery men were Frank Allen and subsequently Leonard 'Pincher' King. At busy times, men from other Weedons depots were brought in to help, and notable among these were two brothers from Wallingford who had no toes or fingers. They are said to have used a shovel with some sort of hook fitted to their hands and are remembered as very hard-working.

Although they had lorries elsewhere, in Watlington Weedons only used horses and carts. Whether not being as up-to-date as their competitors would have been noticeable or not in those days is difficult to judge, but it would have restricted their range. In the 1930s the delivery horses were called 'Major' and 'Chieftain'.

Weedons seem to have sold out to Tappins in 1939 or thereabouts, Mr. Simmonds, the manager, working for Tappins for a while afterwards.

FRED HOAR

Fred Hoar started to trade in coal sometime between 1903 and 1907 when he and later his brother George owned the Black Lion public house at Watlington. He collected coal from the station using a horse and cart. In the early '20s he moved to Hoo Mill in Cuxham Road and by 1928 was in semi-retirement, delivering stone, which he collected from Watlington station, for local road construction, still with just a horse and cart.

STANMORE BROTHERS

Reginald and Frank Stanmore started trading in coal and coke c.1926 and they were also haulage contractors. Coal supplies seem to have come from factors,

Toomers and Dunlops of Reading, most of the coal coming from Coventry for domestic use. Supplies were unloaded at the station and stored at their own premises, 'The Lilacs', Brook Street. At first they ran a Chevrolet lorry and later a Bedford which was painted green with white lettering 'Stanmore Brothers Coal & Coke Merchants and Contractors'. They did not have any of their own railway wagons.

They kept specific days for deliveries to Chalgrove, Pyrton, Shirburn, Christmas Common, Stadhampton, Lewknor, etc. The Earl of Macclesfield is said to have ordered his own coal but hired Stanmores to ferry it from the station to the castle. After Weedon Brothers had ceased trading in Watlington, their premises in Gorwell are said to have been left empty for about two years, before eventually, in 1941, being purchased by Stanmores for coal storage and expansion.

Around 1950 the business was sold to local estate agent Ernest Monk who, in turn, sold it to coal merchant Percy Bush. However, throughout this time the company continued under the name Stanmore Brothers until finally, in 1957, it was taken over by Tappins.

PERCY BUSH

Percy Bush, who came from Thame, started a coal and corn merchants business in Watlington in the late 1930s. He lived in Aylesbury Road, Princes Risborough, and travelled to his small yard in Watlington High Street each day in his lorry. In 1953, following illness, he and his family moved into Watlington to save travelling, and continued in business until 1957 when he sold out to Tappins. By the early 1950s, he had a grey Morris Commercial and later a maroon Dodge, both about 5-ton capacity. The vehicles bore the legend 'P. Bush coal & corn merchant Watlington' in white lettering shaded black. Domestic coal, principally anthracite received directly from South Wales collieries, was bagged straight off the wagon for delivery in and around Watlington, including the villages of Sydenham and Aston Rowant. Some supplies were stored at his yard during the war and also during the summer months.

THE ZONAL LORRY

Under the Zonal scheme, smalls traffic (under 1 ton) was delivered in the area by railway lorries from Thame and Reading. Two 5-ton Thornycroft lorries were based at Thame and driven by Bill Hawthorn and Eddie Smith who, working Monday to Saturday, each spent three days on the Chinnor and Watlington run.

In the mornings, after loading up at the goods shed at Thame, the driver took his lorry over to the station building to pick up any parcels which had arrived by passenger train. The smalls traffic in the goods shed had been received in box vans from London and the North the previous day and sorted ready, whilst the parcels he was collecting arrived that morning. The GWR had its own petrol storage tanks at Thame so the lorry was filled before finally setting out around 8.30–8.45 a.m. The Zonal run is said to have involved about 100 miles, the lorry calling in set order at Tetsworth, Stoke Talmage, Lewknor, Stokenchurch, Watlington, Aston Rowant, Kingston Blount, Sydenham, Chinnor, Bledlow and Bledlow Ridge, finally arriving back at Thame around 5.0 p.m.

Bill Hawthorn recalls how traffic for Aston Rowant was very light in contrast to Chinnor.

Len Breadmore, Zonal driver from Reading, recalls going to Watlington as part of his round from Reading. This included a call at Wallingford which he left at about 10.30. He reached Watlington by about 11.0 and backed into the goods shed to pick up parcels for delivery. He also delivered cigarettes from Reading to several shops. In the meantime, Tappins went out on local deliveries. Cyril Saunders said the lorry called again about 4.0 p.m. for return loads. He got back to Reading at about 5.30.

Bill Hawthorn at Thame.
Cty. Bill Hawthorn

Left: **Eddie's lorry on its rounds in Thame.** ***Right:*** **Eddie Smith at Thame.** ***Cty. Mrs. E. Smith***

ON THE FARMS

Harvesting in 'The Grounds' opposite the Priory. ***Cty. Daphne Roadnight***

Without access to the goods accountancy books for Watlington station, all of which were doubtless destroyed many years ago, it is impossible to establish all the farms in the area which used the railway over the years. However, we have been lucky enough to talk to the descendants of some of those involved and hope that the following notes will give an idea of the businesses involved and examples of the use or otherwise of the railway.

GEORGE ENGLAND

George England came from Kinver, Worcestershire, where he had been a spade and shovel manufacturer. He had also bred pheasants and other exotic birds as a hobby. Around the turn of the century, he decided to develop the pheasant breeding and moved to Christmas Common, where he took over Greenfields Farm and was joined by two of his three sons, and later the third.

The Englands developed Greenfields as a mixed farm with, amongst other things, a large flock of sheep. The pheasant breeding flourished and he became renowned for his gold and silver pheasants.

There had been another pheasant farm in the area run by a Mr. Johnson, but by 1928 he had moved away to Horsham. In the mid '20s, Percy Peyman remembered 30–40 hampers of eggs for hatching being sent out from Watlington station on the afternoon and evening trains. They were apparently left in the waiting room until they could be loaded.

Englands' pheasant farm was at its peak between the wars, when the disappearance of Johnson from the scene was no doubt to their advantage. The farm was equipped with large rearing pens with 10ft high fences, but, as the birds grew, their wings were tied to prevent them flying away. Up to a hundred birds were kept in each pen. Rabbits roamed freely nearby and locals were trusted to shoot them without touching the birds, a code of practice they strictly observed. The pens were occupied between May and September following an October to February breeding season when the chicks were kept in coops. Pheasants' eggs were despatched, between March and June, in hampers packed with straw whilst live pheasants were sent out, twelve to a cage, from July to September. George Howlett recalls the cages being fitted with 'satin covers' whilst porter Charlie Hopkins' son Cyril recalls that if you were lucky, live pheasants being sent out in baskets might lay an egg while they were at the station. If so, it was possible to put your arm through the side of the basket and reach them!

The market for pheasants was threefold, live birds, eggs, and meat. Live birds were sold to other estates, principally in Scotland where they were freed for game shooting. Local customers included the Earl of Macclesfield and Lord Esher. The best eggs were sold to other farms for hatching by other birds, whilst inferior ones were either given away (some went to Messum & Dover, the fishmongers) or hatched and reared for meat. Some eggs were even given to other breeders in the locality, especially if they had a bad season, such was the camaraderie. Customers for the birds sold for meat included Messum & Dover.

Eggs and birds were taken to Watlington station by George England using a horse and cart, and, in the 1930s, a Landrover type vehicle and trailer.

Mr. Pocock recalled live pheasants and pheasants' eggs being sent to all parts of the UK and Ireland and occasionally the continent.

During the war, to meet government requirements, the Englands grew sugar beet and potatoes and virtually abandoned pheasant farming which was never revived on the same scale.

ROADNIGHTS

The 500-600 acre farm, The Priory, in Britwell, just outside Watlington, was bought about 1920 by Sydney Roadnight following the death of former owner Wyndham Stride. Some of the Stride family were employed by Roadnights. At the age of 29, Sydney's nephew, Richard Roadnight, took over in 1936. At this time it was a mixed farm with store cattle (for beef) kept alongside the Priory and in nearby fields, two or three cows for milk for the house, a few chickens and, after the war, sheep for meat.

During the war, potatoes and sugar beet were grown (despite the chalky soil) to meet government needs, and in the mid 1950s some 200 pigs were kept here, each giving two litters a year.

Although Wally Coles could recall sheep for the farm arriving by rail on one occasion, the only really regular use of the railway was sugar beet which was dug up by hand, the top growth cut off and loaded into trailers for hauling by tractor to Watlington station, for despatch to Lincolnshire. When loading into empty coal wagons along the back siding, it was shovelled through the side door to start with, then over the top of the sides. While the men were loading, the tractor went back to the farm for the next trailer. Usually up to four railway wagons were loaded this way during the day, each taking about six trailer loads. During the war years, Mr. Roadnight was issued with permits to requisition railway wagons during a time when they were at a premium. Frank Tredwell recalls that in the early 1950s sugar beet was loaded by Roadnights' men using a mobile elevator.

The refiners produced a sugar beet pulp (sometimes called molasses) for animal feed which was sent back to the farmers. Roadnights again used tractors and trailers to collect the feed from Watlington station, although after the war they had two lorries. At the farm the pulp was mixed with oats and wheat chaff to make "an excellent animal food". Hauliers Hicks of Oxford were sometimes called in to assist if traffic was very heavy. Station staff recall the molasses was received either as large lumps or already crushed.

During and after the war, Roadnights' holding was increased eventually to some 2,500 acres with the purchase of Huntinglands (corn and later pig farming), Upperton Farm (principally corn) and Jones Farm at Britwell Hill (predominantly dairy). Ernie Tappin also farmed at Britwell as a tenant of

Gathering up corn to take to the stacks in 'Little Field' at the back of the Priory.

Loading sheaves of corn. *Photos: Cty. Daphne Roadnight*

Threshing at Roadnights. The straw was collected by Messrs. Ayres and Toomers, both Reading merchants. The machine was hired, probably from Wilders of Wallingford.

Wally Coles, Bert Adams (formerly landlord of The Plough, Britwell), Ted Buckle, Bill Sandford, an unidentified student and Richard Roadnight.

A herd of Hereford beef cattle (usually red and white) being fattened outside 'Chaff Barn' prior to slaughter. The worker in the middle of the yard was Bert Adams.

Joe Sandford loading up manure in the Priory yard. He was an old hand who had come from Essex with the Strides who previously owned the farm.

Photos: Cty. Daphne Roadnight

Electric fencing being laid at tractor speed. The trailer carried posts and reels whilst a prototype Wolseley reel-holder, driven from the trailer's tyre, did the winding or unwinding. In 1954 there were 21 miles of electric fencing on the farm.

The pig shelters for sows and their litters were corrugated iron with timber backs.

Roadnights. When milk production at Jones Farm ceased following the death of the previous owner in 1945, in common with most of the other lands, it was used for arable farming, concentrating on wheat, corn, barley, potatoes, sugar beet, and clover for animal food.

Barley was sold to Morlands Brewery, Abingdon, Simmonds Brewery, Reading, and less often Henley Brewery. Some also went to Dukes of Southampton who owned a large feed mill there. After the war, some was exported via Grimsby Docks, but generally none of this traffic went by rail, although Charlie Rust, one of Roadnights' men, is recalled taking corn to the station about 1950.

When pig farming started in earnest in the mid 1950s, Huntinglands was used, the pigs being kept outside in shelters where the young ones were reared. Roadnights succeeded in producing a cross breed dubbed 'Britwell Blue'.

Moving pigs to Reading market was a two-day affair, involving washing the animals before loading them into Frank Lawrence's lorry. He was a local haulier but, with only one lorry, he hired in extra vehicles.

Beef cattle and sheep were kept near the Priory whilst potatoes and beet were grown in fields known as Foxingtons, Grounds, Coopers, Walled, Cuddington and Pegs Ears. Coopers (Coopers Farm) was used for fattening calves sold on after 12-18 months. A corn drying house was installed alongside the Priory outbuildings and corn was stored in sacks alongside the cattle yard. A combine harvester was purchased in 1941 but threshing machines were still hired in and a couple of horses were retained for chain harrows, corn harvesting and haymaking. Otherwise the stables in the yard were converted for use as garages and tractor stores.

Roadnights, the largest farm in the area, was bounded by mostly mixed farms with, to the north, Harris of Watcombe Manor (who had a few beef cattle), Nixeys in the Easington and Cuxham areas (dairy herd), Christie Millers of Swyncombe (principally corn grower but formerly kept cows and a few sheep) and Phyall of the Grove, Britwell.

During the war, about 7-8 landgirls were employed by Roadnights and, as the war progressed, Italian and sometimes German prisoners of war were also employed. Wally Coles recalls that when supervising them, he "didn't dare get a cigarette out or they all wanted one". Sometimes when this happened, "they would only agree to return to work when they had had a smoke".

Roadnights took on boys from Turners School on the Benson Road. These were deprived lads, but hard workers. Schoolchildren were also employed on Saturday mornings and this was how Wally was introduced to farm work in the 1930s.

The employment of extra labour obviously depended on the crop, but the potato harvest required the most assistance. Potatoes were stored near the Priory and during the war requisitioned by the government as required, but these did not go by rail but were handled by C & G Ayres of Wallingford.

Potatoes and sugar beet were usually harvested from September to January.

One thing regularly received by rail for Roadnights were sacks of artificial manure, which arrived in box vans (often two vehicles), usually just prior to preparing a field for crops. It was either collected with one of Roadnights' trailers or delivered by Tappins. It was spread using a sprinkler affixed to the back of a trailer.

W. R SCHWIER

W. R. Schwier took over the 200-acre Eastfield Farm, near Watlington station in 1932. It was rented from the Earl of Macclesfield and previously occupied by one of the Nixey family. He was a general farmer, keeping a small dairy herd, sheep (before the war) and pigs as well as growing corn. The milk was not sent by rail but sold to the Coop at Wallingford, who picked it up in churns. After the war Jobs Dairy took over the milk.

Schwier also did some dealing in working horses, supplying both local firms like G. E. Stevens of High Wycombe and Aylesbury, and London firms who

Potato planting with a caterpillar D2 tractor driven by Wally Coles. Roadnights had five of these machines. *Photos: Cty. Daphne Roadnight*

sent representatives to Watlington to make a selection. Horses sold were sent to London by train in horse-boxes or cattle wagons, each holding 2-3 animals. Schwier often bought and sold at markets, and occasionally a horse bought at Reading market was delivered by GWR road motor horse-box.

His son Peter remembers incoming horses arriving on the last train or occasionally with the early goods. If the horse-box was at the front of the train, the animals were led away at the side of the station whereas if it was on the rear, they were led out through the pens to avoid disrupting passengers and other activity on the platform.

Schwier also received bagged fertilizer which arrived at Watlington in box vans and was unloaded by his own workers. He also ordered steam coal direct from the colliery and received a 12-ton wagon load about once a year, again unloaded by his workers who took it round to the farm. This steam coal was used for heating and also to power the threshing machine which, after the war, was driven by a diesel engine. Thereafter, Tappins supplied coal for heating.

During the war Schwier employed landgirls from a camp at How Hill.

Maize meal and rice meal arrived by rail in 12-ton opens but brewers grain or wet grain (a biproduct of beer) were roaded to the farm, often weekly, by Tappins and is believed to have come from Henley Brewery. Artificial fertilizer in 2-3cwt sacks was delivered by road from G. E. Stevens of High Wycombe.

After the war, Schwier also sent sugar beet by rail in unsheeted opens and, as with Roadnights, beet pulp was returned for animal feed either in bags or in the form of brickettes or even 'pencils'. Brickettes were popular with some farmers because they took up less room. Peter's father soaked them in an old tin bath kept in one of the outbuildings and worked it into manageable pieces to feed the animals.

We conclude these brief notes on traffic with an extract from an official report which lists traders said to have been using the goods service at Watlington station in 1958:

Government Depot (Command Ordnance Sub Depot)
B. G. Plant, Pyrton Hill House – saw benches
J. Coles & Son, Brook Street, Watlington – hurdles
T. Tappin, Brook Street, Watlington – coal
Valentine Wood & Co. Ltd., Reading – charcoal
Gammon & Woodeard, Brightwell Baldwin – sugar beet
W. M. Harris, Watcomb Manor, Watlington – fertilizer, etc. and sugar beet
R. C. Keen, Manor Farm, South Weston – fertilizer, etc. and sugar beet
E. Nixey, Manor Farm, Cuxham – fertilizer, etc. and sugar beet
R. Roadnight, The Priory, Britwell Salome – fertilizer, etc. and sugar beet
W. R. Schwier, Eastfield Farm, Watlington – fertilizer, etc. and sugar beet
F. H. Stevens, Howe Coombe Farm, Watlington – fertilizer, etc. and sugar beet
G. Strang, Brightwell Farm, Brightwell Baldwin – fertilizer, etc. and sugar beet
Major Whitaker, Britwell House, Watlington – coal
England Bros., The Game Farm, Watlington – live pheasants and pheasants' eggs.

The report also mentioned 'Cake traffic from Birmingham received at Watlington once a week for various consignees' and 'about 40 cartons of tobacco each month are received for H. E. Worley, wholesale tobacconist, Watlington'.

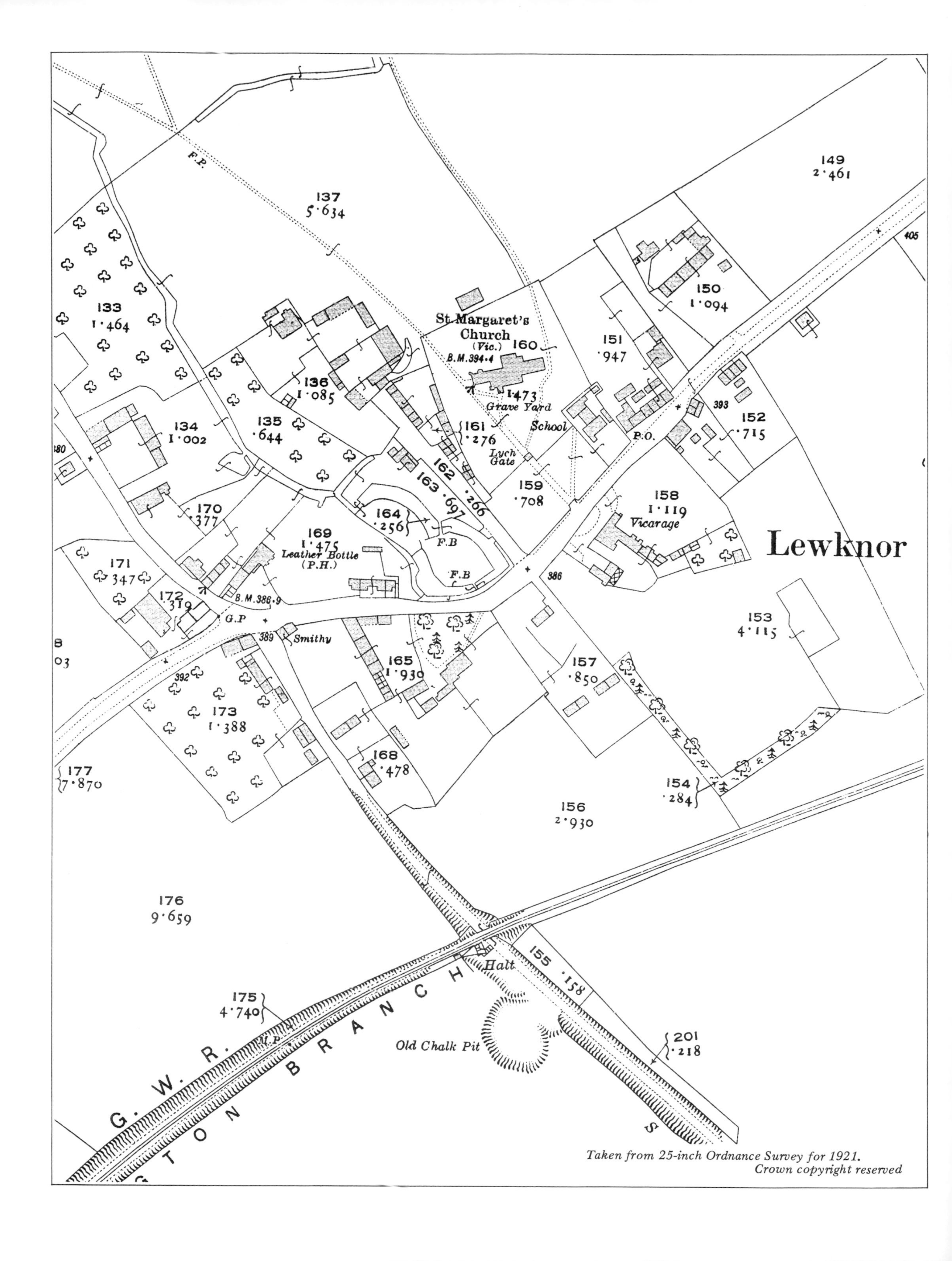

Lewknor
St Margaret's Church (Vic.)
Grave Yard
School
Lych Gate
P.O.
Vicarage
Leather Bottle (P.H.)
Smithy
Halt
Old Chalk Pit
G. W. R.
TON BRANCH
B.M. 394·4
B.M. 386·9
F.B
G.P
F.P.

LEWKNOR BRIDGE HALT 6m 75c

Lewknor Bridge Halt viewed from the roadside in the mid 1950s. The gated approach paths to many halts on the system were provided with boards proclaiming 'Great Western Railway Road Motor Cars will leave this halt [Lewknor?]' etc. and gave times. Whether such a board was originally provided here is not known, but it seems likely. *A. Attewell*

The provision of halts along the Watlington branch, in the longer term at least, did little to dissuade people from the more convenient bus services. In the early 1930s, when Robert Graham was tenant farmer at Linkie Down (sometimes known as Hollybush Farm), above the railway at Lewknor, his three daughters Beryl, Audrey and Molly used the 4.33 p.m. train each day for the return journey from Watlington where they attended a private school. The first train to Watlington in the mornings ran too late to be of any use to them, so they walked down from the farm and under the railway "to the Blacksmiths in Lewknor" where they caught a House Brothers bus which called at the Leather Bottle at 8.31 on its way into Watlington. Of her train ride home, Molly recalls "I was very young at the time and although I cannot remember the journey in detail, I clearly recall seeing Mr Pocock on the train". Reg Pocock would have been making one of his regular visits to Aston Rowant.

Reg's daughter Gwen recalled Mr Hunt, of nearby Manor House, walking up the hill each morning in time for the first train,

Looking south-east away from the village and up the hill towards Linkie Down Farm (now called Hill Farm). The steps to the halt led off to the right on the other side of the bridge. The lane, now truncated by a new road bypassing the village, was known as 'Shiftcutts'. According to official records, this bridge (6m 74c) had 19in wrought iron girders with a square span of 20ft (21ft 6in skew) supported on brick and flint abutments, but subsequent work appears to have obscured the flintwork. The minimum headroom was 15ft 8in. The track was laid on 3in timber decking with ash ballast (1½in on the inside and 3in outside) maintaining the cant on the gentle curve here. This mid-1950s view shows the bridge after some 1950 repairs in which the timber wall plates under the wrought iron plate girders were replaced by concrete bedstones, the timber joists supporting the ends of the floor were replaced by RSJs and the decking renewed. Presumably, the cast stanchions and tubular railings shown here also date from 1950, replacing the timber parapets seen on page 49 of Volume 1. *A. Attewell*

'850' class 0–6–0PT No. 1935 just approaching Lewknor Bridge Halt with the 3.10 p.m. from Watlington on 29th September 1951. A scene for 'My Brother's Keeper', filmed nearby, shows Jack Warner climbing over the lineside fence. Judging from the wobble of the wooden posts, they were certainly in need of replacement by the concrete ones featured here.

Dr. G. D. Parkes

When John Ahern photographed Watlington and Aston Rowant stations in May 1949, the stations were not obviously run down in appearance, but this portrait of Lewknor Bridge Halt gives quite a different impression. During winter months the post at the rear of the platform and the bracket above the entrance of the shelter were used to hold hurricane lamps, which were presumably both lit and extinguished by the late-turn guard.
J. H. Ahern

wearing his 'city gear' complete with bowler hat, briefcase and umbrella.

Certainly in the 1940s, a Lewknor man, who worked at Forest Product Laboratory, Risborough, also caught the first train out and the 5.48 p.m. back, and a Miss Bull from Lewknor often used the halt. Bob Young of Willoughby's Garage, Watlington, occasionally took the train to Lewknor and walked the rest of the way to Adwell when visiting relations.

Looking down to the road from the rear of the tiny platform in the mid-1950s, with the remnants of a former kissing gate still in evidence. *A. Attewell*

'ONE of the most surprising railway stations in our land is that to be found at Aston Rowant, on the little single track ten miles long branch of the GWR from Princes Risborough to Watlington.

'This station is extremely tiny, yet complete in all the ordinary details and equipment of a much larger one. It is very far away from any inhabitation of man, on the high Chiltern Hills, with only one official to act as Station Master, Booking Clerk, Porter, Signalman, navvy and lamplighter all in one. The squirrels come and sit with him in his room, all kinds of birds fly in and out through the doors, open windows and ticket holes of the place. Indeed the whole would serve better as an observation station into the lives of the wild birds and animals of the countryside rather than for a public railway station.

'It would be very interesting to know how many tickets are daily issued at this surprising little station high up against the Chilterns.'

This description, which appeared in the *Thame Gazette* of 22nd April 1924, attributed to the *Weekly Telegraph*, may have been a little tongue-in-cheek, but it was not that much of an exaggeration. In fact, the writer overlooked the chickens opposite the platform, as recalled by Reg Pocock's daughter Gwen in the 1920s, and later, in the 1930s, by Clarence Hailey's daughter.

In the 1920s the station was staffed by just two porters, believed to have been Aubrey Jarmaine, who was certainly there at the time of a break-in in 1914, and Bill Gomme, who

Looking south-west across Aston Rowant station and a winter landscape c.1950. The bridge carrying the busy A40 across the branch was reconstructed and widened in 1925, presumably in connection with road improvements. £3,000 was authorised for the work on 18th December 1925, £2,000 of which was paid for by the Oxfordshire County Council. The road to Stokenchurch climbed away to the left of the picture whilst the Lambert Arms was in the opposite direction some half a mile further along the A40 towards Oxford. The High Wycombe to Oxford bus used to stop, quite unofficially, at the top of the station drive, to pick up passengers. The original bridge (6m 11½c) is officially recorded as having wrought iron girders and curved plate decking, with a span of 14ft (15ft 3in skew) supported on brick and flint abutments (see Volume 1, page 64). The rebuilding of the bridge increased the width between parapets from 34ft 8¼in to 50ft. *J. H. Russell*

ASTON ROWANT STATION

6m 7c

This c.1930 picture, which shows Aston Rowant station after midday, was probably taken on a Sunday when the return of the milk train ran as a goods. The timetable for September 1931 shows the goods leaving Risborough at 9.0 a.m. and calling at Aston Rowant between 9.45 a.m. and 10.0 a.m. Obviously this does not tie in with the shadows but, as this is the most likely explanation for the chaotic spread of items unloaded from a train throughout the length of the platform, we can only assume that, for whatever reason, the goods ran later on this occasion. This scene cannot have been dissimilar to that in the mornings following the unloading of the station truck. The empty baskets at the far end of the platform were being returned from the Lewknor and Tetsworth cress traffic. Tommy Johnson, one-time Watlington sub-ganger, is shown on the right whilst the porter next to him is believed to have been Bill Gomme who transferred to Morris Cowley in 1935. He used to live at Lime Grove, Chinnor, and is said to have left the railway before the war and moved to Norfolk. The other two are thought to have been permanent way men Green and Buckle. The cast iron lamp-post near the nameboard was replaced sometime between 1945 and 1949 when it was replaced by a simple tubular pole on which a hurricane lamp could be hung. These tubular posts, which feature at other stations and halts, may have been old boiler tubes.

Cty. Audrey Griffiths

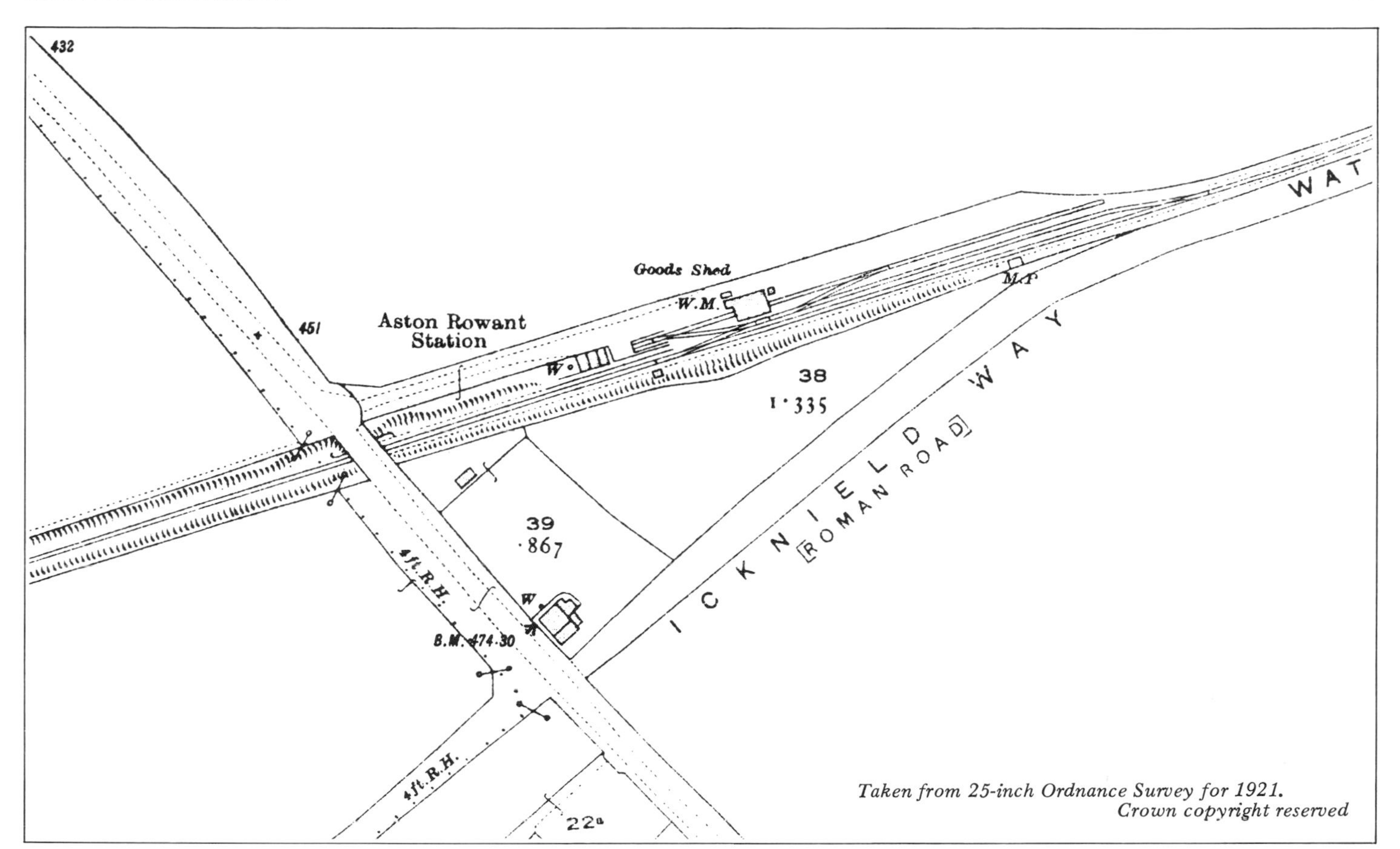

Taken from 25-inch Ordnance Survey for 1921.
Crown copyright reserved

started at Aston Rowant in the 1920s. Aubrey subsequently transferred to Watlington station, possibly in the mid '20s when Harold Blackwell took a porter's vacancy at Aston Rowant.

Born in Carterton, Harold married a Bampton girl c.1920 and moved to Kingston Blount to look after his sister who was ill at the time. They were living above a butcher's shop there by the time he joined the railway. Harold's daughter Joan remembers him taking her to the station on the front of his bicycle on Saturday mornings and watching the breakfast being cooked on the stove in the platelayers hut. She also remembers how it used to taste smoky!

She and her friend used to walk along the track from Kingston to Aston Rowant school 'as there was such a long gap between trains'. When the ground was dry enough, they cut through the gateway on the edge of the goods yard and across the fields to the village. Her father was concerned that she remembered to close the gate across the line at Kingston Crossing.

Ganger Charlie Adby mentioned that Harold used to run an unofficial taxi service as a sideline, leaving the station unattended, but we omitted to ask more about this.

According to local farmer Bill Seymour, some eleven or twelve carts arrived at Aston Rowant station each morning for the milk train, the farmers apparently coming from Crowell, South Weston, etc., and unloading the churns onto the platform through the gateway alongside the station building. As his memories of Aston Rowant stretched as far back as 1912, we cannot pinpoint the date, but occasionally when milk production was high, he had known it to be loaded onto the late goods as well.

A later view from the approach road, showing the gate giving access to the platform. This must have been a busy spot in the mornings when some eleven or twelve carts arrived with churns for the milk train. ***J. H. Ahern***

In the late 1920s, a farmer Browning from Chalford, between Tetsworth and Sydenham, also sent milk to the station in a pony and cart, driven by Cecil Tidmarsh.

Charlie Head of Lewknor gathered sacks of moss — a long grass-like variety — from the hills and brought it to the station on a hand cart. This was sent in the guard's van to

This 1950s portrait of the station features the hand wheel of the pump used to raise water from the well for the station lavatories. When the monogram (on the right) was laid out in chalk in the grass bank opposite the platform, it was flanked by chalk lettering with 'ASTON' on one side and 'ROWANT' on the other, but we have yet to discover a picture of the whole display. It was apparently executed by Charlie Hopkins and Frank Hyde and appeared in the *GWR Magazine* for October 1936. This must have won the approval of Sir Edward Cadogan, a director of the GWR who used to catch the 8.42 a.m. train here each day. He lived above the railway "between the A40 and Kingston Crossing".

Lens of Sutton and GWR Magazine

Another of John Ahern's beautiful photographs, showing Aston Rowant station one Sunday in May 1949, presumably shortly after he had called at Watlington. Sadly, although he continued along the B4009 and photographed Bledlow Bridge Halt, he does not seem to have taken any pictures at Chinnor. ***J. H. Ahern***

London for use in wreaths. Charlie Head was succeeded by Lionel ('Monty') King who, after the war, took moss to the station in a lorry.

When Bill Gomme transferred to Morris Cowley in 1934, his place was taken by Albert Rowe, who moved from Greenford. Harold Blackwell is said to have remained at Aston Rowant until about 1935 when he left the railway. Charlie Hopkins transferred from Watlington that year, presumably taking Harold's place, but we are not sure how long Albert Rowe stayed before his place was taken by Frank Hyde. Both Frank and Charlie Hopkins took great pride in the station garden to the extent of laying out a representation of the newly introduced GWR monogram in pieces of chalk, flanked by lettering for 'Aston' and 'Rowant' in the grass bank opposite the platform. This merited a mention and picture in the *Great Western Magazine* for October 1936.

Frank Hyde was born in Bredwardine, Herefordshire, in 1898 and moved to South Wales when he was 14 years old. After serving in the Royal Marine Artillery, he moved to Watlington with his mother and two sisters, and met his wife Connie. They married in June 1923, by which time he had become a porter at Aylesbury. Connie did not like it there and eventually in 1927 he transferred to Watlington and subsequently to Aston Rowant. From 1928 he lived at The Bungalow, Britwell Road, Watlington, and

Charlie Hopkins at Aston Rowant c.1950. Farmer Leslie Graham recalls "Charlie Hopkins was very helpful and when necessary moved the wagons about for us with a pinchbar." Just after the war, Charlie's son Cyril made wooden lamp stands and sold them at the station. He was proud to say that one was bought by film-star Jack Warner during filming at the station during the 1940s.
Cty. Cyril Hopkins

The station building, another of John Ahern's pictures taken one Sunday in May 1949. Although similar to Watlington, it varied in detail, the most obvious differences being the gable end finials and the absence of shutters securing the forecourt office window. The 1900 timber panelling enclosing the porch appears to have been the same as Watlington, no doubt the work of the same hand. Inside, the accommodation was also similar, with the office on the left being connected to the waiting room/booking hall by a door and a ticket window, a door on the opposite side leading into the ladies waiting room and lavatory. The gentlemen's lavatory was entered through the door in the wall at the near end. As with Chinnor, the standard GWR spear-topped iron railings did much to enhance the scene, but Watlington never received any. Charlie Hopkins was justly proud of the gardens here, and this view gives some idea of how attractive the station must have looked when his prize-winning roses were blooming. The outside-frame goods lock-up in the left background was completed on 12th January 1946 for £16 10s 8d. It was used for parcels, but the sack truck seen here and a broom for sweeping the platform were also kept inside. The corrugated iron shed further left was the lamp shed.

J. H. Ahern

became secretary of Watlington Football Club and the British Legion.

Frank and Charlie made Aston Rowant station very much their own, Frank moving on in 1941 to become a guard, and Charlie remaining there until 1955.

From about 1933, Charlie lived in the High Street in Watlington, cycling to Aston Rowant each day, often with his gun, as he had permission to shoot rabbits in the adjacent fields. He was not only a crack shot, but, having been brought up in the country, he knew how and where to catch rabbits, even by hand, which proved a useful way of supplementing his family's diet.

Before Charlie transferred from Watlington station, his son Cyril remembers, as a boy, visiting his father there. His mother would often send him up with a flask around 11.0 a.m. on Saturday mornings, when Charlie would be doing paperwork in the goods shed office. Cyril was a keen collector of birds' eggs which he found in the trees alongside Watlington station, or even in the goods shed. While he was there, he would also sometimes be given a ride on the footplate during any shunting.

Cyril also collected birds' eggs from the goods shed at Aston Rowant when Charlie moved there, but, with the journey involved, he visited him less often. Incidentally, Cyril recalled that outwards passenger-related traffic at this time included watercress from Edward Smith in Lewknor and honey from Stokenchurch. A farmer Smith from Lewknor, 'near the church', also apparently had beds at Ewelme 'part time', his cress being taken to Aston Rowant station with a pony and coster barrow. Fireman Tom Saunders recalled 'considerable' quantities of watercress from Lewknor and Tetsworth, whilst Fred Collins, who worked for Hopkins coal merchants, said cress went out from Aston at 9.0 a.m., 3.0 p.m. and 'several baskets' at 7.0 p.m.

When the war came and station name-boards were removed all over the system, Charlie and Frank's chalk name and monogram also had to be dug out of the grass embankment. It was never reinstated.

The construction of the MoD at Watlington and the airfield at Chalgrove meant supplies of materials, military vehicles and arms all had to be coped with at Watlington in addition to regular traffic. Such was the congestion that some of the MoD traffic was sent to Aston Rowant yard instead. Tappins, the main Watlington coal merchants, had even been known to receive supplies at Aston Rowant because their wagons just could not be accommodated at the terminus. Sidney Shirley, who also worked for Hopkins, coal merchants, recalls such overflow traffic still appearing at Aston Rowant occasionally in the early 1950s.

Charlie was very conscientious about keeping the goods shed locked, but even more so when boxes for the MoD were in there waiting for collection.

When Frank left to become a guard, Eve Elliot was conscripted as a woman porter to replace him. She was there until 1945 when Laurie Johnson succeeded her.

Laurie had left school in 1935 and worked in the Stokenchurch chair industry, then for Pressed Steel at Cowley. His father was the Watlington ganger, and at some point before the war Laurie was recruited by Mr. Pocock for a porter's vacancy at Watlington. He spent the war years in the RAF and, after being demobbed, approached Reg Pocock for re-employment, which is how he came to take the place of Eve Elliot.

When he was on early turn, Laurie's day began cycling in from Watlington to unlock the station and issue tickets to the five or so regular workers for 'the early train' for

Some of the Watlington branch PW men at Aston Rowant around 1930. As explained on page 238 of Vol. 1, details of PW staff have proved difficult to find but this view shows (from left to right) Walter Hopkins, Paddy Darmody, Tommy Johnson, Bob Johnson, Charlie Adby and Fred Price, the ganger who lived at Wainhill Crossing. A pump trolley was kept at Aston Rowant, but is said to have only been used on Good Fridays. An Edwardian official site plan shows a hut and run-off boarding for a velocipede, to the north of the PW hut. This shed seems to have survived into the 1930s, as Charlie Adby recalled the pump trolley being "kept in a shed alongside the PW hut."

Cty. Charlie Adby

The wooden cabin for Aston Rowant West ground frame was a standard GWR design, presumably provided shortly after the GWR took over the line. A similar one was provided at Chinnor. This view, looking north towards Princes Risborough in glorious sun on 16th August 1955, features the 6 ton military style OW series Bedford owned by Hopkins Brothers, coal merchants. To the right of this scene, the Icknield Way was on higher ground, on the other side of the trees, but the line gradually converged with it, approximately where it can be seen curving to the left in the distance.

J. N. Faulkner

The forecourt elevation of the station building c.1950 showing the main door which, like Watlington, was unused because of a parcels weighing machine blocking it on the other side. Again the office at the far end was fitted with brown lino. A shelf ran across below the forecourt window, beneath which was a safe (in the near corner). There was a cupboard below the other window overlooking the platform, and another one beneath the booking desk which ran along inside the ticket window. There was also a simple table against the south wall. Charlie Hopkins spoke of a drinking trough at the Chinnor end of the station, being used by horses from Aston Stud, but this does not seem to feature in any of the pictures.
J. H. Russell

Risborough. When it left, he sent six beats on the bell, which told Mrs Jarmaine at Kingston Crossing that it was on its way, so that she would open the gates.

During the winter months, he had to light the station fires, one in the office and one in the ladies waiting room, then it was down to the yard to see what wagons had been left by the early goods train. They were generally just coal wagons, perhaps four or five of them left to the north of the goods shed. The wagons had to be checked in and the customers advised of their arrival, but the goods shed office was not used for clerical work and was empty by this time. All the paperwork was done in the station office.

The goods shed itself, dubbed 'the drying shed' by Charlie, was then only used when the crane was needed, to shelter a loading operation, or as a lock-up. The weighbridge was used by local farmers and lorry owners, sometimes to check the weight of their vehicles for relicensing.

The return of the workmen's train was empty stock, but even the second up train, which made the London connection, was of little moment at Aston Rowant where only one or two commuters joined it. Apart from the occasional boarder at the beginning and end of terms, there were not even any schoolchildren. However, the return train, the 10.22 ex Risborough, conveyed the station truck, which Laurie remembers at the rear of the train.

Anything for Aston Rowant was unloaded on the platform and typically included castings for the chair industry at Stokenchurch, Wills cigarettes from Bristol for the Red Lion at Stokenchurch, and bottled beer for the Lambert Arms, half a mile down the A40. In earlier years, beer arrived in casks. As with his predecessors, Laurie delivered the beer to the Lambert Arms on a sack truck and, in time-honoured tradition, was rewarded with a free pint for his trouble. Charlie was similarly rewarded for cycling out to Stokenchurch to deliver cigarettes to the Red Lion.

As traffic was gradually lost to the roads, there was less traffic for the branch to handle, but nowhere was this more obvious than at Aston Rowant station. As Laurie remarked, 'It was so far away from some of the villages'. After the hustle and bustle at Watlington when he first joined the railway, he found the inactivity at Aston Rowant in the postwar years deadly. 'It could be very boring'.

As there were so few passengers and not much in the way of goods to deal with, interruptions like the arrival of the permanent way gang, local farmers, or the coal merchants, provided a welcome break from the monotony. Charlie Hopkins often made a cup of tea and took it out to Hopkins' coalmen. He was always helpful and sometimes even loaded bags for them. Whenever their employer, 'Nibbo', was on the lorry, he would go up to the office with Charlie and enjoy a good natter, but, knowing how difficult it could be to get away afterwards, he forbade his employees to do the same!

Charlie and Laurie only saw each other briefly each day when they changed shifts at 2.0 p.m. Any loading in the yard was normally carried out single-handed, often in the goods shed in the case of a sheeted load. The porters managed to get the heavy sheets into position themselves but the roping was done between them at hand-over time. They do not appear to have had an overlap in hours, so this may have been an unofficial arrangement.

Looking north towards the goods shed from the end loading dock c.1950. The 15 ton weighbridge, GW No. 292, measured 16ft x 8ft and dated from 1917 when it replaced a smaller 33 year old 5 ton machine at a cost of about £90. Although the goods shed was extremely similar to the one at Watlington, the weighbridge at Aston Rowant was sited at the south end of the building and just shows on the edge of this picture. The weigh office must have projected inside the goods shed like the one at Watlington. The sleeper-built enclosure in front of the lean-to office was used for station coal. An earlier official site plan shows a similar enclosure at the opposite end of the building instead. The end loading dock in the foreground had been used for loading horses from Aston Stud. An index book in the divisional office at Reading listed a drawing for Aston Rowant horse dock on 30th December 1932, which presumably dates the concrete and blue brickwork evident in this and other pictures. This ties in conveniently with the prior establishment of Aston Stud. Lengthman Charlie Adby recalled pit props from Stokenchurch being loaded here in earlier years. It is believed that the last cattle to be unloaded at Aston Rowant (sometime during the early 1950s) were for farmer Robert Graham of Church Farm, Lewknor. The consignment was destined for Chinnor for collection by farmer Hill of Crowell, but because his farm had not been tested for TB at the time, they were instead purchased by Robert Graham. *J. H. Russell*

Another view of the goods shed in May 1949, showing how similar it was to the one at Watlington. The hinged door on the near end (see page 54) had been removed since 1941. Of the days when wagons were collected in the evenings by the up goods, Harry Humphreys recalled that they would "fetch the wagons, put them in the loop, run round them and put them on the train".

J. H. Ahern

In Laurie's time, wheat, straw and sugar beet were loaded in the yard for despatch, whilst incoming goods included sugar beet pulp which arrived in opens.

Neither porter saw the goods trains as the yard was serviced before the early-turn man was on duty, and the evening goods, which rarely called anyway, went through after the station was closed.

In Laurie's time, Reg Pocock only visited about once a week to look at the books and have a cup of tea with the late-turn man. Evidently, the lack of business in the postwar years would have made a more frequent check on the books pretty pointless. Apart from this inspection, the porters were on their own, so anything like the amount to charge for unusual fares was obtained over the telephone from Risborough.

It is difficult to describe any more of a typical working day, simply because the main problem for the porter in charge at Aston Rowant was passing the time during long periods of inactivity. It could be a lonely vigil.

Even the arduous task of pumping water from the well to fill the tank in the roof which supplied the station lavatories with 'not drinking water', was only necessary about once a fortnight, because there were so few passengers. According to Laurie, it was just as well, because 'it took a hell of a long time to get water'. The staff did not trust the supply for tea-making, so they took flasks in with them.

In the winter months, besides the two fires, there were the oil lamps to tend. There had been a proper one mounted on a cast-iron post at the Chinnor end of the platform, but this became defective in Laurie's time and was replaced by hurricane lamps, two hung on rather more utilitarian posts on the platform, one above the seat inside the porch and one in the office. They often blew out in bad weather. If anyone wanted to use the lavatories during the hours of darkness, they borrowed the hand-signal lamp which was used to give the 'right away'.

The late-turn porter locked up and went home around 8.30 p.m.

The introduction of the Zonal delivery system in 1947 replaced the station truck and removed the lingering 'smalls' traffic from Aston Rowant. Thereafter it was delivered by the Zonal lorry from Thame, which,

The north end of the goods shed in May 1949. Unfortunately, we have not discovered any photos of the forecourt elevation of this building.

J. H. Ahern

driven by Eddie Smith, called at the station each day.

In the postwar years, the station was used for scenes in at least four British films, *The Captive Heart* (1946) with Michael Redgrave, Mervyn Johns, Basil Radford, Jack Warner, Jimmy Hanley, Gordon Jackson and Guy Middleton; *My Brother Jonathan* (1947) with Michael Denison, Ronald Howard, Dulcie Gray, Stephen Murray, Finlay Currie, Beatrice Varley, James Robertson Justice, James Hayter, Wilfred Hyde White and Thora Hird; *My Brother's Keeper* (1948) with Jack Warner, George Cole, David Tomlinson, Bill Owen, Brenda Bruce, Beatrice Varley, Wilfred Hyde White, Maurice Denham, Valentine Dyall and Christopher Lee; and *Portrait of Clare* (1950) with Margaret Johnson, Ronald Howard and Richard Todd.

The filming took place on Sundays when there were no public services. Frank Tredwell was the driver on 4th September 1949 for *Portrait of Clare*.

Perhaps prompted by a vacancy at Chinnor, it was eventually decided to dispense with one of the porters' positions at Aston Rowant, and in 1949 Laurie Johnson was transferred to Chinnor, leaving Charlie Hopkins as the sole member of staff, working from 7.0 a.m. to mid afternoon. After he had gone home, the guard collected

the tickets and attended to the platform lamps.

Charlie must have realised that the paucity of traffic was leading towards the inevitable end. Nevertheless, he still took pride in keeping the station immaculate and was very protective of his territory to the extent that he would never allow the coal merchants access to the weighbridge office in the goods shed. In short, even with his friends, he made sure that everything was in order and remained protective towards the station which he had lovingly tended for all those years. Laurie remembers him as 'a solid, dependable man of long standing.'

GOODS TRAFFIC

Aston Rowant station was used to receive traffic for Lewknor, Postcombe, Tetsworth and Stokenchurch. Predictably, outgoing goods traffic was largely hay and straw whilst incoming traffic included animal feed, fertilizer, seed potatoes, and. of course, coal.

As with Watlington and Chinnor, there are memories of locally-cut timber being sent out from Aston Rowant station during the Great War. Daniel Moore, who had a sawmill at Stokenchurch, supplied the cottage industry of furniture making, and was very busy at the time providing trench props which local farmhand Bill Seymour recalls being brought in with a team of two or three horses. The props were piled high in the goods yard for despatch to the ports, a rail-mounted crane being stationed there for loading. The goods yard was apparently so full with stacked timber at one time that the gate to the field on the western boundary of

This c.1950 view of the site clearly shows the dip under the bridge and climb on the other side towards Watlington. The five-bar gate in the western boundary, as mentioned in the text, was further down the yard to the right of this picture. Opening onto the adjoining fields, it is said to have been provided for manure traffic, but, whatever the reason, it was certainly useful as a quiet access for racehorse traffic. Farmer Leslie Graham recalls "Towards the end of the war, some crates of parts arrived for a combined harvester but they were too heavy for the crane, so they were diverted to Thame". As the only crane at the site was the 30 cwt one in the goods shed, a larger rail-mounted crane had to be sent for to handle exceptional loads. Random surviving CME Department paperwork reveals three such occasions: 'Lend 12 ton steam crane to the Goods Department for use at Aston Rowant', on 13th, 14th and 27th February 1946. *J. H. Russell*

A companion view to the picture on the previous page, this time looking towards Kingston Crossing and showing the end of the sidings and the permanent way hut. The loop siding was lengthened and connected to the running line in 1912. Fireman Tony Benham said one of the few occasions when the northern loop entry was used during the late 1940s/early 1950s was either when the auto-trailer, with passengers on board, was backed onto the loop to collect a horse-box from the dock, or when running round a Watlington-bound train to put the whole formation into the loop in order to place a horse-box in the dock. Horse-boxes were invariably put on the front of the trailer in the bay at Risborough, but in his time there were only two or three a year.
J. H. Russell

the yard was pushed open to ease movement past it all.

Bates, a furniture manufacturer at Stokenchurch, also sent out tables and chairs, apparently bundled in sizes with appropriate packing. Much of his output, however, went by road to High Wycombe.

Charlie Adby, who started in the Watlington permanent way gang in 1929, also recalls pit props from Stokenchurch, and more locally from woods belonging to John Clerke-Brown, being loaded at the dock.

The main farmer in the area seems to have been Harry Blake, who, having sold land in Chinnor to W.E. Benton c.1912, then moved to Woodway Farm at Aston Rowant. This had formerly been part of the Thomas Taylor estate and included Woodway Cottages where the Aston Rowant station master was living. Bill Seymour and his father, who had worked with Blake at Chinnor, also moved to live in Woodway Cottages.

Bill recalls taking hay and straw to the station by horse and cart and loading it into wagons there ready for the porter to sheet and rope. It was sent out on the evening goods, much of it apparently to the GWR stables at Paddington, which sent return loads of manure in open wagons. Bill believes the gate in the western boundary fence was installed in connection with the distribution of manure to local farmers, but this is difficult to establish.

Bill did not recall any regular flow of animals using the station, and his employer, who also had land at Eynsham, found it more expedient when moving his cows there for grazing, to drive the 300-strong herd along the road for loading at Thame station. They set out around 4.0 a.m. with Mr. Blake following behind in his 'tin lizzie'.

Farmer Brown of Town Farm, Lewknor (near the watercress beds), took milk to the station each day, but he appears to have been succeeded at Town Farm by the Jones family. Other farmers using Aston Rowant station included Browning of Chalford Manor, Holmes of Hill Farm, Lewknor, Robert ('Bing') Graham of Church Farm, Lewknor, and Green, who had two farms, one at South Weston and the other along the main road between Lewknor and Watlington. Robert Graham had been the tenant of Linkie Down Farm, to the east of Lewknor Bridge Halt, but in 1935 he moved to take over Church Farm from the Smith family, and around 1947 additionally took over Field Farm between Lewknor and Shirburn.

Robert Graham's son Leslie recalls collecting fertilizer from the station, as did farmers Browning and Holmes. 'Each farmer had his own van which was positioned in the siding beyond the goods shed so we could back our tractor and trailer up to them. It took several trips to and from the farm to clear it.' The trailer held about 3 tons. 'Sometimes the bags had slipped in transit and it was difficult to open the sliding door when they had got wedged against it.' Occasionally, the fertilizer arrived in sheeted opens 'but the rain often got in'. The fertilizer was produced by ICI and ordered from Donaldsons in Watlington. There were three main types which all arrived in paper sacks: potash in 2cwt bags, basic slag 1cwt bags and sulphate of ammonia 1cwt bags.

Farmer Frank Holmes remembers that before the war they also received imported animal feed by rail. There were two types, cotton seed from Egypt, and linseed cake.

'During the war we had to become largely self-sufficient and afterwards we purchased it from Donaldsons and collected it from Watlington.'

He also recalls that during the war, 'we were more than encouraged to grow sugar beet or potatoes . . . our soil was really only suitable for the beet. It was taken down to Aston Rowant station and forked into empty coal wagons and sent away for refining. I believe it went to Kidderminster'. Despatch was strictly regulated by a government department and farmers were issued with loading permits to avoid congestion at the refineries. Frank Holmes devoted about 20 acres a year to beet, which yielded about 15–20 tons per acre. Farmers Jones and Browning also grew sugar beet, most of which was loaded away in January. 'Charlie Hopkins let us warm ourselves around his fire and made us all a cup of tea.'

Frank also remembered calves arriving from Wiltshire c.1946 but 'we didn't send cattle away . . . they were sold locally for slaughter'. Sheepdogs arrived in the passenger brake van. 'We always tried to get Scottish sheepdogs because they are the best.'

In the immediate postwar years, Art Paris of Stockwells timber merchants recalled calves arriving in the guard's compartment of the auto-trailer. These small creatures for farmer Will Hodges of Gordons Farm, Aston Hill, 'travelled in sacks with their heads poking out'.

Laurie Johnson confirmed that during this period, there was still some hay and straw traffic despatched in one or two sheeted opens at a time, whilst incoming traffic again included sugar beet pulp for animal feed.

In the early 1950s, some farmers also received bags of seed potatoes from Ireland and Scotland, which arrived in box vans. Blue-dyed stock potatoes also arrived in unsheeted wagons, all this traffic usually being unloaded and collected by the farmers, although Hopkins were sometimes hired to deliver it to the farms.

TIMBER

In the mid-1950s, G.C. Stockwell (Hardwood) Ltd, who traded from Mill Road, Stokenchurch, received rough-cut planks of beech from Bucksburn, Aberdeen. Apparently from storm-damaged forests, the timber arrived in 12ft lengths stacked in

Aston Rowant East ground frame, provided in 1912, controlled entry to the north end of the loop and was locked by a key on the train staff. The simple wooden cover would originally have been fitted with a hinged door. ***M. Wallen***

Cecil Tutty at the side of the Fleur de Lys public house, Stokenchurch, in the early 1930s, with the second-hand Chevrolet.

The Dodge lorry used by Daniel Moore.

Daniel Moore with a bow bending bench template at the back of the Fleur de Lys.

open wagons which arrived two or three at a time. Art and Roy Paris and Terry Sears unloaded the planks from wagons on the coal road to a lorry backed up to the wagon.

COAL MERCHANTS

JARMAINE & SON

William Thomas Jarmaine, known as 'Gerry', was a coal merchant at Aston Rowant, near the Lambert Arms, from about 1893, around the time his son Aubrey was born. He had previously been a farm labourer but borrowed £50 from his wife to start the business.

Bill Seymour said Jarmaine collected coal from Aston Rowant station and ran a carrier's service in connection with local markets and events like the Watlington Fair and the Thame Show. He had a horse and cart and a wagonette, which apparently doubled for passenger carrying by placing forms inside for seating. He even ran an unofficial bus service to Oxford and High Wycombe carrying six passengers, three along each side.

The coal cart was painted black with white lettering 'Jarmaine & Son, Coal Contractors'.

According to the bankruptcy report in the *Thame Gazette* for 13th June 1905, the coal and cartage business led him into debt with his supplier W.V. Baines & Co. Ltd. and Weedon Brothers, who must also have helped him out. He had apparently struggled to make ends meet for some time because in 1902 he had attempted to supplement his income by farming 5 acres of land at Lewknor and 5 acres at Postcombe. However, the crops failed due to wire worm.

He was very obliging and was helped out by his young son Aubrey. However, fate was certainly not kind to him because shortly before going bankrupt he had even lost an eye from a stray splinter while he was chopping wood.

It is not clear whether William Thomas did any more work in the coal or cartage business afterwards, but Aubrey joined the GWR as a porter at Aston Rowant, and in the 1920s lived at No. 2 The Council Houses, Lewknor, still dealing with coal from his father's yard near the Lambert Arms. Aubrey also ran a carrier service, taking chickens to market in Maidenhead.

This 1930s Bedford belonged to Hopkins Brothers and besides the coal business was used for cartage work. It is seen here well loaded with chairs from one of the local manufacturers.
Cty. Mrs. C. Hopkins

DANIEL MOORE

By 1903, Daniel Moore, landlord of the Fleur de Lys in Stokenchurch, was listed as a coal merchant. For many years he collected supplies from Aston Rowant station, using a pony and cart. The steep climb up Stokenchurch Hill restricted him to loads of 1 ton at a time, and even then he would stop part way up to give the pony 'Topsy' a rest. When stationary, the weight of the cart was taken from the pony by the use of 'skids' placed under the rear wheels. These 'skids' were stowed on the side of the cart. Moore delivered to Stokenchurch, Ibstone, Ewelme, Stoke Talmage, Adwell, etc. His regular customers ordered coal from the pub but it was also hawked from door to door.

Coal was kept at the Fleur de Lys where there were also stables. Furthermore, wood, gathered from the large estates in and around Stokenchurch, and cut up on site using hand saws, was taken for storage behind the pub using a trailer hauled by a team of two or three horses. Other pieces were carted there by lorry. This wood was sold to the local furniture industry, for which walnut was particularly popular. Walnut trees were sometimes literally bought and cut down from the front lawns of local houses and manhandled onto the lorry or trailer, several men pushing them up 'skids'.

The Moore family were evidently skilled craftsmen, for Daniel's son Jacky (Ernest John) made furniture at the back of the pub and was an expert at 'bow bending' for chairbacks, a skill he learned from his father. Daniel's other son Harold made tennis rackets in London.

By the 1920s, the horses were supplemented by lorries, starting with a secondhand Chevrolet, PP 7651, bought from Towersey coal merchant Banbrook. In the 1930s this was supplemented by a new Dodge, APP 759, purchased from Mr Leverett of Suckling Garage, Stokenchurch. Cecil Tutty, who ran the coal side of the business, drove the Dodge, which his son Cyril recalls enabled larger quantities to be collected from Aston Rowant station. Cecil, who lived at Postcombe, used to cycle to Stokenchurch each day, but subsequently took the Dodge home with him each night and started the day by going direct to Aston Rowant to collect supplies. Cyril remembers helping his father bag the coal and being given chocolate from the machine in the station as a reward. He also recalls how windy it was in the yard, particularly in the winter when 'it paid to keep your head below solebar level to avoid the bitter winds'.

Other lorry drivers for Moores were Ernie Hay, Tom Pollett and Dan Ayres.

Moores received about two or three wagons of coal a week, supplies including 'Coventry nuts', a small shiny coal.

When Daniel Moore died in the late 1930s, he bequeathed the business to Cecil Tutty, but he declined to take it on and so it passed to Daniel's son Jacky. Cecil continued to handle the coal but Jacky appears to have been more interested in expanding the timber merchants side of the business, investing in a sawmill at Stokenchurch, along the Oxford Road, near to the Police Station. In 1939, E.J. Moore was listed as a coal and timber merchant.

Moore and others at Stokenchurch also produced chair components which were despatched by rail from either West Wycombe or High Wycombe stations. They were taken there by a carrier called Simmonds.

In 1945, the whole business was taken over by a Theodore Gillett, who operated from the same premises, Cecil Tutty continuing to work for him until his retirement. Gillett had a 3 ton Commer Lorry which doubled for timber and coal, but during the 1950s he phased out the coal sales and concentrated on timber.

HOPKINS BROTHERS

Herbert Hopkins, one of several brothers, came from Highbury in North London, where his father had a brewers engineering company making bottle-washing plant and associated equipment. After suffering bouts of tuberculosis, Herbert was advised by his doctor to move to the country.

By 1911 he had taken over Ye Olde Kings Arms Hotel at Stokenchurch where the local directory also listed him as a coal merchant and contractor, with 'motor accommodation and petrol stocked'. He had also taken a small farm at nearby Coopers Court.

Coal deliveries were made by horse and cart, and Hopkins ran a Landau service between Stokenchurch and Aston Rowant station. He is also said to have been one of the first in Stokenchurch to own a car.

Around 1920 his health was failing, so his eldest son Cyril left Borlase School in Marlow to help him run the business. By this time, he had relinquished the Kings Arms to concentrate on coal. Herbert died shortly afterwards and by 1928 the business was under the name of his wife Alice. She was helped by Cyril who, by 1931, took control, but only under the strong influence of his mother.

When Cyril became involved, the delivery area was limited by the horse and cart, so in 1924 he bought a lorry from London, testing it around the streets before he brought it home. The motor lorry not only increased the area for coal deliveries but also enabled him to take on deliveries and removals. He also served the chair and furniture industry and even carried pit props to the station.

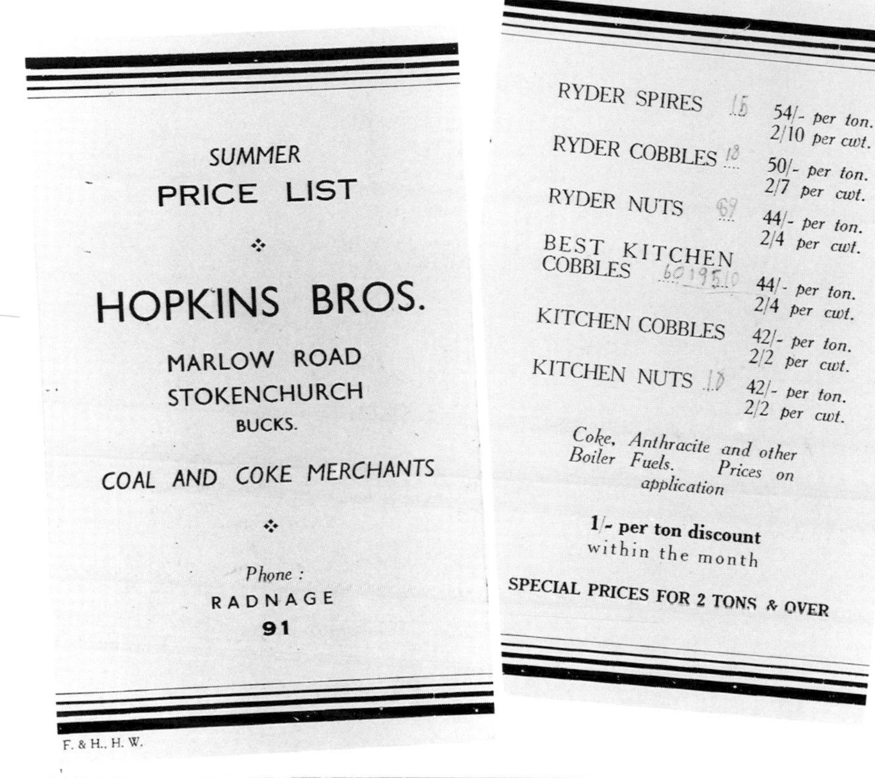

SUMMER
PRICE LIST

HOPKINS BROS.

MARLOW ROAD
STOKENCHURCH
BUCKS.

COAL AND COKE MERCHANTS

Phone:
RADNAGE
91

F. & H., H. W.

RYDER SPIRES	54/- per ton.	2/10 per cwt.
RYDER COBBLES	50/- per ton.	2/7 per cwt.
RYDER NUTS	44/- per ton.	2/4 per cwt.
BEST KITCHEN COBBLES	44/- per ton.	2/4 per cwt.
KITCHEN COBBLES	42/- per ton.	2/2 per cwt.
KITCHEN NUTS	42/- per ton.	2/2 per cwt.

Coke, Anthracite and other Boiler Fuels. Prices on application

1/- per ton discount
within the month

SPECIAL PRICES FOR 2 TONS & OVER

When Fred ('Bacca') Collins joined the firm as a driver in the 1920s, coal was stored behind the Barley Mow, but by 1935 Cyril's youngest brother Eric had joined him, and Hopkins Brothers had an office and yard at Dunroamin in Marlow Road, Stokenchurch. Hopkins also rented 60 sq yds of wharfage at Aston Rowant station, where a large bunker alongside the north end of the sidings held some 300 tons. The earliest lorry recalled was a 30 cwt Chevrolet. This was joined by what 'Bacca' referred to as a 5-ton 'bullnose' Bedford. These were replaced by Austins.

Hopkins brought some of their coal from factors, Browns of Oxford, who also sold them two wagons. These were different colours, one a reddish (bauxite?) colour and the other grey, but they were both signwritten 'HOPKINS' with black lettering shaded grey (could this have been white lettering shaded black?) which might indicate that they were purchased before the company became Hopkins Brothers. Browns' own wagons also continued to appear with deliveries.

Cyril suffered ill health and left the company in 1949, when he moved to Folkestone and bought a guest house.

'Bacca' Collins also retired in 1948 and was replaced by Bob Bird, who was asked to help Eric during two weeks demob leave and stayed for eighteen years! The other driver during the early 1950s was Sidney Shirley.

At this time, Hopkins had two Bedford lorries, a 5-ton tipper used for bulk deliveries, and a 6-ton military style O series, an ex-Army vehicle, which had a horizontal bar across the front. This was unofficially used to nudge wagons along the siding if they were not positioned conveniently — 'but only if Charlie Hopkins wasn't around!' More conventionally, such moves were made using a towing chain secured to the wagon coupling. At this time, the lorries were painted dark blue but apparently without any signwriting.

Sid and Bob worked from 8.0 a.m. to 5.0 p.m. or sometimes later, and enjoyed a good working relationship. They had a happy time on their rounds and were always busy; even in slack periods they repaired coal sacks or did gardening for the Hopkins family.

Coal arrived in large quantities, especially in the summer when they took advantage of lower prices — £1 a ton cheaper (it was sold for four shillings a hundredweight). Hopkins often received about four wagons a week, but there could be anything up to ten wagons on hand at any one time.

Supplies came principally from Birley, Arley and Birch Coppice Collieries and hard coal from Spiers and Deep Main, Coventry. They also received Yorkshire coal, Welsh anthracite, Derby Brights, Coalite, Phurnacite, nutty slack (which, 'basically dust', was bought by the older generation for small fires) and Donkey Nobbles (compressed coal dust for overnight boilers). They also received coke by rail from Birmingham Gas Works, although later this was delivered to their yard at Stokenchurch by road from High Wycombe Gas Works.

When setting out on their rounds in the morning, Sid and Bob usually went to Lewknor, Kingston Blount, Chinnor and Stokenchurch, then, after an hour for lunch, they would cover the Stokenchurch and Lewknor areas in reverse, depending, of course, on requirements. They could

This picture shows what is thought to have been a model T Ford, perhaps the lorry bought from London in 1924. ***Cty. Mrs. C. Hopkins***

deliver about 12 tons a day. Hopkins successfully tendered for schools and had the occasional wagon load order for large houses in the area including Aston House where the tipper lorry was useful for delivering coal to the cellar. During the wartime rationing, the larger houses had been restricted. Bulk deliveries, made with the tipper lorry, were checked on the weighbridge at the station by Charlie Hopkins.

Normally coal was bagged straight off the wagon, each 1 cwt sack being checked on the portable scales, then being lifted into the lorry. When enough coal had been shovelled out, the scales were lifted inside the wagon so the sacks could be weighed there and transferred to the back of the lorry. This avoided having to lift them from the ground. By Sid's time, the steel-bodied mineral wagons had become fairly commonplace and were much easier to shovel supplies from, compared to the ageing planked floors of the traditional wooden ones. The larger 20-ton steel mineral wagons were even more popular with Sid and Bob.

In the mornings, Charlie Hopkins would remove the wagon labels and chalk the names of the merchants on the side, before disappearing back into the station to do the paperwork. On one occasion Kingston Merchant Don Benning's wagon was mistakenly marked up for Hopkins, who took most of the contents before the error was realised! However, it was remedied by letting Benning have one of theirs, presumably of a similar grade.

Sid and Bob were keen enough on bagging game to carry a 12-bore shotgun in the cab of the lorry in case something turned up on their rounds. Sid remembers the Icknield Way was particularly rich in game. They also shot the occasional rabbit in the field alongside the goods yard, but this did not seem to go down all that well with Charlie, who had permission to shoot there. One day when Sid and Bob found a stuffed pheasant on a rubbish tip, they propped it up securely in a convincing manner and waited for Charlie to spot it. As already mentioned, he was quite a marksman, and, unsuspecting their little joke, could not understand why the bird would not fall when he shot it!

They all got on well together and Sid and Bob never hesitated to help out with any deliveries for the railway. They even carted some basic slag fertilizer to a farmer in the Tetsworth/Postcombe area. This was not a popular load because it proved just as dusty as coal and gave off a bad smell!

Eric Hopkins died in 1964

Hopkins' Bedford delivery lorry at Jubilee Road, Stokenchurch, in the 1950s, with Bob Bob Bird and Sid Shirley on the pavement. ***Cty. Bob Bird***

Mares in the stable yard.

ASTON PARK STUD

Aston Stud was started in 1928 by Clarence Hailey, who came from Clare in Suffolk. He was born in 1867 and is said to have been the first racehorse photographer in the country. He owned a bloodstock agency based at Jermyn Street in the City of London and travelled all over the world to view horses for clients. He specialised in buying sprinters and stayers for flat racing.

It was therefore with considerable skills that he set up a new stud farm at Aston Rowant. It was established on part of the Aston House Estate, close to the church, the existing stables buildings having been part of the farm. Clarence had lived at Surbiton for many years, but was living at Epsom while their new home at Aston Rowant was being prepared.

From the outset it enjoyed success with the stallion Trigo, which won the Derby for Barnett in 1929. Barnett, a bachelor, bought Aston Stud in the early 1930s apparently as something of a hobby. He even bequeathed it back to the Hailey family, but unfortunately omitted to sign the will.

At one time Cecil Tidmarsh was a groom, and his son Jim also worked there, but not at the same time. In the 1920s, Cecil had worked for Mr Head,

Trigo in the stallion's paddock. *Photos cty. Peter Norman*

The stud manager's cottage.

Saunders and Criss Cross on their daily walk in the local lanes.

a cockney who lived at Lewknor (Head, incidentally, sent sacks of moss to London). He subsequently took various farming jobs and, in the early 1930s, seasonal work at Attington Stud, which was situated between the Lambert Arms and Tetsworth. Afterwards he worked for Clarence Hailey as stud groom before and after the war. When he was laid off at the stud farm, he worked on the land, spending a long time on the Beechwood Estate.

When Jim worked there as one of four stable lads in the 1930s, the stud was managed by Clarence Hailey Junior and the groom was Harry Horne. Jim's day was from 7.0 a.m. until 5.0 p.m. and his first job was to feed the mares. There were usually between 30 and 40 of them in their own boxes in the main stable block. Harry Horne dished out the food in buckets and the lads fed it to the animals. The food was mainly oatmeal, supplemented once a week with linseed oil which was mixed in with it. The lads also replenished the feed nets which hung from the rafters and ensured the mares exercised their neck muscles while reaching for it.

After feeding, they were exercised, great care being taken to ensure the ground was suitable; if it was too frosty, there was a danger of them falling. This was never done later than about 2.0 p.m. and, while the boxes were empty, the lads could muck them out and line the floor with fresh straw. The mares were fed again in the afternoon.

Food and straw were supplied by Mr. Britnell of Sydenham, who also disposed of the manure and soiled straw.

The mares and colts were given the freedom of the 'running paddocks' but they were not usually groomed, unless they were to be shown to a potential buyer.

Any yearling which showed potential was kept separate, about six usually being kept for training, whilst the others were sold through the bloodstock agency. Clarence Junior's daughter Sally remembers becoming attached to some of them, and was often saddened to see them go.

The stallion Trigo was kept quite separate in his own box and paddock some distance away. He was in the charge of a stallion groom who was the only one allowed to exercise him. Trigo was walked outside at about 10.0 a.m. each day, usually around Aston Rowant and perhaps out to Kingston Blount, but never near the A40 which was very busy. Trigo was frisky and not always easy to keep under control, but most of the local roads were quiet. Other stallions were also sometimes hired in.

Jim remembered a special train when some 8–10 mares were sent to Ireland for auction. He was proud to be chosen to ride in the groom's compartment accompanying the horses to Holyhead where Irish grooms took over.

Jim remembers the horses were fed before being led along the wide grass verge on the north side of the A40 to Aston Rowant station. Harry Horne led the way in a car with straw and food for their journey. The lads led each horse individually without blinkers.

It seems likely this was done on a Sunday morning when the A40 would have been quiet and a special train easier to arrange, but we cannot be certain now.

Reg Pocock was waiting at the station to receive them and the horse-boxes, which had been cleaned out, were apparently in the short dock with the doors open. It is not clear how many vehicles were involved, it may have been three or four, but as the dock was so short, they would have needed shunting as they were loaded.

The delicate operation began after one of the lads had lined the horse-box with straw, then they had to coax the animals inside. This could take anything up to an hour. Getting the first one loaded was the most difficult, as once it was inside, the others were more inclined to follow. Jim remembers how they pulled the front legs forcibly onto the flap door, using rope if necessary, then two of the lads linked arms under its rump and pushed the animal forward. He thinks they may have travelled four to a box on that occasion but they certainly stood alongside each other facing opposite directions with a feeding tray at one end and a bar behind the hind legs to stop the horses kicking too much. Once they were inside, the door was shut quickly, then it was the railway staff's responsibility to make sure each vehicle was bolted and secured.

Sally Hailey recalls a special trainload of mares arriving at Aston Rowant during the breeding season (14th February–30th June). This apparently involved a dozen or so horse-boxes, each with its own attendant. She remembers them being unloaded onto the platform under her father's supervision. As the platform was not long enough, the train had to move up when the front vehicles had been emptied. The mares were led through the gate on the edge of the yard and across the fields to the village in order to avoid the A40, whilst the

Left: The park cottage. *Right:* Mr. & Mrs. Hailey senior and junior in 1933. Clarence junior was known as Jim; his wife was Sheila
Cty. Peter Norman

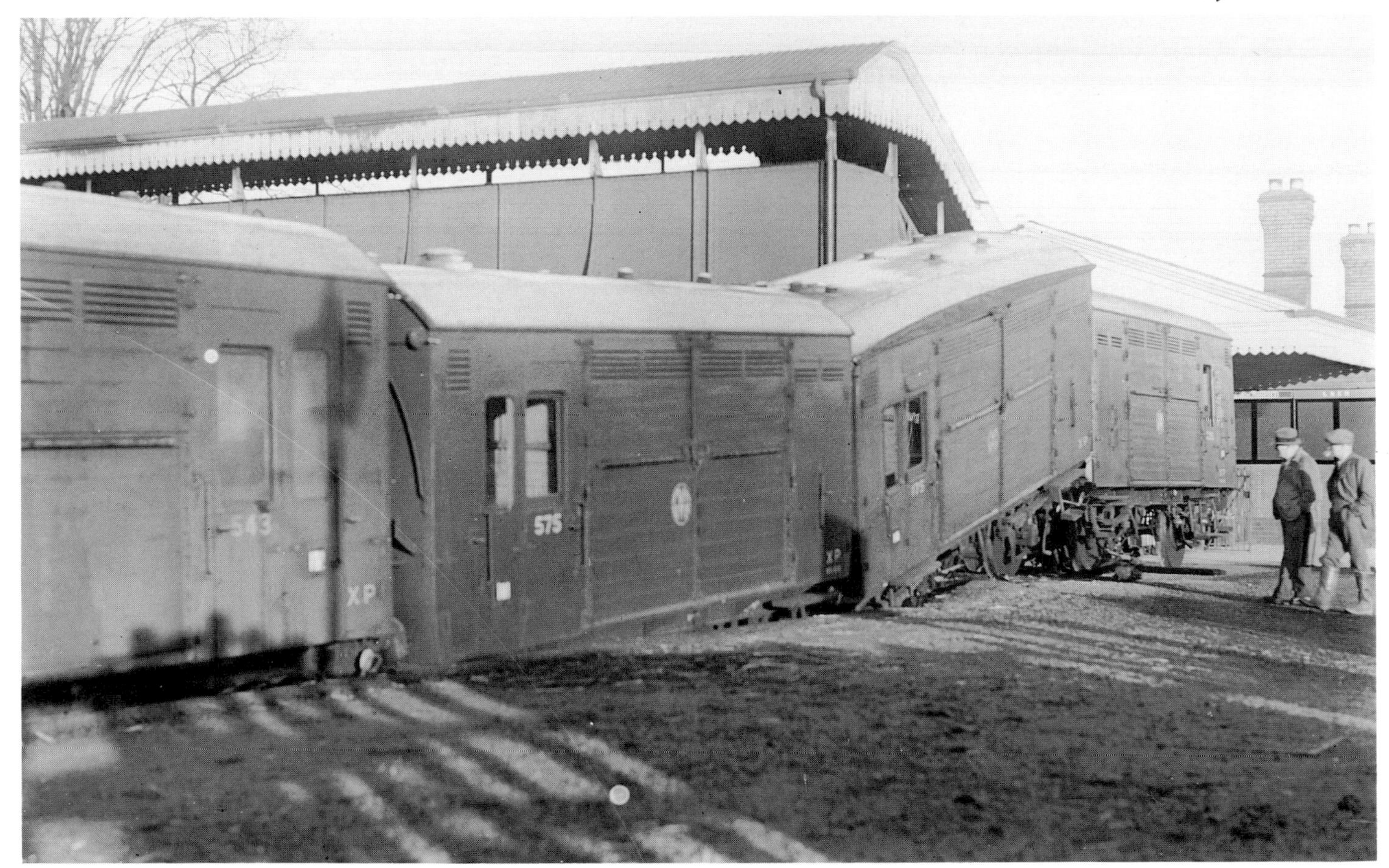

These empty horse-boxes at Princes Risborough in the 1930s are said to have been to Aston Rowant and were stabled in the end loading dock awaiting collection. However, they were hit by a train of wagons supposedly being backed into the up platform but mistakenly propelled into the dock. The figures on the right were Clement East, director of Timothy East Ltd, coal merchants, and Garnet East, manager of Brimmers Farm when Timothy East Ltd. farmed there between the wars.
Hugh Harman

Horse-boxes for Aston Stud were ordered in advance and taken through to Watlington where, as seen here in June 1951, they were held on the spare road ready for a special working. *Derek Clayton*

train of empty stock continued on to Watlington afterwards.

Such trains were well organised in advance and Sally remembers her father finding out who the driver would be, then going to see him personally to plead for exceptionally careful handling of the train in view of the delicate state of the mares.

Sally thinks the railway was only used when a quantity of animals had to be moved, single horses being sent by road. However, Bill Seymour and Laurie Johnson both recalled horse-boxes attached to the branch passenger train at various times in connection with Aston Stud. Laurie remembers two or three boxes on the back of the branch trailer being loaded on the platform. Bill Seymour also remembered the horses being led across the fields, particularly in bad weather when the A40 was slippery.

At Risborough, horse-boxes collected from Aston Rowant and Watlington were taken to the bay platform and coupled in front of the trailer. This c.1955 view shows one shortly after arrival at Watlington, whilst the view on page 127 features a number of horse-boxes being conveyed on the 5.48 p.m. from Risborough. *Gregory*

Laurie also remembered when 15 or 16 horses were sent off to Newmarket on a Sunday. It took a little while to collect the vehicles which were ordered in advance and arrived over several days. They were held in the loop. The branch engine was steamed specially for the train, everyone no doubt being glad of the extra overtime. It seems likely that Sundays were encouraged because such a special would have been difficult to accommodate in the weekday timetable.

Laurie remembered the horses being 'loose boxed', i.e. one per vehicle and, with any number of vehicles, the train had to pull up several times along the short platform.

During the war, Clarence Hailey Junior served with the RAF and later BOAC in the Gulf. His father stood in as manager of the stud farm in his absence, food production taking priority over the breeding. Clarence Junior resumed management when he returned from the war in 1945, his father, keen as ever, subsequently resuming his bloodstock agency in the City at the age of 78!

Clarence Senior regularly travelled to London on the train and was well-known to the Aston Rowant porter. He was taken to the station and met by his chauffeur Mills, who also assisted at the stud. If Clarence Senior was running late in the morning, the train was held for his and anyone else's arrival.

The family were also well-known at the Lambert Arms where they often dined. The landlord was 'a great character' and at times the hotel became something of a social centre for those from the racing world visiting the area. The Lambert Arms was also a focal point for the local hunt.

Clarence Senior died in 1949, followed by Barnett shortly afterwards. In 1950 the stud was sold to Mr Allnut. It subsequently had several owners including the Wright and Wilder families. Clarence Junior meanwhile had moved to the Mentmor Stud at Leighton Buzzard where he worked as stud manager to Lord Rosebery for twenty years.

Even in the 1950s, Watlington porter Cyril Saunders remembers a Newmarket sale special being run for Aston Stud. He went to Aston Rowant to help Charlie Hopkins deal with it. He thinks the fourteen horse-boxes were worked empty through to Watlington first, where the engine ran round and probably took water. At Aston Rowant the horses were loaded along the passenger platform, the train being moved up as the operation progressed.

There was one stallion and thirteen mares, the stallion being loaded first in the leading vehicle. However, despite the care taken, it sensed the mares which were being led to the station and jumped out of the horse-box onto the platform. Cyril remembers the 'pandemonium' that followed until the stable lads got the stallion under control, whilst Charlie Hopkins sensibly shut himself out of the way in the station building until it was safe.

KINGSTON CROSSING

5m 8c

THE earliest recollections we have of life at Kingston Crossing come from Audrey Griffiths, whose parents, Aubrey and Ethel Jarmaine, moved there from a council house in Lewknor in 1934, when she was eight years old. The previous occupants were the Bill family. Her father, Aubrey, son of Aston Rowant coal merchant William Jarmaine, had joined the GWR and by 1914 was working as a porter at Aston Rowant. By the time they came to the crossing, he was working as a porter at Watlington station.

Unlike Wainhill, where the gates were kept closed across a quiet lane, at Kingston they were normally closed across the railway, allowing traffic free passage between Kingston village and the B4009 from Chinnor, and Stokenchurch on the main A40.

It was therefore necessary for Ethel Jarmaine to close the gates across the road prior to the arrival of each train. As with Wainhill Crossing, she knew when the train

Kingston Crossing in 1919.

L & GRP

was due, but in this case the porters at Chinnor and Aston Rowant were more inclined to ring her to say the train was on its way, although "it all depended on who was on". The crossing was provided with lattice post distant signals on the approach from each direction but they were not interlocked with the gates. Ethel pulled the relevant one to the 'off' position to indicate the gates were safely open for the train.

The signal lamps were trimmed and filled once a week by the porter from Chinnor who would arrive at 2.0 p.m. and drop into the house for a cup of tea during the hour or so he had to wait for the 3.20 to take him back. He was also responsible for cleaning the lamps on the gates, which were otherwise tended by Ethel, who also looked after the oil light at the halt.

The permanent way gang also dropped in for a cup of tea — "We'd brew up for them whatever time they came and they'd all sit inside for a chat."

The village was some way from the line, so the crossing house was quite isolated; the nearest neighbours were Mr & Mrs Jones and their son Leslie, who lived in a cottage ¾ mile away. They occasionally received parcels which were dropped off at the crossing and delivered by one of the Jarmaines. Incidentally, parcels were also delivered to Kingston Blount by request of Chinnor. Their next nearest neighbours were the Clerke-Browns "from the farm up the road".

The cottage itself was very basic, a stable-type door at the back of the building leading into a wooden scullery, with a sink and copper on the right, and shelves and a cupboard on the left-hand wall. A door straight ahead led through to a living room equipped with a 'Kitchener' range for cooking and heating. There was also just room for a piano which Ethel played. A door on the left led off to Aubrey and Ethel's bedroom, which was situated in a small extension, which Aubrey thinks once served as a sitting room.

A door and wooden partition wall in the living room enclosed the staircase, which led up to a very small 'room' on the landing and a 'large' bedroom with two beds where Audrey and her sister Esme slept. When Ethel Jarmaine's mother went to visit them, Audrey had to sleep on the landing where there was just room for a camp bed.

There was no mains water or electricity; the house was lit with oil lamps downstairs and "you took a candle upstairs with you". The water was "lovely" and came from a well which used to get so low in the summer that the family had a job to reach it.

The Jarmaines collected milk from a farm in Kingston village and kept it cool in a bucket of water. Butter was kept in an earthenware cooler and meat was stored in a mesh-fronted safe hung on an outside wall.

The lavatory was a primitive bucket in a shed, "round the back, behind the scullery", emptied into holes dug in the garden — "We grew prize spuds". At night they used to take a hurricane lamp round there with them and hope it would not blow out on the way.

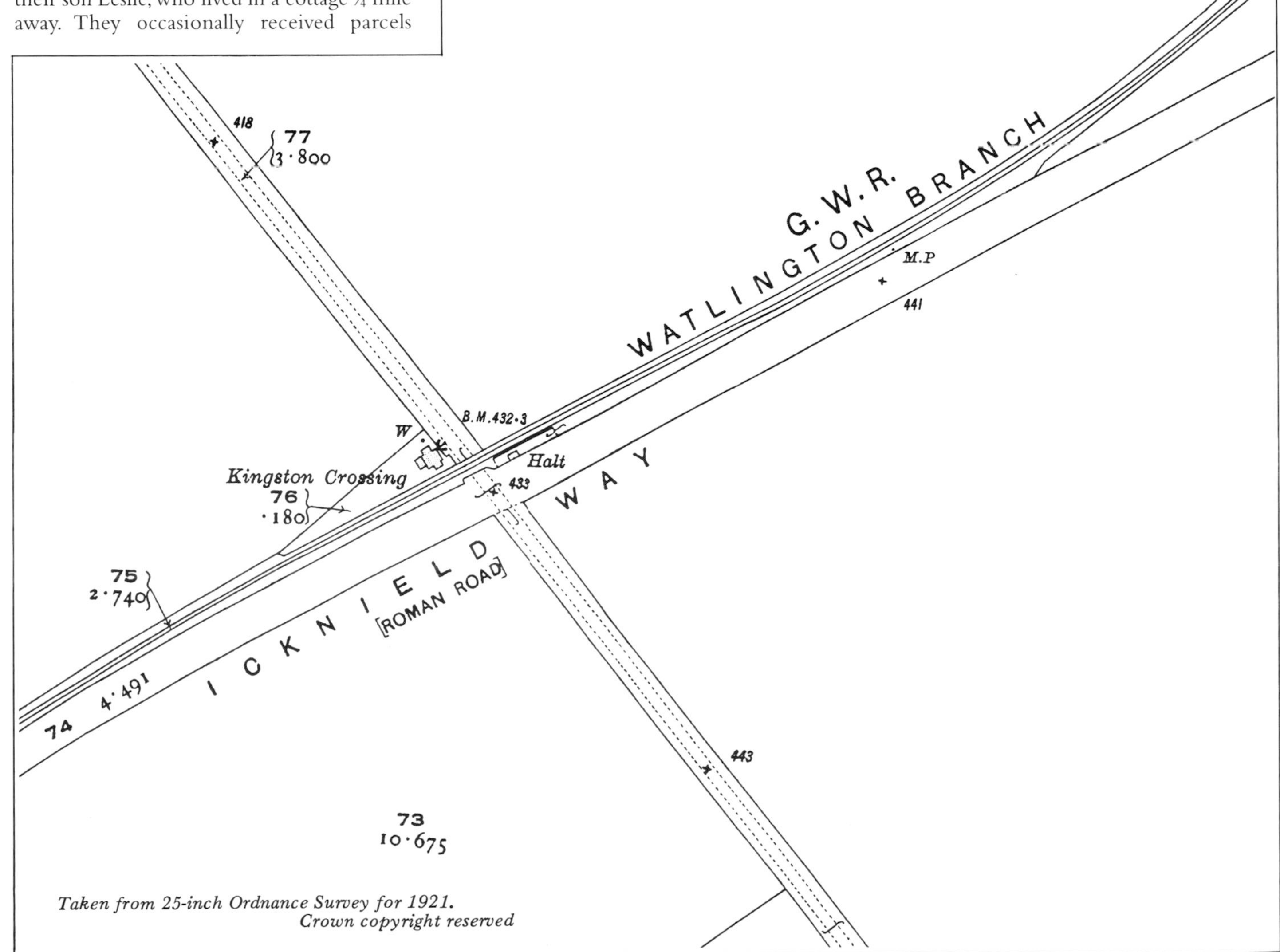

Taken from 25-inch Ordnance Survey for 1921.
Crown copyright reserved

As with Lewknor, the proper post-mounted glass-cased oil lamps were replaced with simple tubular posts from which hurricane lamps were hung. This picture was taken on 16th August 1955. *J. N. Faulkner*

Audrey used to enjoy listening to Radio Luxembourg but the accumulator always seemed to run down on Sundays when she was listening to the Ovaltinees! The family never had any holidays and never went away.

Both of the girls went to school at Chinnor, travelling in on the 9.0 a.m. and returning about 4.0 p.m., but later, when her older sister Esme left school, Audrey did not want to stay there at lunchtimes and walked home along the track. There were no trains between 12.15 and 2.0 p.m. "so I was perfectly safe".

The two girls also used to walk along the line on Sundays when they would "go coaling", picking up all the lumps of coal which had fallen off the engine or been thrown at rabbits by the crew. They also picked up wooden track keys. Very often they gathered so much that they could not carry it all and had to go and get their father.

If they ran short of coal, they would cadge some from the engine crews, but whereas Audrey found the conscientious Harry Humphreys was "mean", Geoff Pearson "threw no end out for you".

Tradesmen calling included Ken Saw, the butcher (and later Ken Parslowe), Jack Turner, Chinnor greengrocer, Mr Kimberley from Risborough who delivered oil and polishes, and Mr May, baker from Kingston Blount. There was only one other shop at Kingston, and that was run by Mr & Mrs Clarke.

Aubrey died in 1938 when Audrey was twelve years old. After that they coped as well as they could, and the rest of the branch staff were good to them. Very often they had not got the gates open when the train reached the crossing, especially if it was before time,

Left: Esme and Audrey Jarmaine in the 1930s when they were in the Girl Guides and Brownies. Meetings were held at the reading rooms at Kingston Blount. *Right:* Sally Matheson, who lived at the Wainhill end of Chinnor, and Ethel Jarmaine, at Kingston Crossing. During the 1940s, Sally worked as a clerk at Watlington station, travelling in from Wainhill Crossing Halt each day on the empty stock return of the 7.25 a.m. *Cty. Audrey Griffiths*

and they could not always hold them in a strong wind "no matter how hard you tried", even with two of them, so the fireman would climb down to help. Geoff Pearson and George were very friendly and waved whenever they passed.

When Audrey was thirteen, she recalls "I was only a kid but George Nicholson was my favourite", "I worshipped him". Her sister liked his brother Joe who, by that time, was a porter at Watlington. She remembers that if the engine crew were in a jovial mood "they'd stop the train and come and have a chat".

As explained, the normal position of the gates was across the railway and, officially at least, after the passing of the last passenger train, they were supposed to be padlocked. Audrey says she does not remember them ever being locked. For the passing of the early morning goods and late goods (when run), the guard opened the gates to allow the train to pass, so the Jarmaines were undisturbed. Therefore imagine their surprise when at 10.5 p.m. on Boxing Day 1940, they heard the 10.0 p.m. goods from Risborough run into the down side gate, "breaking the top bar and one spar". The driver was Geoff Pearson.

In 1940, when Audrey was 14½, she left school and did housework at Kingston House for 18 months, until she was 16, when she was able to earn more money at the Belling & Lee aircraft component factory in Risborough. "There were eight of us from Kingston" all joining the 7.25 from Watlington at the halt. Belling & Lee employees included Freda Ludlum, Gladys Quartermaine, who lived between Kingston Blount and Kingston Sturt, and Cis Munday, daughter of the landlord of the Shoulder of Lamb at Kingston, who walked up to the crossing. Two other women from Kingston worked at the Cheverton & Laidler Stationery Co. "City gents" usually travelled on the later train, but when they caught the 7.25 there could be up to twelve people on

A passenger's view of the line veering away from the Icknield Way, (behind the halt) towards Chinnor, where the cement works dominates the landscape. *J. H. Venn*

Jean Saunders operating one of the signal levers. *Wilf Stevens*

This 1956 view of the crossing shows the corrugated iron shed used to store lamp oil, which was sent in gallon cans from Chinnor. The lever frame controlling the up and down distant signals just features behind the Kingston Crossing nameplate. *M. Wallen*

This picture of Jean Saunders in the wooden porch annexed to the kitchen lean-to also provides a closer view of the cast-iron nameplate. *Wilf Stevens*

the halt and, if it was raining, the tiny shelter was packed!

Audrey remembers how the guards "used to heave you up the steps", it was "a heck of a job" to get up into the trailer. She and her workmates used to sit in a gang on their own and did not mix with the other workers. At night they returned on the 5.55 p.m. from Risborough, "cutting across the park" to get to the station. Instead of using the trailer, Audrey travelled in the extra coach and jumped to the ground when they reached Kingston. Towards the end of the war, production increased, so she worked late and travelled home on the last train.

Audrey used to enjoy going to the pictures and remembers going to Watlington one night and Thame the next to see George Formby. However, the branch train was no help to her as the last one was at 8.0 p.m. and, although more buses started to run to Thame when she was 16 or 17, the last one left at 9.40 p.m. "so you couldn't see the end of a picture" as the film finished at 10.0 p.m.! She used to walk to Watlington and back — "We used to walk miles in those days". If she wanted to go into High Wycombe, she walked along the railway line to Aston Rowant, then down the A40 to the Lambert Arms, because the bus did not stop at the station.

At the end of the war, when she was 19, the Belling & Lee factory closed and moved back to London.

In 1943 her sister Esme became a clerk at Watlington station and got married the same year. Esme and her husband also lived at the crossing cottage. They had the upstairs and Audrey slept downstairs in her mother's bedroom, until she left home in 1949, later getting married herself. When Esme and her husband eventually managed to get a council house, Esme visited her mother every day, but Ethel was lonely at the isolated spot and eventually the Clerke-Browns found her a house down in the village.

After Ethel had vacated the crossing house, Cyril Saunders, porter at Watlington, was posted there on relief duty. He got married in October 1952 and subsequently applied for the tenancy of the primitive cottage, even though there was no mains water, sewage or electricity. His wife Jean was to be employed as crossing keeper, but, before they were accepted, she had to go to Paddington for a colour vision test which a previous applicant had apparently failed.

They moved to the crossing in May 1953 and enjoyed their time there. Jean says "I loved it" and was not worried about being there on her own, until she started listening to Dick Barton on the wireless at 6.45 p.m. before the 7.15 from Watlington went through. On dark nights she used to rush back indoors afterwards, feeling really scared!

Jean Saunders closing the gates across the railway. *Wilf Stevens*

A passenger's view of a Watlington-bound train continuing on its journey. *Wilf Stevens*

Cyril Saunders closing the gates across the road on 13th February 1954. *M. Wallen*

Kingston Crossing Halt on 13th February 1954. *M. Wallen*

Another wintry portrait, this time looking along the road from Kingston Blount towards the hills. Although the location was subject to few changes, this 1950s view makes an interesting comparison with the one on page 69 in Volume 1. ***Cty. Cyril and Jean Saunders***

The Saunders did not mind that they had to fetch their water from the well, and remembered that whereas it was within easy reach during the winter months, in the summer it took 3½ clothes lines (33ft each) to reach it. Like the Jarmaines, they found "the water was lovely". Cyril used to joke that even the cattle in the nearby fields were provided with mains water to their troughs! However, around 1956 when the water main was being laid to an American radar station on Kingston Hill, the crossing house was connected to a supply but "we never did get electricity".

Lighting was by paraffin oil lamps but candles upstairs, whilst cooking and heating were still dependent on a combustion stove and a small Primus. The railway gave them 30cwt of coal a year, but, sent to Chinnor, they had to pay ten shillings for Jim Plumridge to deliver it!

Jean boiled water in a copper for washing clothes on Mondays, or for filling the galvanised bath which hung on the wall. There was a soakaway for the sink waste but the contents of the bucket used in the lavatory were still buried in the garden. Because the cottage had no loft, "it was worse than a greenhouse in summer, and like an ice box in winter".

Jean rarely went down to the village and remembers a van from the International Stores, Watlington, calling on Tuesdays and Fridays.

If she was away, a relief man was sent out to look after the gates. Between trains he based himself in the PW hut on the Chinnor side of the crossing, where he could keep warm by the fire and make tea.

Cyril left the railway in January 1955, but remained living at the crossing, with his wife as gatekeeper, until 1962.

Anne Saunders at the crossing with Rover, their Welsh Collie. Rover would bark when six bells ran on the telephone; this was the code for calling Kingston. ***Cty. Cyril & Jean Saunders***

CHINNOR STATION

3m 48c

Judging from the state of construction of the new cement works, this picture of Chinnor station was taken about 1928 and makes an interesting comparison with the view on page 44/45 in Volume 1.
C. L. Mowat

WHEN Arthur George Harmsworth went to Chinnor in 1921 to take up the station master's post, he was a 41-year-old widower with two children. At first he lodged in Station Road but in January 1922 he married Florence Ginger from Bledlow and purchased No.1 Station Road. He remained station master for twelve years and was also responsible for Wainhill, Kingston and Bledlow Bridge Halts.

Joe Bateman and Alf Taylor were porters at Chinnor for many years and served George Harmsworth loyally. Joe, the senior porter, had previously been employed at the corn mill in Mill Lane, and his wife's father, Joe Reynolds, had been one of the first booking porters at Chinnor. Joe Bateman joined the staff on the Watlington branch in 1915, and is remembered around the village delivering all manner of goods using the GWR two-wheeled hand cart. Local bus driver Fred Seymour even recalls Joe struggling all the way out to Sydenham with a couple of heavy suitcases on the railway delivery bike. Rather than use the brakes, he used to stop the bike by putting his feet on the ground, much to the fascination of the local children. Several people have said he was a great character.

Alf Taylor, who had started as a weighbridge lad at Newbury, became lad porter at Chinnor around 1920. In order to gain promotion to porter, he moved to Alvescot for a short time around 1926–7, but returned to Chinnor as soon as a vacancy arose in 1928, and married Maude, the daughter of Watlington branch ganger Walter Hopkins. The staff were well aware of their romance, and the local newspaper boy carried messages between the station and the Post Office where she worked. When they were married in Chinnor church, the staff laid detonators on the line and these were exploded by the Chinnor Goods around 1.0 p.m., just as they were signing the register.

Alf's place as lad porter was probably taken by Jack Rutland who spent about twelve months at Chinnor around that time. His father, Frank, was a porter at Risborough from the early years of the century and by the 1930s became foreman there. Jack cycled

Porter Joe Bateman and station master Harmsworth at Chinnor station platform in the 1920s when the proper oil lamps were still in use. These were later replaced with simple posts and hurricane lamps, one being hung by the gate, as shown here, and one by the steps leading down from the road bridge. The interior of the building was lit with ordinary oil lamps stood on tables. We have not discovered a date for the rendering applied to the east-facing gable ends but it looks reasonably fresh here. *Cty. Eric Harmsworth*

to Chinnor and back each day from his home in Risborough and recalls the two porters were Joe Bateman and Albert Hemmings. Albert died during Jack's year there and he remembers Alf Taylor replacing him.

While he was at Chinnor, Jack remembers Mr Saw, the butcher, receiving a side of beef each morning. This was sent from Watlington in the guard's compartment of the 11.30 a.m., and Mr Saw, who would be waiting for it, took it away on a horse and cart.

During the same period, Ernie Forte, who as a youngster worked for farmer Tom Nixey from 1924–29, took milk to Chinnor station each morning with a pony and milk float. "If you were late and the station master saw you coming, they'd stop the train and wait." As at Watlington, everyone would help with the loading, even the ganger. Ernie said "In them days life was different — you don't realize the niceness of people years ago; today they'd go off and leave you."

George Howlett also recalls farmers from Sydenham taking milk to the station and loading it onto the rear of the train. From 1929–32, while George was still at school, he used to sit in the waiting room each night talking to either Joe Bateman or Alf Taylor while he was waiting for the arrival of the 8.0 p.m. from Risborough which conveyed the *Evening Standard*. George delivered about a quire (25) around the village and local pubs, and two quires on Saturday nights when there would often be a queue of people at the station waiting to buy a paper from him for the football results.

Sadly, George Harmsworth suffered ill health, but they all pulled together as a team. There was no relief clerk available to cover his duties so the porters did the paperwork between them and Maude remembers her husband was praised for his accountancy work.

George died in October 1933 at the age of 52, the *Thame Gazette* recording that he was 'widely respected for his general courtesy' — a sentiment which agrees with the experience of those who remember him.

Reg Pocock, who would have known him for eleven years, attended the funeral and no doubt felt the loss of a good colleague and friend. He may even have been instrumental in recommending the placid and conscientious Watlington station clerk, 41-

Porter Alf Taylor, station master Harmsworth, porter Joe Bateman and Rita Carter "who lived near the Batemans".
Cty. Eric Harmsworth

George Harmsworth's son Eric on the station delivery cart in the 1920s.
Cty. Eric Harmsworth

year-old Sydney Pratley, as Harmsworth's successor.

Pratley had joined the GWR in 1906 as a lamp boy and became a signalman at Old Oak. Although he had volunteered for service in the Great War, he was retained on the railway and in order to avoid shift work, went on to study for the GWR's clerical exam. Around 1920 he had become a booking clerk at Llandovery where his three daughters were born, but as his wife's family were in the Wycombe area, they were keen to move back to the locality, so he took the booking clerk's post at Watlington in 1928.

While they were in Watlington, they lived in Love Lane 'just round the corner from driver Geoff Pearson', but when they moved to Chinnor, they lived at 9 Wykeham Rise.

Station master Harmsworth on the base of the goods yard crane in the 1920s.
Cty. Eric Harmsworth

Porter Percy Smith and station master Sydney Pratley in the 1930s.
Cty. Gwyneth Russell

On the run-up to the Second World War, Syd Pratley's daughter Freda remembers the local billeting officer visiting each home to check the availability of spare bedrooms. As one of their daughters was away, the Pratleys were able to offer accommodation for one schoolgirl, Minnie Farley. It seems that Dr Leverkus was the main instigator of the local scheme for the reception of evacuees, whilst Mrs Nixey of Manor Farm met the children and took them round to their billets. Jim Clark said the evacuees who arrived were Roman Catholics originally intended for somewhere in Gloucestershire rather than Chinnor where there was no Catholic church. Despite the mix-up, they stayed in Chinnor and held services in Crowell church which at that time was apparently hardly used.

The influx of these evacuees meant there were too many children for the school, and Freda remembers this was overcome by dividing the pupils into morning and afternoon shifts.

In 1942 Sydney Pratley moved on to a higher grade post at Wooburn Green. He had got on well with everyone and was held in the highest esteem by all who worked under him. Having worked on the Watlington branch for some fourteen years, he no doubt missed all his colleagues.

In the early 1930s, Alf Taylor had also moved on to Maidenhead to become a porter/guard, his place being taken by (we think) Percy Smith, who was certainly there from at least 1935–37, and in turn was replaced by Joe Bateman's wife Ivy, who served as a woman porter during the war.

Guard Tom Bowler's son Bryan worked at Chinnor as a junior porter from 1943–45, cycling in from Watlington each day. He remembers Ivy and Joe covering the early and late shifts between them, with Pratley's successor, station master E. Davies, covering the office from about 8.30 a.m. until 5.0 p.m. As Ivy and Joe covered the early and late trains, the books were balanced three times each day, i.e. before each hand-over and at the end of the late shift.

As the junior, one of Bryan's main responsibilities was keeping the station spotless, Mr Davies being particularly fastidious about the brasswork in the ladies lavatory.

This portrait of Sydney Pratley at Chinnor station in the 1930s was taken from the approach road to the cement works.
Cty. Gwyneth Russell

The railway was a very prominent feature when it first came to Chinnor, but as this view shows, the modern cement works grew to dominate the landscape, until the tiny station was barely significant. This rather bleak view was taken around 1950. *J. H. Russell*

When Joe Bateman retired in 1945, Bryan became a Grade 2 porter, alternating with Ivy Bateman, who stayed on after the war. Bryan cycled in each morning from his parents' home in Hill Road, Watlington, in time to book on at 7.30 a.m. The journey took about half an hour and so he was glad of the company when a friend of his, Alfie Britten, got a job at Chinnor cement works and rode in with him.

Bryan left his bike against the station building and, after unlocking the doors, he lit all the paraffin lamps and the fire in the office ready to book the first train which left Watlington at 7.25.

One morning when Bryan was running late, the 7.25 overtook him while he was still cycling through Kingston. His father Tom, who was usually on the same shift as him, was guard and, on arrival at Chinnor, was faced with writing out sixpenny paper tickets for the 30–40 workers who were travelling to Risborough at that time. Bryan said "I never heard the last of that", but "It only happened once!"

As mentioned in Volume 1, this first train was strengthened by an extra coach coupled behind the branch trailer to accommodate the increased number of workers travelling to Risborough at this time. It was also used again at night for workers returning on the 5.55 p.m. ex-Risborough.

The first train returned empty stock except for Sally Matheson who, working as a clerk at Watlington, was unofficially picked up at Wainhill Halt.

When station master Davies booked on at 8.30, in time to book passengers for the 8.40 ex-Watlington, the office would be nice and warm for him. He lived in Thame and drove to Chinnor each day in his little Austin Seven, which he left along the forecourt side of the station building. Davies, "a proper chapel man", was "regimental" — "a boss who wanted things done properly". He

A closer view of the station building and platform on the same occasion. The corrugated iron goods lock-up on the platform was provided in 1912 in lieu of the goods shed which was swept away during improvements to the layout of the sidings in the goods yard. The station 'not drinking water' supply came from a well enclosed by the wooden palings at this end of the station building; part of the large pump wheel just shows by the corner of the goods lock-up. Porter Bryan Bowler recalled that pumping water to fill the supply tank in the lavatories took a long time as he had to keep running round to the opposite end of the building to see if it was full. He pumped the water until the tank overflowed. He also recalled that when the porters made tea, they collected water from nearby houses and spent their break in the PW hut. *J. H. Russell*

Lady porter Ivy Bateman on the station platform with the railway's delivery bicycle, probably in the early postwar years. *Cty. Sylvia Guntrip*

would leave the station for his lunch hour, which was spent at Mrs Bateman's.

When the station master arrived, it released Bryan to go over to the cement works to take the numbers of the wagons there and write out labels for vans of cement which, at that time, were being sent out to Greenford, Chalford and Taunton. "It was a fair old way to walk round the cement works." Bryan looked at the 'breeze wagons' first at the lime kilns, then he cut through to the coal wagons waiting to go "over the tip", then "down the bottom" to the empties in the outwards sidings, and finally back up to the box vans being loaded with cement.

Incidentally, Bryan remembers bags of cement were loaded into the vans with a chute whilst the gypsum was unloaded on the same line using a mobile crane with rubber tyres.

If it was raining, Bryan would be pretty wet by this time and he would dry himself under the rotary kiln. After finishing at the cement works, he made his way over to the

Interior of the office at Chinnor in the 1950s. *Wilf Stevens*

After Eric Humphrey was promoted to Challow, the post was covered by a Mr. Barrett from Bristol, and for a lengthy period by relief station master Ron Cox, although we have not been able to establish the order in which they served. The station master in 1956 was J. G. Williams who is believed to be the subject of this photograph. Relief station master Keith Lewis covered during the final months. *Wilf Stephens*

goods yard to record the wagons there. He would often see coal merchant, Jess Rogers, bagging coal from the wagons, using an old 5-gallon oil drum with the bottom removed to hold the sacks while he was filling them. This simple device, fitted with hooks or handles to hold the sacks, was stood on his cart when the wagon doors were first opened, but put inside where he was shovelling as soon as there was room, so that loaded sacks could be transferred directly onto the cart instead of being lifted from the ground. "I felt sorry for him sometimes when he used to get great lumps which had to be broken up with a pick." Jess had some deliveries in wagons "without side flaps" but only end doors. This made unloading very difficult and time-consuming, so station master Davies had a word with the rolling stock office who waived the demurrage charges.

After his round, Bryan went back to the station office to write up the details of all the wagons, sheets and ropes. He was always back in time to unload the 10.22 ex-Risborough which conveyed the station truck "on the back of the trailer". Goods for Chinnor were unloaded into the goods shed on the platform and this train also carried large numbers of parcels which were taken into the waiting room. Before the war, the station truck had been conveyed down the branch on the early goods, but as there were no staff on duty at Chinnor at that time of the morning, it is tempting to speculate that the guard probably locked any items for Chinnor in the goods shed on the platform.

After the train had gone, the parcels and smalls traffic was delivered around the village using the two-wheeled hand cart. Items regularly included sides of bacon, flour, Lyons cakes to Hicks and rolls of leather to "the shoe repairs shop round by the church". Sometimes there were two barrow loads. Once Bryan even pushed a heavy galvanised water tank all the way to Wainhill on the two-wheeled barrow.

Larger items were collected from the goods shed by "old Mr Lacey" with his horse and cart, or A.A. King who ran a small van for deliveries to Kingston Blount and Sydenham. Both men were farmers and regular cartage contractors. William Lacey,

A view from the platform, looking towards Watlington. Although probably taken about 1957 after the major expansion of the cement works, the scene is very much that experienced by passengers since the 1930s, as they watched the branch train dip and rise along the switchback approach.

BRIXHAM

Although very similar to the buildings at Watlington and Aston Rowant, the one at Chinnor varied in that the accommodation was reversed and the lavatories were at the south end of the building and the office at the north. The 'waiting room' inside the porch still served as a booking hall/parcels office with a weighing machine against a sealed forecourt entrance. Inside the office, the station master sat near the platform window facing the north wall with the clerk to his left and a small ticket window behind him. The office door was in the far corner near the weighing machine. For some reason, with the exception of the southernmost wall, the building was rendered some time in the 1920s whereas those at Watlington and Aston Rowant survived unscathed. The British Automatic Co. had a chocolate machine stationed at Chinnor, on the left just inside the station building. It dispensed one-penny bars of chocolate, apparently purchased by the station master who made a small profit on the sales. The path leading up the side of the embankment to the wicket gate by the bridge was a later addition dating from the 1920s or 30s. Although there were a number of steps in the path, the descent was only illuminated by a single Tilley lamp which was hung from the nearby post adjacent to the roadside fence. The garden allotment beyond the end of the platform was kept by the station master whilst Joe Bateman kept an allotment near the former foundry site. *H. A. Vallance*

who had 9 or 10 horses, stopped carting just before the Second World War in order to concentrate on farming.

Other jobs included pumping water using a large hand wheel to fill the tank for the station lavatories. As there was no drinking water at the station, Bryan used to get some from "the houses across the road" at the back of the station.

There were also truck loads of hay to sheet and rope for the provender store at Didcot. This was done when the opposite turn porter, Ivy Bateman, was there with him. "She couldn't carry the heavy sacks up the ladder and I was only just strong enough." Hay needed two sheets and Bryan had to climb onto the top of the wagon with each rope after securing one end, then hand the other end down to Mrs Bateman below.

The highlight of the day was the Chinnor goods which came out from Risborough at lunch time. Before it arrived, Bryan and Ivy Bateman went round putting the flaps up on the wagons, ready for the shunt. Bryan said "I used to do all the shunting because Mrs Bateman never did" "My Dad taught me how to use a shunting pole before I was sixteen."

Bryan's memories of the Chinnor goods are particularly valuable because they tell us how his father, Tom, handled the train. As he had been a guard at Watlington since 1934, it is tempting to believe that this is how it had been done during those years, whereas changes in guards and other staff after the war brought a host of variations, some of which are discussed later.

Tom apparently arranged it with Risborough to marshall the train with the coke breeze on the front, followed by coal and empty vans for the cement works, and the yard traffic, mainly coal for the local merchants, at the rear.

On arrival at Chinnor, the whole train was taken into the cement works private sidings and run round on the loop there. Then, after uncoupling the leading wagons of breeze, it

was all pushed towards the lime kilns, all the vehicles of the train giving a reach beyond the engine stop board. The wagons of breeze had to ascend the inclined siding, so, Bryan recalled, "we used to belt it up there at a fast gallop and chase it to stop it".

Coal for the works and empty vans were then "pushed down the straight road" and left for the cement works staff to distribute. Coal was gravitated over the tip whilst vans were pushed to the loading area. The remaining portion of the train was then drawn out of the works and back through the station clear of the yard entry points. It was then propelled onto the loop, or 'long road' as it was known, and left there while the empties were collected from the siding or 'short road'. The empties were then also put into the loop and coupled onto the rear of the train left there, the whole lot then being drawn back towards the station and into the short siding again, where the yard traffic was uncoupled and left.

The brake van was now at the Watlington end of the yard empties ready for the return journey and it only remained to go down to the other end of the cement works and collect the outwards traffic. Incidentally, any empties ordered for Siareys timber traffic were left on the loop and pushed northwards towards the dock later by the porters using a pinch bar. Bryan recalled how, very unofficially, they had used the small yard crane to pull the wagons into the dock, but this was strictly off the record!

When going to the south or 'bottom end' of the cement works, the empty yard traffic and brake van were 'kicked off' down the gradient towards Kingston, the guard bringing them to a stand beyond the lower connection into the works. The engine then ran inside there to pick up coal empties and any vans of cement, which were then coupled onto the train waiting on the running line and taken back to Risborough.

Mrs Bateman's daughter Sylvia would sometimes go into work with her mother and sit in the booking office. She recalls the open fire in there and the 'musty smell'. Ivy used to wear a uniform skirt and jacket with brass buttons. Her mother 'dealt with everything', including the deliveries to the local shops using the station bicycle.

The parcels which came in on many of the trains were handed to the porters to deal with, but on 9th January 1946 when Ivy picked up two from the 5.55 p.m. ex-Risborough, she did not notice a pram

The midday Chinnor goods, which appears to have been formed of empties from the cement works and coal yard,, about to leave for Risborough on 16th August 1955. ***J. N. Faulkner***

GW traffic minutes for 1905 and 1914 record approval for a station master's house at Chinnor at a cost of £345 plus land and £384 respectively. In the event, just like the proposal for Aston Rowant, this was not proceeded with and station masters had to find their own lodgings. This picture shows Eric Humphrey's son and wife outside the house they rented at No. 9 Wykeham Rise, just over the bridge from the station. It is believed to have been owned by Siareys. This picture was taken c.1950.
Cty. Eric Humphrey

which had been sent from Thame. The guard had left it on the platform against the platform seat because of 'the gale then blowing'. Unnoticed by anyone in the dark, the pram blew across the platform and fell onto the track. It was later run over by the 7.15 p.m. Watlington to Princes Risborough, 'the driver noticing an unusual crunching noise under the footplate as the train was leaving the station and finding the pram wedged beneath the engine'.

When station master Davies transferred away to Wallingford in 1946, his place was taken by J.W. ('Jerry') Pearce who only stayed at Chinnor for about a year before moving on to High Wycombe. He had previously worked in the goods department at Aylesbury with Eric R. Humphrey who had in the meantime taken a clerk's position at Twyford while awaiting promotion. By coincidence, when Jerry Pearce left Chinnor in 1947, Eric took his place.

Eric Humphrey recalls that when taking or leaving a station master's post on the Great Western, the hand-over procedure included a full inventory, so when he went to Chinnor one Monday in October 1947, he was met by a relief station master who showed him over the station and the three halts, including the two crossing keepers' houses at Wainhill and Kingston Blount. He also introduced him to the management at the cement works which was a large and very important account for the railway.

The hand-over generally took about 2–3 days, during which time he was taken through a detailed inventory which ranged from balanced accounts and tickets to all items of furniture, platform barrows, lamps and other equipment. It was all over by Wednesday night.

On his first morning, Mrs Baldwin, a vicar's widow, went to the station to introduce herself. She then enquired whether he had anywhere to live, which he had not, and by 3.0 p.m. she reappeared at the station having arranged three rooms for him at the house of Mrs White, another vicar's widow. He and his family stayed there for some time before eventually renting a house in Wykeham Rise on the east side of the railway bridge.

Although the impression is sometimes given that the GWR arranged accommodation for station masters, if this was ever the case on the Watlington branch, then by this time they were evidently left to make their own arrangements.

When Mr Humphrey first went to Chinnor, Ivy Bateman was still employed as a porter. Her husband Joe died in October 1947 which must have been a bitter blow, but although this almost coincided with Mr Humphrey's arrival, he could not recall the situation or who the other porter was at the time. As Ivy could not do the shunting, Mr Humphrey had to stand in on the porter's duty while the yard or cement works was being sorted, unless the opposite-turn porter was on duty. The guards were apparently uneasy about the situation, especially, they argued, when so many men were looking for employment. Ivy was therefore soon replaced by young Ike Ford, who Mr Humphrey recalls as "a bit of a lad". The other porter at the time came from Wycombe but his name is not recalled.

The clerk was Norman Stratford, Mrs Bateman's nephew, but he was not there long before being replaced by Alan Rich (for a short time) and then Bryan Rich, his brother.

Eric Humphrey worked from 9.0 a.m. to 5.0 p.m. and began each day with any "phone work" and sorting out any "more pressing matters" before making his way over to the cement works, usually about 10.0 a.m., to see the foreman, and sort out the papers and bookwork for the numerous wagons there, and any demurrage charges.

When he first went to Chinnor, the paperwork was six weeks behind, so he was keen to keep on top of it all. He was usually at the works for 1–1½ hours, and even helped with labelling the wagons. Later on, perhaps when Mr Humphrey was upgraded from class 4 to class 3 and put in charge of the whole line, it would appear that the porters resumed this duty instead.

Yard traffic was relatively quiet but Eric recalls that at harvest time, farmer Joe Hill would ring up on a Monday and order "something like 15 wagons" for the despatch of wheat which was "sent to driers in the Midlands". This could go on for several days depending on the success of the crop. He also recalls a number of farm implements being handled at Chinnor. The occasional pig, and crates of chicks and ducks which arrived, were often looked after by Eric and his wife at their home overnight.

In 1948 Ralph Cann went to work as a porter at Chinnor on the opposite shift to Ike Ford. Ralph's brother was a fitter and turner in the cement industry, moving in the early 1940s from his last job at Rhoose in Wales to take up employment at Chinnor cement works. His parents were Londoners and when visiting Chinnor, liked it so much that they moved there *c.*1941.

Ralph was keen on railways and during school lunch hours used to race to the station with his friends to watch the Chinnor goods shunting. They were often so engrossed that they completely forgot the time and were late back to school.

His first job was cutting firewood for a local dealer, but as soon as a porter's vacancy arose at the station, he applied and was interviewed by station master Humphrey, who at that time was in charge of the whole branch.

This view, looking along Hill Road towards Chinnor Hill from the railway bridge, was very similar to the outlook from the Humphreys' house in nearby Wykeham Rise. It was also the prospect beckoning ramblers from the Bluebell specials. The bluebells could be found in Marlow Wood and Vernice Wood beyond Goose Neck.

Looking towards the road bridge from the station platform one sunny afternoon in the 1950s while the branch train was being held for departure time. The line climbed quite steeply through the cutting beyond, levelling out at Donkey Lane Crossing. Chinnor resident Ruth Woodward recalls "I used to catch the early train from Chinnor to Princes Risborough – they always gave a toot on the whistle when around Kingston to gee us up! We never missed the train, it always waited for us." *M. J. Esau*

Subsequently, Ralph had to go to Paddington for a test with Inspector Honeybone and was soon on the platform at Chinnor and assisting with the shunting he had watched with his friends.

He and Ike alternated each week on shifts of 7.0 a.m. to 4.0 p.m. and 1.0 p.m. to 9. p.m. Monday to Saturday. The early-turn porter unlocked the gates and doors, and on dark mornings lit the two hanging-type outside Tilley lamps, one of which was on the western side of the road approach to the bridge, near the wicket gate. The other one was by the platform entrance gate at the Watlington end of the station building. The first one not only illuminated the entrance near the bridge, but also the steps leading down the side of the embankment.

The interior of the building was also lit by oil lamps, the two in the booking office standing on tables near the ticket window and at the back of the room. On cold mornings, the early-turn man also lit the station fire.

At around 7.30 a.m., the first passengers started to arrive for the 7.25 from Watlington, usually somewhere between six and ten workers for Princes Risborough. They were all issued with grey-coloured workmen's tickets.

After the first train had left, Ralph used to clean the station and pump water from the tank wagon to fill the tank which supplied the station lavatories. The well, at the Risborough end of the building, had become unreliable by this time so a water tank wagon, refilled at Risborough every four weeks, was stationed in the end loading dock.

Although the first train officially returned empty stock from Risborough, it usually brought two regular passengers, one returning from night work and the other, Charlie Rogers, who worked at Siarey's saw mills.

Station master Humphrey and the clerk, Bryan Rich, arrived some time between 8.30 and 9.0 in time to book the second up train. Their arrival released Ralph to go over to the cement works to check and label the wagons. Although the 9.0 a.m. was the busiest train of the day, there were only about a dozen or so passengers, a few of whom were city workers ('the bowler hat brigade') and the others mainly shoppers on their way to Risborough or High Wycombe. The remaining trains were much more lightly used. The 8.58 also conveyed the travelling safe, the previous day's takings being posted through the slot for conveyance to the cashier at Paddington. Incidentally, paybills were sent to Paddington on Mondays in a cash bag which returned on Thursdays with the wages.

While he was over at the cement works, Ralph called in to see Jim Rumbelow, the stores man, to confirm what traffic was to go. He also called in to see Charlie Rutland, the canteen manager, who provided him with a cup of tea and a sandwich.

By Ralph's time, the station truck no longer ran, having been superseded by the Zonal delivery scheme. Even so, George Howlett, relief guard in the late 1940s, remembers that the guard's compartment of the 10.22 could be virtually full with parcels transferred from both up and down trains at Risborough.

The Thame Zonal lorry arrived around 10.30–11.0 a.m. each day on its rounds, which included Aston Rowant (Watlington was served from Reading). The lorry, driven by Eddie Smith or, more occasionally, Bill Hawthorn, collected bulky parcels or items for delivery outside the village which had accumulated in the small corrugated iron goods shed on the platform (after the demise of the station truck, the shed was soon relegated for use as a store for firewood). Smaller items for the village, like Lyon's cakes from Greenford, for instance, were delivered on the station bicycle which Ralph remembers looked like a butcher's bike with a large carrying basket on the front. In earlier years, deliveries are said to have been made with a low four-wheeled trolley.

The Chinnor goods arrived at lunchtime. This primarily conveyed coal and gypsum for the cement works, but also coal for the local traders and goods for the village. As most of the cement from the works was despatched by road, the return working was mainly empties with only one or two outwards vans of cement.

Ralph Cann assisted the guards who, he recalls, each had different ideas of how to tackle the job. Coal for the works was usually marshalled at the front of the train and traffic for the yard at the back. A common procedure was that on arrival, the engine ran round the train using the loop adjacent to the goods yard. The brake van was then detached and propelled through the loop and left on the running line at the Watlington end of the train. The loco then returned through the loop and went into the works to collect the empty coal wagons. These were drawn out onto the running line, then propelled through the loop and onto the brake van left at the south of the station. The loco then returned to the Risborough end of the train and delivered the loaded wagons into the works and yard respectively. Ralph Cann remembers that local traders' coal tended to arrive in batches, so whilst on some days there was nothing at all for the yard, on other occasions there might be two or three wagons.

In another common procedure recalled by Ralph, after the train had arrived from Risborough and been run round in the loop, it was drawn back through the platform, clear of the cement works sidings, then propelled inside towards the coal drop where the loaded coal was secured and uncoupled. The traders' coal was then propelled into the goods yard and coupled to the empties which were drawn out and left on the loop. The coal was then placed in the siding, after which the brake van, which had been next to the engine throughout these movements, was propelled down the running line towards Kingston where it was left while the yard empties were collected from the loop and coupled on to it.

The engine then ran back into the cement works and down the loading road where the occasional van of cement was often standing. This was coupled to the engine and propelled down to the outwards spur ('the hole'), to collect the empty coal wagons waiting there. These were drawn back up through the works, then pushed down onto the yard empties and van waiting on the running line where the return train was now complete.

There were many permutations, not least involving the use of the new connection into the south end of the works to collect outwards traffic, but in order not to disrupt the account of Ralph's day any further, these are detailed separately (see page 206). However, one uniting theme is that if all the work had been completed in time, the engine and train were abandoned on the running line while the crew went over to the cement works canteen before returning to Risborough.

When the late-turn porter arrived at 1.0 p.m., the station master was usually at lunch, the clerk was in the office and the other porter was out in the yard assisting the guard of the Chinnor goods with shunting.

Invariably there were parcels to deliver to the village, so when Ralph Cann was on late turn, he began the afternoon on the railway bicycle. Very occasionally, if an item was too large or heavy for the bike, it was delivered by both porters using the 4-wheel trolley.

When Ralph returned, the whole team was usually at the station, the early-turn porter probably sorting out the paperwork from the goods train. The empties and occasional van of cement had already been recorded in the morning when the porter went over to the works at about 9.0 a.m.

Because he was in charge of the whole branch, Mr Humphrey travelled out to Watlington each afternoon on the 2.5 p.m. and did not return until the 7.15 p.m. train, leaving the clerk in charge. Most of Ralph's afternoon shift was not at all demanding, even the cleaning had been done in the morning. Besides the despatch of the few trains, there was only the occasional parcel to deal with and, in the winter months, Tilley lamps to prepare.

After the clerk had gone home, the late-turn porter was based in the office where tickets and an excess pad were left out for him, together with a cash float. However, not many tickets were sold in the evening.

Prior to going off duty, the tickets, excess pad and the cash were put in the safe, the key to which was left in a drawer. The date stamp was changed ready for the morning and the lights extinguished before locking the office and main entrance doors. Incidentally, when the Tilley lamp in the parcels office was extinguished, it was brought into the booking hall to cool down and remained there until the morning.

The routine differed on Saturdays when people travelled into Risborough in the morning for the matinee at the cinema. The clerk had a half day and the porter dealt with the exceptionally busy extra train around midday for football supporters and shoppers to Princes Risborough or High Wycombe. The 12.25, easily the busiest of the week, was so crowded that many people had to stand or sit on each other's laps. Eric Humphrey remembered Sid Jarvis (Watlington's last station master) returning home on this train. When he enquired if it was possible to find an extra coach for this one train, it transpired that an auto-trailer used for a mid-week service to RAF Bicester was stabled at Risborough over the weekend, so for a time *c.*1948 that one train ran with two trailers. The problem did not recur in the evening because returning passengers seemed to be staggered over various trains back from Risborough. When George Howlett was guard on a Saturday, he spent the whole journey from Chinnor to Risborough booking tickets, and was still taking money when they arrived in the bay platform, but there was no anxiety — "I knew most of the people . . . they were very honest." Because of this extra train, the Chinnor goods ran later on Saturdays, but the procedure in handling it was the same.

Ralph played football for Chinnor on Saturday afternoons, so, with Mr Humphrey's blessing, the opposite-turn porter, Mick Turvey, covered the earlier part of the late shift for a portion of his wages.

GOODS TRAFFIC

As with Watlington, the main outwards traffic from Chinnor for many years was predictably hay, straw, grain, agricultural produce, livestock and timber. Although the cement works became easily the largest industry in the area, most of its output went by road.

One of the farmers who used the railway was Tom Nixey, from Sussex, who bought Manor Farm, Chinnor, in 1913 when his son Henry was eight years old. When making the journey to view the farm, Henry remembers the two of them walking four miles from Cuckfield in Sussex to Haywards Heath station where they just missed a train. Then when they eventually reached Risborough, they just missed the Watlington train and had to walk again. As they were strangers, Henry remembers his father tipping a local man 6d for explaining the best route for them to reach Chinnor.

Manor Farm was mainly arable, the rest of the land being used for sheep, until 1923 when they also started a small dairy herd. About thirty gallons of milk were sent to the United Dairy in Kensington each day on the 8.55, as already recalled by Ernie Forte on page 91. By the late 1930s, the milk was sent by road using haulage contractor Crocketts of Askett.

Corn was sent to Goodeys of Reading, the sacks being loaded directly off the cart into box vans or sheeted opens whilst cattle cake was received from Goodeys. While Ernie Forte worked as a farmhand for Nixey from 1924–29, he recalled linseed cake and cotton cake arriving by rail in box vans. "We'd collect it with a big horse and wagon." Nixeys also received the occasional wagon load of coal (13 shillings per ton) for their steam-driven threshing machine. The coal was ferried round to the farm in a two-wheeled horse-drawn tipping cart.

A glimpse of the goods yard from the cement works approach. *M. J. Esau*

No. 5755 pulling away from Chinnor on its way to Watlington in 1957. The simple barricade on the weighing machine in the yard saved it from the pounding of vehicles driving over it on their way in and out of the yard. *N. C. Simmons*

The forecourt of Chinnor station on 12th June 1957 with a drinking water wagon in the end loading dock. The well was unreliable by this time so water was sent from Risborough. In November 1934, official records show that tank No. 39 was despatched to Chinnor when the water supplies at Wainhill Cottage and Chinnor station had failed. In the 1930s, a timber-built loading platform was built alongside the dock siding for loading timber. According to Eric Harmsworth, the station master's son, the dock was used for loading hay, straw and grain whilst cattle and horses were received and despatched here. George Howlett recalled two or three vans of fertilizer at a time being unloaded here by workers from Hill Farm. The inlaid narrow gauge track, still in situ in the foreground, had connected with Siarey's timber yard, details of which are given on page 111.

R. M. Casserley

By 1929 times were hard on the farm so Mr Nixey advised Ernie to find another job and here we have a slight but most interesting diversion which throws light on other traffic. For twelve months Ernie worked for Mr Knight, a builder from Chinnor Hill, but as the Depression had set in, he could not sell one of his houses. Things were looking pretty bleak until one day when Ernie was on his motorbike and called at Surman's garage in Crowell for petrol. He was greeted with the question, "Here, Ern, want to buy a lorry?" They had just built an 'open wagon' on a 'Chev Six' chassis and offered it to him for £50. He said he could give them £25, and they said "That'll do, pay the rest when you can". That night in the Black Boy public house, a foreman for the South Oxfordshire Council said he had heard that Ernie was in the contracting business and asked if he would move 29 tons of granite chippings which had arrived at Chinnor station. It was required for tarmacking Chinnor Hill but the council could not find anyone to move it and the wagons were already incurring demurrage charges.

Ernie had yet to learn to drive so he taught himself on the Sunday afternoon prior to carting the 6-ton loads up Chinnor Hill the next day!

The goods yard crane FM139 probably dated from the 1912 yard improvements when the goods shed and its internal crane were swept away. The 20-ton weighbridge, No. 4182, again obstructed to prevent traffic passing over it, was moved from South Lambeth in 1928 to replace an older machine which was obsolete and subsequently condemned. This work cost £155.

A. E. Smith

The siding in the foreground of this view of the goods yard was known as 'the short road', whilst the one behind, which incorporated a crossover connection with the running line, was known as 'the long road'. This 1957 view featuring 5755 with a Watlington-bound train, also shows the permanent way hut on the edge of the yard. A velocipede was dumped alongside the gangers hut at one time. It is said to have been difficult to use because of the gradients. In later years, the gang only used the hand trolley, but Charlie Adby said that at one time the velocipede had been used on Good Fridays and Boxing Day "when there was only one train". *N. C. Simmons*

He completed the delivery over the following three days and afterwards was offered successive 29-ton consignments and 'clearing up work' behind the roadworks gang. Following this, he was also offered carting for the cement works, and farmer Henry Hill asked Ernie if he was willing to handle trusses of hay and straw to both Chinnor and Aston Rowant stations. Ernie was only too pleased to accept, and over the years moved "tons and tons for him", mostly destined for the horses which worked in London.

Ernie enjoyed his work — "It was nice to be alive in them days. As soon as you pulled into the station they'd ask if you were on your own, then say, 'Come on, I'll give you a hand'. Today they'd just say that's not my job."

If there was anything to be delivered, the station master would ask him to take it and Ernie would send the bill in afterwards. He also helped out Chinnor coal merchant Jess Rogers when he was taken ill, and Hopkins brothers who, based at Aston Rowant, "delivered for miles around". "I carted hundreds of tons for them." During the war, Ernie returned to the land because it was more profitable, so a 5-ton Bedford, he had run using casual labour, was sold back to Surmans, but he kept the Chevrolet.

Jack Rutland remembered Joe Hill sending out hay which was loaded by the farmer and sheeted by Alf Taylor and Joe Bateman. The Hill family are said to have farmed in the area for 300 years. Joe's father, Henry, lived at Ellwood House, alongside the main road at Crowell, just outside Chinnor, whilst Joe lived at Woodway Farm. The farm itself was principally arable with, at one time, wheat and barley being sent to Henley Brewery on a steam lorry.

Even into the 1950s, the Hills used Chinnor station to receive and despatch animals. Cattle came from Devon and sheep from Scotland, sometimes in wagons attached to the last passenger train, and were unloaded in the platform at Chinnor. This was not popular with the station staff as the vans would, by that stage of the journey, carry a considerable amount of dung which was trampled all round the station, making a lot of work for the porters who had to clear it all up. When animals for Hills arrived after dark, they were kept in Mr Eggleton's field, near Siareys, by arrangement, and driven to Hill's farm the following morning.

During the Second World War, Hill, in common with so many other farmers, was compelled to grow sugar beet, which was shovelled into open wagons at Chinnor station by farm hands and again sheeted by railway staff.

Bryan Bowler recalls that in the 1940s the principal farmers using Chinnor station were Bill Lacey and A.A. King from Sydenham, who were both also haulage contractors. They both sent out hay, some of which went to the GWR provender store at Didcot, as did some of Joe Hill's. Absalom Lacey had run a carrier's service for many years, his son Bill, who left school around 1910, taking ducks to Campbell and Langley, distributors for the hotel trade in London. Other services included a run to Thame market on Tuesdays, often with passengers seated on forms put inside the cart. However, in the 1920s when other carriers began to use lorries, Laceys concentrated more on farming although they still carted some items for the railway until at least the 1940s. Bill Lacey carted gravel for the council, using lorries driven by Jim Holland and Reuben Giles who were employed as farm hands and drivers. They also carried hay and straw for Joe Hill who sent straw to High Wycombe for use as packing in the despatch of furniture.

Other agricultural traffic arriving by rail in the 1940s included an annual van of seed potatoes from Scotland for the local allotment association, and Bryan Rich recalled potatoes dyed blue for animal feed. These were also collected by local farmers.

COAL MERCHANTS

FRENCH, BALL, TWYMAN

G. French lived at the King's Head public house (Landlord Mr Barnacle) and traded in coal from some time between 1903 and 1907. This appears to have been rather a hand-to-mouth set-up because he neither stored coal at the King's Head, nor, as far as we know, did he rent wharfage at the station. He is said to have taken orders before the coal arrived at the station and is recalled making deliveries using buckets and a hand trolley. He received about a wagon load per week.

By 1911, the business was taken over by Charles Ball, who delivered larger quantities using a horse and cart, which he kept at the Lord Nelson where he was landlord. He also had his own railway wagon (lettered 'C. Ball') which he was so proud of that he made a point of watching it in service in goods trains. Because of the shortage of men in the area during the Great War, Charlie was helped out by Clifford Price, son of the Watlington branch ganger, who unloaded large quantities of coal in the goods yard, assisted by porter Joe Bateman. They shovelled it into 1cwt bags which were stored at the Lord Nelson. Much of Ball's supply is said to have come from Baddesley Colliery.

Around 1920, Ball retired and the business transferred to John Henry Twyman, a Londoner and ex-Navy stoker, who also took over the Lord Nelson. Assisted by his son, he is said to have received one wagon a week and used a horse and cart for deliveries. It is not clear for how long he traded but he is said to have given up following the tragic death of his son on the crossroads below the station, where he rode a new bicycle into a horse and cart. Twyman is not listed in the local 1928 trade directory.

FRY, SHRIMPTON

Shortly after the Great War, Miss Ella Fry ran a coal business which trade directories for 1920 and 1924 list as John Fry based at the Royal Oak. The horse and cart, driven by Gerry Seymour, covered not only Chinnor itself but outlying villages such as Sydenham. Again they received about one wagon a week.

Fry's business was taken over in the 1920s by Charlie Shrimpton, operating from the Bledlow Road with a horse and cart. He is said to have had one of the first lorries in Chinnor, and traded until the 1930s.

CARTER

Another coal business operating in Chinnor around the Great War was run by Joe Carter of the Wheatsheaf public house, but he is said to have handled only a small amount of coal and is remembered pushing 1cwt barrow loads (sold for one shilling) from the Wheatsheaf into Chinnor.

COLE/PLUMRIDGE

Arthur Charles Cole came to Chinnor during the First War, and started his coal business from Four Ways

Ernie Forte with, in the foreground, Bill Stopps, Jimmy Quater and a colleague whose name is not recalled. This picture was taken c.1932/3 when Ernie was involved in carting granite chippings from Chinnor station with his green 'Chevvy'. ***Cty. Ernie Forte***

in lower Station Road about 1920. He is listed in trade directories from 1924. He started with a single horse and cart, then later, after he had purchased another, he sometimes used the two horses together as a team. These were superseded by a 1-ton lorry bought from Horace Horton, a local miller who went out of business. Cole was the first Chinnor merchant to use a lorry, which enabled him to cover Chinnor, Bledlow Ridge, Sydenham, Horsenden, Aston Rowant, Stokenchurch, Ipstone, Haddenham, Long Crendon and Thame.

Cole did not have an office in the station yard but he did rent wharfage there, penned with old sleepers along the back of the yard. Even so, most coal was bagged straight off the wagon, and his main supplies were kept in his own yard in lower Station Road. Most of his coal came from London factor, Frank Butt, supplies arriving in various colliery wagons, apparently up to three a week.

Cole retired shortly before the Second War, when the business was taken over by Jim Plumridge, who married Cole's daughter and operated from Chinnor Hill. He replaced the lorry with a 3-tonner and expanded the business, taking over some other local merchants. Ernie Forte said Plumridge received between eight and ten wagons a week. "It was a big business." Plumridge became the last Chinnor-based coal merchant to use the railway.

ROGERS

Jess Rogers was trading from premises in the High Street by 1928. Eric Harmsworth said that in the early 1930s Rogers was the main merchant at Chinnor and apparently also rented wharfage along the back of the yard. During the 1930s when Rogers was taken ill, local haulage contractor Ernie Forte used his lorry to do the coal round for him. During this time, Rogers received about 2–3 wagons a week, and Ernie remembers Ted Fortnam, who worked for Rogers filling the bags ready for him to collect from the station. Supplies were kept both there and at Rogers' own yard. During this time, Jess asked Ernie if he would take the business on, but he declined. However, his health must have improved because Bryan Bowler remembers Jess unloading his own wagons during the war. When Jess died, his wife continued the business, employing Ted Fortnam who also drove the horse and cart. Incidentally, trade directories for 1911 and 1915 list a coal merchant by the name of Fortnum operating from the Black Dog public house, but whether this was Ted Fortnam is not clear. However, Ted Fortnam subsequently took over the business from Jess Rogers' wife, and eventually sold out to Plumridge about 1950.

Ted Fortnam, who had worked for Jess Rogers, seen here from the window of a branch train passing Chinnor goods yard in the mid-1950s when he was presumably employed by Jim Plumridge. *A. Attewell*

W.H. SIAREY

Siarey's business dated at least as far back as the 1840s when William Siarey was listed simply as a mason at Kingston. By 1877 the business was based at Aston Rowant under Mrs Susannah Siarey's name. In 1903 William Howard Siarey was listed as 'general builder, contractor, decorator, undertaker and sanitary engineer', and by 1915, 'timber merchant'. Siarey is believed to have handled timber for the Great War when the government controlled supplies, and during this time he established a timber yard and sawmill in the Oakley Road.

Towards the end of the Great War, a 180 acre wood was felled and the timber was loaded at Chinnor station for despatch to Walkers, a timber wholesaler in London. Farmer Henry Nixey's father helped transport it all to the station, but whether Siareys had any involvement is not known.

By the time Arthur Sherwood became an employee in 1931, Messrs W.H. Siarey were trading as general builders, with the occasional load of timber received by rail from Osborn Stevens of Uxbridge. This was mainly softwood used in house construction and apparently arrived in Osborn Stevens' own wagons. Other suppliers included Davis of West Drayton, who imported softwood, Gosnell, and Norlsons.

During the Second World War, the yard was enlarged to serve as a Ministry storage area for timber. The Ministry maintained strict control over stocks and used its own lorries to move supplies around the country as required. Stocks were frequently replenished from other similar depots.

The sawmill was powered by a Blaxstone stationary steam engine which was connected to the machine via an overhead shaft. During the war, the yard was manned throughout day and night but, because of the blackout, the steam engine was not used after dark because of the sparks.

Besides the saw mill, there were also two timber drying kilns which produced kilned elm. This was particularly useful for ammunition boxes used in the desert because it was the only wood not affected by the heat. Siareys had the best kilns in the area and during the 1950s installed another two. Other wartime products included pit props, whilst Chinnor porter Bryan Bowler recalled some timber being sent out in sheeted wagons and also truckloads of wooden track keys destined for the GWR creosote works at Hayes.

All this traffic was handled at the wooden platform by the crane in the goods yard and was ferried there from the sawmill by local motor haulier Horace Horton of Mill Road, Chinnor.

In the early postwar years, the company owned two Fordson tractors for hauling timber 'bobs' (open-frame trailers) used to collect locally felled timber. Although they handled elm and oak, the main supplies were beech, some of which at this period came from Stonor Park and Amersham and even as far afield as Surrey. Each tractor was accompanied by a team of men to cut and fell, but the tractors were later superseded by Commer articulated lorries driven by, among others, Bob Gee and Alf Stanley.

W.H. Siarey's son Ronald, who joined the company straight from school in 1934, took over in 1947 and expanded the business by supplementing locally grown beech and oak logs with imported beech from France. Initially this arrived as logs, but later it arrived already sawn into planks. The wood was seasoned, 'put in stick', at the back of the goods yard on both their own land and the railway company's.

In order to handle all of this timber, W.H. Siarey & Son Ltd laid narrow gauge rails from the rear of the loading dock in the goods yard, across the station approach, across Meadow Road and into their premises. The rail system served the log stacks, sawmill and timber seasoning stacks and was laid across railway property under an agreement dated 16th May 1949. The Jubilee track and 18 bogies which ran on it were purchased from George Cohen of Shepherds Bush whilst the line was laid by Miles of Long Crendon.

As business increased, the timber was moved into the yard on lorries instead; one of them, an 8-wheeled AEC, could only turn at the bottom of the yard. Siareys also came to use their own mobile crane instead of the fixed one in the goods yard. Thus the tramway fell out of use and the agreement with British Railways was eventually terminated on 31st December 1958.

Incidentally, offcuts and shavings were collected by Horace Horton in his Ford lorry. He took the dust to a pit near the Icknield Way at Crowell and disposed of offcuts, which he purchased for a nominal sum, by hawking them around Chinnor for sale as firewood.

Siareys actually ran two businesses from the site, the other, the Grovelands Building Co., run by Jim Wise, fronting onto Oakley Road. This was a general builders merchants, builders and undertakers. The funeral director was Vernon Croxford. Until the early 1950s, they offered elm coffins made by Frank Beckenham who travelled in each day on the 7.25 a.m. from Watlington. His place was later taken by Tony Smith.

This group of workers at Siareys in 1942/3 shows (from left to right): *Back row:* Frank Neighbour, Henry Smith, Bernard Croxford, Arthur Sherwood, Horace Horton, Harry Witney. *Second row:* Jack Britnell (standing to the left), Ted White, Alf Stanley, John Goodchild (boy), Wilf Spiller (man in trilby), Derek Cattlin (standing), Tony Benham (standing). *Third row:* Clem White, Bert Hopkins, Peter Graffy, Percy Harris, Henry Gray (laughing). *Fourth row:* (three heads close together) Albert Bishop, Walter Crowdy, John Barndon, Doug Gibbs, Cliff Rumbelow, Norman Gibbs, Michael Harman, Ted Newitt, Les Gibbs, Unknown, Sam Pullin. *Fifth row:* Bill Harman, Jim Wise, Victor Stroud (with arms folded), Frank Bishop, Charlie Gibbs, Arthur Rodgers, Joe Cox, Charlie Rodgers, Vernon Croxford, Will Stroud. *Front row:* Frank Beckenham (standing), Bert Horton (standing), Joe Collins, Tommy State (seated on ground), ? Coward, Ron Siarey, W. H. Siarey, John Adnett (kneeling), Charlie Chapels (seated on ground). *Cty. Victor Stroud*

A wonderful panoramic view west from the hills, showing Wainhill Crossing on the left halfway down the print, and the line's approach from Risborough, in the 1930s. Crossing keeper Jessie Smith's son David said "It was the best place to be brought up". *Ronald Goodearl*

WAINHILL CROSSING 2m 66c

Violet ('Girlie') Price pictured by the garden gate at Wainhill Crossing in the 1920s. *Cty. Violet Saw*

WE are not sure when Fred Price and his family first moved into Wainhill Crossing House, but it was probably around 1912 when he was appointed Watlington branch ganger. He succeeded a Mr Drummond who, like his predecessor Blackhall, had occupied the cottage, their wives serving as crossing keepers.

Fred, who had started out as a farmhand for Fred North, moved to Marlow after he was married in 1903. However, his wife Louisa suffered ill health, so they moved back to Chinnor in order that her mother could look after her. By 1905 he had become a platelayer at Chinnor, and by the time he was appointed ganger, they had three children, Violet, Wilfred and Clifford. A fourth child died in infancy.

Louisa looked after the crossing, where the gates were normally across the lane. There was no warning of the approach of trains, they just knew the timetable, but the railway telephone provided in the house was particularly useful in fog. Normally, with a good view from the crossing in both directions, trains were "easily seen" although apparently

Ganger Frederick Price at Bledlow Bridge in the 1920s. *Cty. Violet Saw*

The Chinnor PW gang at Wainhill in the 1920s. They were (left to right) unidentified, Bob Johnson, Monty, unidentified, Reg Gibbons, Fred Seymour and Frederick Price, the ganger. The unidentified men are said to have been employed as carpenters.

Frederick Price and one of his dogs.

Violet and one of the enginemen, as yet unidentified, in the 1920s.

Louisa Price and her daughter Violet.

"during gales the gates had to be closed three minutes beforehand."

Fred left the house every morning at 6.30 a.m. and walked to Chinnor, where his men assembled at the hut on the edge of the goods yard to collect tools and instructions. Two members of the gang recalled were Walter Hopkins and Bob Johnson. The sub ganger for many years was Fred Seymour, who usually walked to Watlington and back on his daily inspection. Fred Price walked to Risborough and returned on the 10.22 a.m.

Fred and his family kept pigs, goats and dogs at the crossing, and in the 1920s one of the dogs, a black retriever or labrador called Monty, became very much part of the scene to staff and passengers. He apparently knew the times of the trains and used to wait on the halt platform to collect Mr Price's newspaper off the 10.22 a.m. ex-Risborough each morning. However, on one occasion, a note, which had been placed in the paper, blew away and, in his attempt to retrieve it, he ran under the train and tragically was killed. The *Daily Mail* even carried a feature on him.

Sadly, Louisa died around 1930, the family remaining at the crossing and the children manning the gates until around 1933. Fred subsequently moved to Station Road, Chinnor, "opposite his daughter Violet", and later, after marrying a Mrs Ball, moved near the Bird in Hand public house.

It is not clear who occupied the crossing directly after them, but a train is said to have run through the gates shortly after they left, something which did not happen during the tenure of the next known occupant, Mrs Daisy Walker, who seems to have been there from at least December 1933 to early 1937. Her husband Steve was not on the permanent way, but served as a porter at Chinnor on the opposite shift to Joe Bateman. The Walkers had previously lived at Risborough above the tailor's shop. She remembers Wainhill as "a beautiful place".

The lane over the railway at this point deteriorated further on as it led up the hillside to the Leather Bottle public house. As it

This picture of Monty at Wainhill Crossing appeared in the *Daily Mail*.

Mrs. Louisa Price and Monty.

This snapshot of Monty also gives a precious view of the lane which led from the B4009.

Photos: cty. Violet Saw

was not suitable for road vehicles, traffic over the crossing was solely for the few houses on the eastern side of the line.

The nearest property, just up the road on the right, was occupied by Mrs Ludgate who had a big family. Her children played together with Mrs Walker's. The next property was a wooden building occupied by an old couple, followed by the 'fly house', so called because it was unoccupied and the windows were "always covered in flies". Above that were "the big houses", one of them occupied by a lady who had been an actress. Mrs Walker worked for her on Sundays.

These properties did not attract much traffic, only the occasional horse and cart and the odd car. Pedestrians used the small wicket gates, but the main ones were kept across the lane. People would open the gates themselves, but "I had to be alert when I knew a train was due" because some would leave the gates across the line. However, it was very quiet at Wainhill and sometimes Mrs Walker did not see anyone from one week to another.

When she went to live at the crossing, Mrs Walker had four children (John and Pat from her first marriage, and Diana and Doreen from Steve), whilst a fifth, Tony, was born while she was there, her father-in-law, a signalman at Risborough, using a week's holiday to cover the gatekeeper's duty while she was away for the birth.

This view looking across Hill Field was taken from Keens Lane, or Donkey Lane Level Crossing as it was known, between Chinnor and Wainhill. In the early 1800s, wood cut from the hillside for chairmaking was carried along the ancient 'hollow ways' by donkeys fitted with panniers. These animals were kept in a building just off the right-hand edge of the picture. The land on both sides of the railway from Wainhill to Chinnor was farmed by W. Eggleton. The two detached houses in the centre of the picture, Stepping Hills and Greenways, were built alongside the Icknield Way for Miss Chance and Miss Cobb. Both properties were later acquired by the Cement Company, Stepping Hills for use as a hostel for Polish workers, and Greenways for a warden's house. The scar on the hillside on the right of this picture, above the end of Keens Lane, was known as 'The Horseshoe'. This was a popular play area with children sliding down the slope in rubber tyres and on scraps of corrugated iron.

Accommodation at the crossing was extremely modest, especially for a family with four children, two Alsatians and a cat. As built, it was basically two rooms on the ground floor and one upstairs, whilst a lean-to, which was almost certainly a later addition, provided a scullery. Mr and Mrs Walker had the bedroom whilst the children slept in the two downstairs rooms, and a landing at the top of the stairs also provided a site for a single bed. An old sleeper-built hut at the back of the cottage is said to have been built by ganger Drummond.

There was no mains water, gas or electricity, cooking and heating being provided by a "huge, great kitchen range", and washing was done using an old-fashioned copper heated by wood or "anything that would burn". Water for washing was collected in a large rainwater tank at the front of the house and drinking water from a well, a full bucket of each being kept in the scullery. It took many buckets to fill the copper for washing or a bath, and even the sink drained into another bucket which had to be emptied. Lighting was provided downstairs by a large brass paraffin lamp bolted to the middle of the ceiling, an oil lamp in the scullery and candles upstairs.

The lavatory in the shed was yet another simple galvanised bucket positioned under a wooden seat with a hole in it. It was emptied at night into holes dug alongside the line

with John holding the lamp, "when no-one was about". "It was jolly heavy to carry".

The family lived on rabbits shot by Mr Walker or an aitch-bone of beef bought from the occasional trip in to Wycombe when Mr Walker could stand in for his wife's duty. This aitch-bone was "a cheap cut if you took the lot" and, kept in a meat safe on the outside wall of the cottage, it lasted the family all week, also providing dripping and soup.

They had "quite a nice little bit of garden" and never bought any vegetables, although her husband wasn't much of a gardener, "but his father was very good". "We grew what

The line climbed almost continuously from just over a mile outside Risborough to a summit before Chinnor, so the progress of trains could usually be heard very clearly all the way. George Nicholson recalled that on occasions they tried to take too many wagons and would get stuck. When this occurred, they left some of the vehicles secured on the bank with the brake van and took the front part of the train on to Chinnor with the guard on the footplate, returning for the rest of the train as soon as they had run round. This picture was taken looking down the bank towards Risborough on 12th June 1957. *R. M. Casserley*

we could". There was also a greengage tree in the garden outside the sitting room, and a Magnum Blue plum tree.

Milk was bought from Eggletons Farm, the children taking an empty 2-pint can down the track with them to Donkey Lane on their way to school. They left it at the farm entrance and collected the full can on their way home. "They never spilled any."

Daisy did not do much shopping in Chinnor, and did not go into Watlington. She was "very tied and couldn't move hardly at all — once a week was your limit." Money was very tight, Steve Walker earning £1 10s 0d a week whilst she received ten shillings for crossing keeper duties. There were no luxuries, "no butter — only margarine". Her son Pat remembers how the family furniture "had to be returned because we couldn't afford it".

They were allowed a certain amount of coal each year from the railway, but the loco crews were always dropping some off for her out of the bunker and often stopped for a chat if she was outside.

To supplement their income, Mrs Walker took in washing from porter Joe Bateman's wife Ivy, who took in lodgers at their home in Station Road, Chinnor. Daisy earned a shilling a week for laundry, regularly sent (unofficially) on the train to and from the crossing "providing no-one was about". The money was also sent on the train. "We were all very poor, and used to help one another." "It was hard work but I was very happy." "Life is not as sweet as it was."

"On Friday nights we used to boil the copper and have baths in the galvanised bath which was kept on the wall." A fish and chip cart used to come up the lane on Fridays and, if the children were well behaved, she bought them a penny worth of chips each

Even though the halt at Wainhill was not opened until 1925, it was still equipped with conventional oil lamp standards and cases similar to those shown in the pictures of the other halts. However, in the 1930s, these were replaced by the utilitarian tubular posts with hooks for hurricane lamps, as seen here. The wooden steps alongside the lamp posts were made specially to enable Jessie Smith to reach the hook when hanging the lamps, but they also doubled as boarding steps for the spare coach. 16th August 1955. *J. N. Faulkner*

and occasionally a piece of fish between her and her husband.

Other treats recalled by her son Pat included nut brittle sold at the Tuck Shop at the foot of Chinnor Hill, and occasional visits by train to see their grandmother at Marlow, the children travelling on their own.

Daisy's duties at the halt included lighting the platform lamp and looking after the ones on the gates. These were all trimmed in the scullery with oil kept in the shed. She was issued with a hand signal lamp so that she could see what she was doing.

As there was no train service on Sundays, they were free to go out, and, just like Audrey Griffiths at Kingston Crossing, Mrs Walker recalls "We walked for miles in those days."

Her husband Steve spent many hours studying to become a signalman which was his dearest ambition and, in the course of bettering himself, they moved away to Marlow. She would like to have stayed at Wainhill — "We were so carefree and happy." As things turned out, he was killed in an accident after taking his signalling exam and never saw the letter which arrived the morning after his death, telling him that he had passed.

The next occupants, Percy Smith and his wife Jessie, stayed rather longer, moving in early 1937 and remaining there for 24½ years. Percy, whose father was station master at Bledlow on the Thame line, was born in 1911 and served as a porter at Saunderton from 1927, then Chinnor from 1931 to 1937–8, presumably taking Steve Walker's place on the opposite shift to Joe Bateman. He married Jessie in October 1935.

Jessie recalled the railway telephone but said that, as they knew the times of the passenger trains, Risborough or Chinnor staff

Percy Smith on the halt platform in the late 1930s. When he was working at Chinnor and on relief work elsewhere, he used his bicycle and later a motorbike. *Cty. Jessie Smith*

Looking north towards Risborough on 12th June 1957. *R. M. Casserley*

Jessie Smith and her children, David, Colin and Jean, at Wainhill shortly after the war. *Cty. Jessie Smith*

would only ring to let her know when a goods train was on its way as the time for these varied. If the Watlington goods was running some way behind schedule because of work at Risborough, she often rang them to find out where it was.

She could see at least half a mile down the line in each direction and recalls how the sometimes heavily-laden goods trains took so much longer to reach the crossing, but she could not remember one stalling on the bank.

Motorists usually sounded their horns, and cyclists their bells, to summon her to open the gate and let them across.

With only nine or ten houses beyond the crossing, the gates were not used much, but, as Mrs Walker had found, people "would get themselves through but leave the gate swinging". When Jessie first went there, "it used to be horses and carts", but there were gradually more cars. Besides local inhabitants, regular motor vehicles in her time included Mr Mackintosh, the milkman, who called just after 9.0 a.m. He had a dairy at Little Horsenden, and in the 1930s deliveries to Wainhill were usually made by horse and cart driven by Horace Bowler. In later years deliveries were made by Frank Neighbour, a milkman from High Street, Chinnor. Other tradesmen included Percy Seymour, a baker based in the High Street, whose deliveries were also made by Bill Rutland (and later a girl), Ken Parslowe, a butcher based at the corner of Thame Road and Lower Road, Chinnor, and Arthur Witney, a grocer from Bledlow, who also sold paraffin for lighting.

Regular visitors included the permanent way gang who would call in for a cup of tea when they were passing.

Jessie's duties at the crossing included keeping the lamps alight on the gates (they showed red one way and green the other) and trimming and lighting the oil lamps hung on a post to illuminate the platform. To

The Smiths' eldest son David c.1938. *Cty. Jessie Smith*

The crossing viewed from the rear of a Risborough-bound train. *Hugh Davies*

reach them, she had a wooden step made from old wooden sleeper offcuts nailed together. Sometimes there were such gales that the platform lamp had to be put inside the shelter instead, whilst, if the gates banged, the lamps mounted on them would go out.

It was not until about 1950 that mains water and electricity were finally laid on to the crossing cottage, so Jessie, who raised three children there, shared much the same experience of living there as her predecessors, with oil lighting, a kitchen range for cooking and heating, and unofficial coal from the branch engine to supplement their allowance. In the summer she used to put the milk down the well to keep it cool. She said the water in the well "was nice until a nest of ants dropped in the water". Rainwater collected in "the big tank" was still boiled in the copper for washing and baths and "never seemed to run out".

Jessie found "it was a tie" to look after the crossing, but managed to get into Chinnor between 3.30 and 6.0 p.m. when there was a gap in the timetable while the Watlington engine worked a trip to Thame. Otherwise her neighbour, Mrs Ludgate, looked after the crossing for her — "You don't realize how pally it was", and reinforced this throughout her recollections with sentiments like "You'd do anything for anyone" and "I'm sure it was a better time".

On her way to Chinnor, Jessie used to cycle in the cess alongside the track as far as Donkey Lane when she was taking her children to school, but, after the ganger caught her doing this, she had to cycle across the fields instead. Mr Neighbour, the milkman, sometimes took the children to school for her.

Jessie also recalls Mrs Connie Croxford from Chinnor who took an old pram to Wycombe to do other people's shopping. She would come back on the 6.0 p.m. with cakes, buns and fish and chips. "The train had even been known to shunt back to Risborough when they realised they'd left without her."

Some of the winters were hard; the snow in 1941–2 blocked the road and was so deep at Wainhill that it was level with the tops of the hedges. They managed to keep the trains running, so milk, bread and papers for the nearby houses were dropped off at the crossing and delivered by Jessie.

By this time, Percy Smith had become a relief porter/guard, travelling to wherever he was required on his motorbike. When he was needed at Watlington, where he is said to have covered guard's duties following Tom Bowler's accident, he used to have to get up early enough to reach Watlington in time for the 4.20 a.m. goods. However, sometimes, particularly if he was running late, he would telephone the driver to tell him to wait at the crossing and they would pick him up on their way out to Risborough.

Jessie recalls flags and detonators at the house, but she never had to use them. However, the gates were run through twice during her time there. On one of these occasions, a group of young people, expected back late at night on their way home from a dance, assured her they would close the gates behind them. However, while their taxi went across the line to drop them off and turn, at sometime between 11.0 and 11.30 p.m., they forgot and left the gates across the track. Inevitably, the late goods returning from Risborough ran through both gates before the car had returned.

This upset Jessie who felt she had failed the railway — "You knew you were in charge". The gates were replaced within a day.

On the other occasion, although a friend was entrusted to look after the gates one morning, they were left across the track and run through by Geoff Pearson with the early morning goods.

The children would help out and take it in turns to work the gates, but, if the family were away, the Chinnor station master would arrange for a porter to cover the duty. He would take a flask with him and sit in the hut all day, but if the Smiths were away on their week's holiday, the porter could not sit outside all that time, so he based himself in the house and looked after the animals.

BLEDLOW BRIDGE HALT

1m 43c

Certainly by the 1940s, Bledlow Bridge Halt was only used by a handful of people, although fireman Tony Benham recalls a few extras once a month for a children's home that was "just up the hill" to the south of the bridge, opposite the road to the village. A parents afternoon there brought extra passengers who travelled out on the 1.55 p.m. from Risborough and returned on the 7.15 from Watlington. Otherwise Tony regarded it as "a very poor halt".

The responsibility for the halt was given to the station master at the nearby Bledlow station on the Oxford line. For many years this was Percy Smith, whose son Percy lived at Wainhill Crossing. During the late 1930s and 40s, Les Smith, another son, served as porter

A train from Watlington approaching Bledlow Bridge Halt on 25th July 1955. *H. C. Casserley*

BLEDLOW BRIDGE

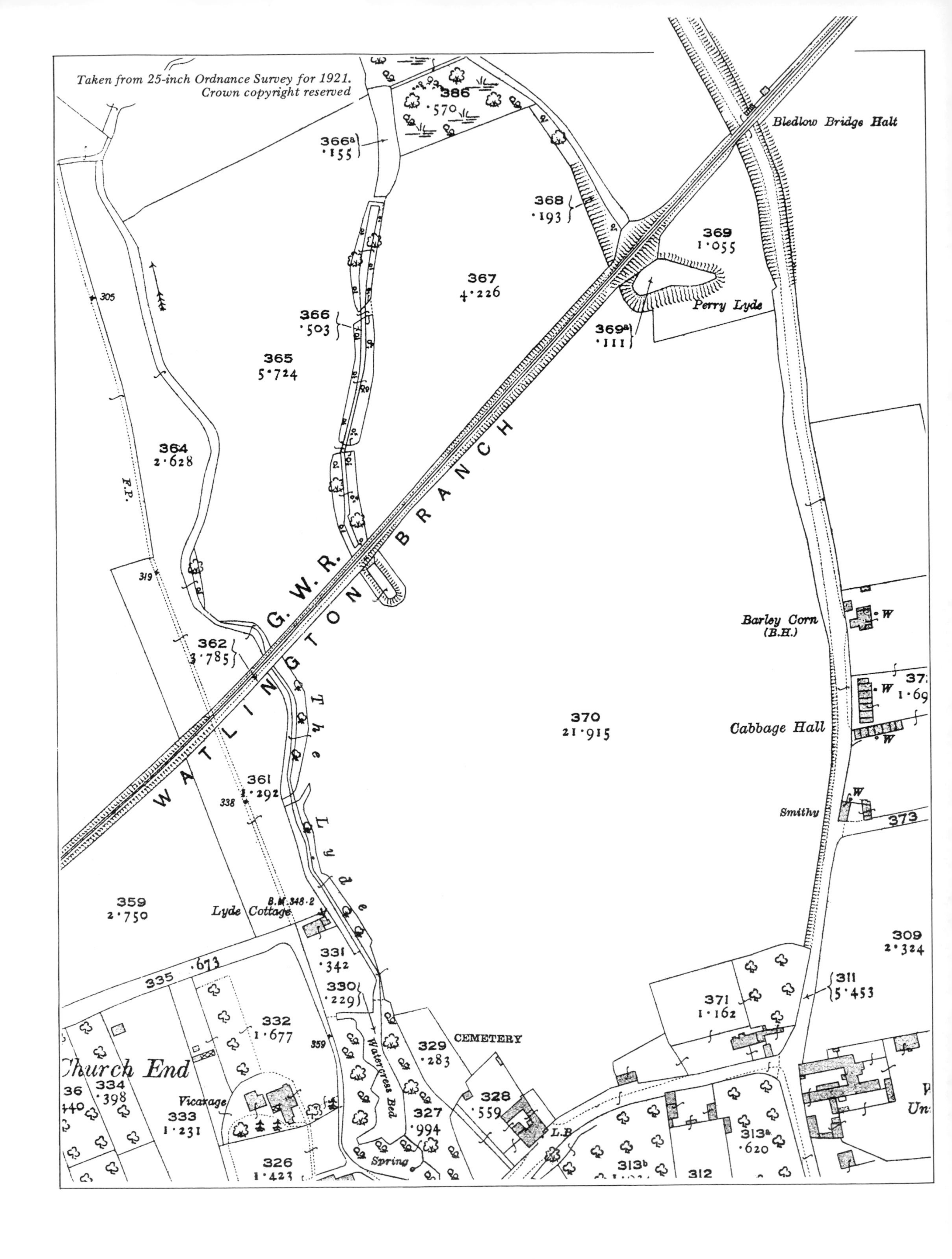

Taken from 25-inch Ordnance Survey for 1921.
Crown copyright reserved
Bledlow Bridge Halt
Perry Lyde
G.W.R. WATLINGTON BRANCH
The Lyde
Lyde Cottage
B.M. 348·2
Barley Corn (B.H.)
Cabbage Hall
Smithy
CEMETERY
Church End
Vicarage
Watercress Bed
Spring
F.P.

there, cycling out to Bledlow Bridge on Mondays with the supply of paraffin to refill the lamps, including the down distant for Wainhill. This lasted the week and during the winter months Les called at the halt each afternoon to light the lamps, which by this time were extinguished by the guard of the last train. One of his predecessors, Gerry Carpenter, had incurred an extra journey each night to put them out himself. The two lamps on the platform were reached by steps left at each base but the one over the entrance to the shelter needed a ladder which was stowed inside the shelter across the back wall. There was also a light at the bottom of the approach steps.

A passenger's view down onto the tiny platform on 10th September 1954. We have failed to discover a photograph of the steps leading up from the road. The 7 sq yds of land for the shelter were acquired from Lord Carrington in 1909. *R. M. Casserley*

No. 7442 arriving at Bledlow Bridge Halt with the 5.48 ex-Risborough which, on this occasion, 21st June 1951, evidently was conveying a number of horse-boxes ahead of the auto-trailer. *R. H. G. Simpson*

The steps of auto-trailer No. 190 photographed in the boarding position alongside the low platform at Bledlow Bridge Halt. In a report of a minor incident, relief guard Percy Smith wrote "The warning I give to passengers [descending from the trailer] is 'Mind the steps, please, they are a bit steep', and I always help them down". After giving the 'right away' to the engine crew, it was easy for the guard to close the door and forget to pull the lever which retracted the steps. If the driver or fireman noticed them still out, they would tug on the whistle several times to attract the guard's attention, then point to the steps. However, they sometimes went unnoticed and relief guard Len Howse recalls "It was always said you were never a guard on the Watlington branch until you'd broken the steps of a trailer after forgetting to retract them!" He remembers in the 1940s watching a train arrive at Risborough with the steps still out from Bledlow Bridge . . . "then there was a loud bang!" "It never happened when Harry Humphreys was driving". Tony Benham recalls "Whenever this happened, a chair was borrowed from the nearest station and used until a spare trailer could be had". According to porter Bryan Bowler, spare trailers came from Slough. They were maintained by a Carriage and Wagon Department man at Risborough and, apart from being sent for step repairs, they were changed from time to time, sometimes because the batteries went flat and there were hardly any lights at all. "Many times Slough slipped up and sent us a gas one . . . we had no gas, so they had to change it." Porter Frank Saunders could not remember the steps being broken in his time (1937-9) but he does recall how Slough had sent a gas-lit one as a temporary stand-in. *M. Wallen*

WE have already explained how the construction of the GW/GC Joint main line through Risborough radically transformed the station into such a busy junction, with expresses speeding through on their way between London and Manchester, Bradford, Birkenhead and Shrewsbury. The *Railway Observer* for March 1952 said 'Like many junctions it has spasms of activity when trains converge from all sides, followed by periods of comparative calm'.

Of course, the working of such a busy main line junction and the traffic over each line is well beyond the scope of this branch line history, but we could not resist attempting to record something of the scene which greeted passengers stepping off the little Watlington branch train. Indeed, the sharp contrast portrayed in this chapter only serves to emphasise the insignificance of the Watlington branch and all its rural charms against the greater scheme of things.

What follows is a mere summary of trains and traffic through Risborough during the immediate pre- and post-war years, to complement the period under review in our examination of the stations along the branch.

By the summer of 1937, Great Western expresses routed over the GW/GC Joint route were largely hauled by the prestigious and powerful 'King' class 4–6–0s, which were scheduled for use on the 6.30 a.m. Birkenhead, 6.55 a.m. Wolverhampton, 7.40 a.m. Shrewsbury, 9.5 a.m. Birkenhead, 3.55 p.m. Birmingham, and the return trains from Paddington at 4.5 p.m., 11.5 a.m., 2.10 p.m., 6.10 p.m. and 7.10 p.m. respectively. The 9.10 a.m. Paddington to Birkenhead was also worked by a 'King' as far as Wolverhampton, where the engine was taken off and worked back to Paddington with the 11.55 a.m. from Birkenhead. The 6.55 a.m. Wolverhampton called at Risborough and provided an excellent run to Paddington. Passenger clerk Hugh Harman recalls it as "without a doubt one of the most popular trains", whilst the 7.10 p.m. from Paddington conveyed a slip portion for Risborough, this being recalled with up to three vehicles.

The only conventional GW stopping train over the GW/GC Joint route north to Banbury was the 4.40 p.m. Paddington to Banbury, the rest of the services being provided by the Banbury and Aylesbury auto-trains, both worked by 54XX 0–6–0PTs or 48XX 0–4–2Ts. The Aylesbury auto worked two return trips from Risborough to Banbury whilst the Banbury car worked three, also conveying the slip coaches on its last down journey to serve stations north of Risborough.

Stations to the south of Risborough were served by Paddington–Aylesbury and Paddington–Oxford outer suburban trains,

PRINCES RISBOROUGH

Looking south through Princes Risborough station during the late afternoon of Monday, 2nd June 1952, with what may have been the 4.48 p.m. Aylesbury to Paddington train at the up platform, and the 5.48 p.m. to Watlington in the bay on the right. By this time, most local services from Risborough ran to Marylebone station, with only a couple of trains each from Aylesbury and Oxford using Paddington, which was reached via Maidenhead. *G. A. Hookham*

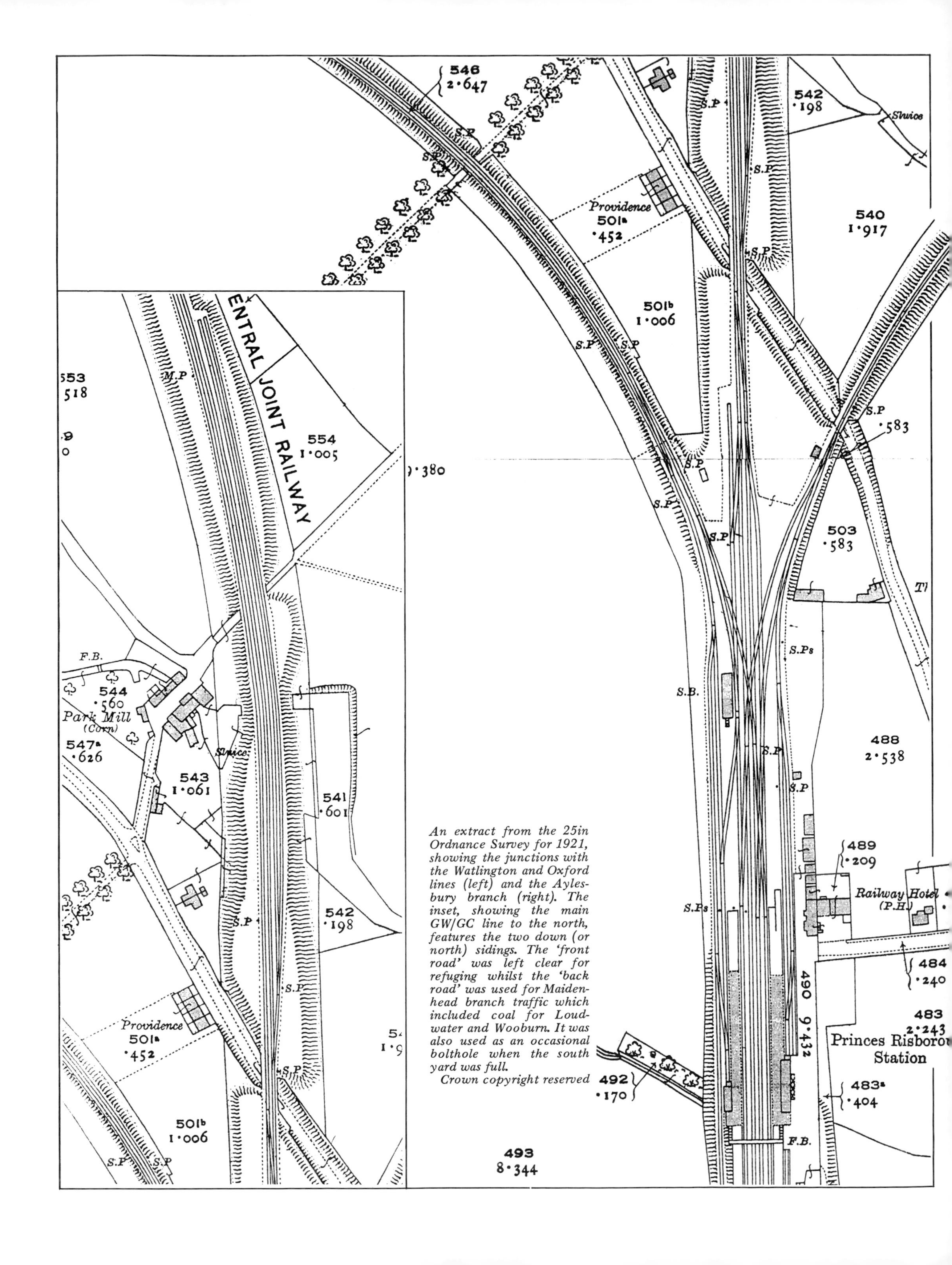

An extract from the 25in Ordnance Survey for 1921, showing the junctions with the Watlington and Oxford lines (left) and the Aylesbury branch (right). The inset, showing the main GW/GC line to the north, features the two down (or north) sidings. The 'front road' was left clear for refuging whilst the 'back road' was used for Maidenhead branch traffic which included coal for Loudwater and Wooburn. It was also used as an occasional bolthole when the south yard was full.

Crown copyright reserved

five up and six down trains worked between Aylesbury and Paddington and four return trains between Oxford and Paddington. The Aylesbury trains were run with four-coach 'A' sets (van third, first, third, van third, strengthened by up to three extras at peak times) hauled by 61XX 2–6–2Ts.

The Oxford trains were also run with four-coach 'A' sets, largely hauled by 'Hall' class 4–6–0s, although the 2.38 p.m. Oxford–Paddington was hauled by an Old Oak 'Castle' and occasionally other 4–6–0s. At this time, an Oxford diesel railcar ran two return trips over the branch, incorporating a short trip to Thame at 5.42 p.m. The Aylesbury auto also ran a trip to Thame at 8.2 p.m.

The 8.18 a.m. and 6.38 p.m. from Oxford conveyed loaded siphons for Paddington whilst the 8.10 a.m. Paddington ran with a head of milk vehicles for Watlington, Aylesbury and Oxford, and another on the rear for Thame.

On Tuesdays only, the 9.20 a.m. Paddington ran with two 61XX 2–6–2Ts, the pilot engine being uncoupled and run clear at Risborough while the train engine detached two front coaches which the pilot worked forward as the 11.15 a.m. to Thame. This engine returned with the 5.55 p.m. cattle train from Thame, and then continued on with a 6.25 p.m. Risborough to Slough cattle train.

The LNER ran three down and one up Manchester and Bradford expresses over the joint line, which up to this time had been hauled by D11 4–4–0s and C4 4–4–2s. However, by 1936–7 the ex-Great Central classes were being superseded by B17 4–6–0s, and from 1938–9 A3s and V2s were used on the 10.0 a.m. and 6.20 p.m. Marylebone to Bradford.

The 10.0 a.m. Marylebone to Bradford, the 12.15 Marylebone to Manchester and the 5.0 p.m. Bradford to Marylebone each comprised five or six coaches including a restaurant first and open third dining pair, plus one or two extra coaches at weekends, whilst the 6.20 p.m. Marylebone to Bradford had six coaches, seven on Thursdays and Saturdays, and, until December 1935, slip brakes for Stratford-on-Avon (detached at Woodford) and Brackley (detached at Finmere). The 12.15 p.m. Marylebone called at Risborough but the others passed through at high speed on the middle roads.

Three LNER local trains from Marylebone served Risborough each day, the 6.10 a.m. to Wotton, the 4.50 p.m. to Brackley and the 5.35 p.m. to Risborough, plus, on Wednesdays and Saturdays, 11.35 to Risborough which returned empty stock to Neasden Junction.

The only other local provided by the LNER was an early morning auto-train from Aylesbury to High Wycombe and back, which had been worked variously by E8 2–4–0Ts and F1 and F7 2–4–2Ts.

Until the outbreak of the Second World War, all Great Western goods trains using the GW/GC Joint line between Ashendon Junction and Northolt Junction (including those using the line between Risborough and High Wycombe, e.g. an Oxford to Taplow goods) were stopped at Risborough in both directions for numbertakers to log

This view north on 13th June 1947 shows No. 6682 of Oxford shed which had probably arrived at 1.3 p.m. with the 11.40 Oxford to Taplow freight pictured here collecting Maidenhead branch traffic left in the north siding by the up Woodford before continuing its journey at 1.50 p.m. This picture also shows the two parallel single lines for Watlington and Oxford diverging to the left and the Aylesbury branch curving off to the right. The north signal box, on the left, controlled this end of the station. ***J. H. Russell***

The interior of the impressive Princes Risborough North signal box, showing the 126-lever frame which, at 22 yards (the length of a cricket pitch), was one of the longest on the GWR. The bench on the left held the train register whilst the control telephones can be seen above the cupboard immediately beyond the small window overlooking the Watlington and Oxford lines from the west bay. The northernmost of the two fireplaces can also just be seen flanked by the two wooden chairs. Both north and south boxes were oil-lit until 1921 when gas lighting was installed, and this was superseded by electric lighting and heating in 1948. During the final years when the Watlington branch was worked by engines and crews from Slough, after the day's services when the engine returned to Slough, the single-line train staff was handed to the north box signalman who hung it over the lever for the Watlington branch starting signal. *Wilf Stevens*

the vehicles. This information was used to determine payment due to the GW/GC Joint Committee by the GWR. No similar records were made of LNER trains.

With trains of some 50–70 wagons, this task took about half an hour, which, as Hugh Harman remarked, was "all very well in the summer, but on a dark night, heavy rain, galeforce winds, snow and ice underfoot, peering at wagon labels with an oil hand lamp and writing in a notebook with pencil (copying pencils and ink would have run in wet weather) could be an arduous task indeed".

During this time most engines took water, and even after the number taking was no longer required, many trains still stopped for the purpose as evidenced by the 1944 summary reproduced on pages 210–213.

The following summary gives some idea of the Great Western goods trains which called at Risborough throughout the 24 hours each weekday in the summer of 1937. They are listed in the sequence in which they arrived.

This summary appears overleaf.

No. 6925 *Hackness Hall* from Oxford shed crossing over to the up platform line with what was probably the 2.40 p.m. Oxford to Thame service, c.1947. This engine would have been scheduled to work back to Oxford that evening with the 6.55 p.m. Paddington via Reading. Tail traffic on Thame line services was quite common until the early 1950s. *H. K. Harman*

Dave Pinfold making an entry in one of the train registers. There was a separate register for the one-engine-in-steam-worked Watlington branch. The projecting cubicle behind him housed a WC. *Wilf Stevens*

The single-line token instrument for the Aylesbury branch can be seen in the left background (partly hidden by the levers) of this picture of Dave Pinfold standing by the frame. The token instrument for the Oxford line was on the opposite side of the box, obscured in this view by the wooden walls of the WC. *Wilf Stevens*

No. 5900 *Hinderton Hall* (of Tyseley) speeding through Risborough on the up main shortly before midday on 23rd July 1955 with the 10.10 a.m. Birmingham to Margate through train (via Kensington). Apart from occasional excursions to Kent or Sussex running via Kensington (Addison Road), trains between the Midlands and the Southern Railway (or Region) had traditionally been routed via Reading, but in the summer of 1950, two up and one down Saturday trains between Wolverhampton or Birmingham and Hastings or Margate were introduced, with Southern and Western coach stock alternating. These were joined the following year by Saturday through trains from the Eastern Region, between Nottingham or Leicester and Ramsgate or Margate. The auto-trailer in the west bay had formed the 11.30 a.m. Watlington, whilst the east bay (on the right) was for Aylesbury services.

H. C. Casserley

SUMMARY OF GWR GOODS TRAINS CALLING AT RISBOROUGH – Summer 1937

12.35 a.m.–1.10 a.m.	UP	10.15 a.m. Banbury–Old Oak Common.
1.2 a.m.–3.15 a.m.	UP	11.30 p.m. Banbury–Park Royal. Put off coal loadeds into up refuge.
1.18 a.m.–2.36 a.m.	UP	12.1 a.m. Oxford–Taplow called to pick up traffic from up side.
2.43 a.m.–3.3. a.m.	DOWN	1.10 a.m. Old Oak–Tyseley.
4.31 a.m.–4.51 a.m.	DOWN	2.10 a.m. Paddington–Bordesley.
4.59 a.m.–5.10 a.m.	DOWN	3.35 a.m. Acton–Oxford. Covered cars.
5.40 a.m.–6.25 a.m.	DOWN	2.0 a.m. Paddington–Aylesbury. Stopped on down main to detach station trucks which were reversed over to headshunt, then pinchbarred to goods shed. Also station trucks for Watlington and Thame left on down side.
7.17 a.m.–8.0 a.m.	DOWN	4.55 a.m. Old Oak Common–Banbury. Empties.
8.15 a.m.–10.0 a.m.	DOWN	3.55 a.m. Slough–Oxford, dropped off traffic on down side for Risborough, Oxford and Watlington branch including empty vans from Greenford for Chinnor. Also collected. Waited for path to Oxford. Watlington/Oxford traffic sorted later by pilot. [61XX and 56XX]
10.25 a.m.–11.0 a.m.	DOWN	7.25 a.m. Old Oak–Bordesley.
11.15 a.m.–11.40 a.m.	UP	8.30 a.m. Banbury–Old Oak. [2301 and 2251] [8.30 Banbury–Acton coal ex Coventry area plus Thomas & Green traffic for 11.30 a.m. (11.42) Oxford–Taplow]
11.44 a.m.–12.36 a.m.	UP	9.40 a.m. Banbury–Old Oak, put off loaded coal in up refuge.
12.55 p.m.–2.6 p.m.	UP	11.42 a.m. Oxford–Taplow ran to up refuge to pick up and detach. [61XX and 56XX]
1.9 p.m.–4.18 p.m.	UP	12.47 p.m. Aylesbury–Risborough ran to yard and remained as pilot for shunting. Duties included sorting up and down sidings for onward transit, the down sidings at the south or London end for traffic for Watlington and Oxford, the up refuge to the north of the station (delivery and collection), bringing coal to goods yard, and serving both private sidings.
3.22 p.m.–3.40 p.m.	DOWN	9.45 a.m. Acton–Banbury picked up on down side – mainly empties.
4.19 p.m.–4.45 p.m.	UP	2.40 p.m. Banbury–Old Oak.
4.22 p.m.–4.59 p.m.	DOWN	2.45 p.m. Acton–Tyseley coal empties.
5.15 p.m.–5.45 p.m.	DOWN	3.20 p.m. Old Oak Common–Banbury, stopped for examination.
8.24 p.m.–9.39 p.m.	UP	2.30 p.m. Bordesley–Hanwell Bridge. Coal.
9.20 p.m.–9.50 p.m.	DOWN	5.45 p.m. Taplow–Oxford.
10.58 p.m.–11.12 p.m.	DOWN (SO)	9.35 p.m. Old Oak Common–Cannock Road. For examination.
11.30 p.m.–11.45 p.m.	DOWN	7.45 p.m. West Drayton–Oxley meat train.

Goods trains working between Old Oak, West Drayton or Acton and Banbury or Bordesley were normally worked by 28XX, 30XX or 43XX whilst those between Paddington and Aylesbury were worked by 31XX or 61XX.

The LNER used the GW/GC Joint route for their overnight express goods services to and from Ardwick (Manchester), York or Dewsnap (Guide Bridge). These were mainly worked by former Great Central 4–6–0s (B7s) and LNER K3s. Eight or nine mineral goods or empties also ran each way (total 16) throughout the 24-hour weekday timetable, many of them scheduled to take water at Risborough, whilst a local goods was run in each direction between Neasden and Woodford, the northbound train calling at 7.0 a.m. and the southbound train at 10.15 a.m. After the war, their arrival at Risborough coincided and crews changed over there.

After an initial reduction of services at the outbreak of the Second World War, the Great Western maintained four expresses each way between Paddington and the North. From 1940 there was an additional express in each direction between Paddington and Shrewsbury but no LNER expresses over the GW/GC Joint, the surviving service being routed over the old Metropolitan/GC line. Local services were covered by three Oxford to Paddington, and five Aylesbury to Maidenhead or Paddington trains each way, plus a through train from Banbury via Oxford to Risborough and back. The

The Aylesbury branch auto was normally worked as a push-pull, but evidently on this sunny day c.1955, an auto-fitted engine was not available and the unidentified pannier tank had to run round to the opposite end of the trailer at each end of its journey. The Railway Hotel and Witchens garage, where some passengers left their cars, can be seen in the background. Acetylene gas lighting had been provided to illuminate the station in 1905, but around 1921 this seems to have been superseded by conventional coal gas supplied by the local Princes Risborough Gas Light & Coke Co. Later, in March 1947, £1,313 was authorised for the provision and installation of electric lighting and heating in the station buildings, signal boxes, goods shed and yard in lieu of gas. The stylish concrete-posted platform lamps were provided as part of the scheme, but a report of a minor incident mentions electricity in the course of being installed in October 1948. *T. B. Sands*

The Aylesbury auto-train in the east bay and, in the background, the Watlington branch train waiting in the west bay in the mid-1950s. The 'bay spur' alongside was often used to hold stock. In October 1946, the Aylesbury auto was scheduled for two return trips to Banbury, one to Thame, and a total of four single trips over the Aylesbury branch itself. By 1953, the Thame trip had been withdrawn, but by 1959 two auto-trains were operating seven return trips over the branch, two return journeys to Banbury and two to High Wycombe, plus trips on the ex-GC line. *Real Photographs*

Oxford and Aylesbury trains were third class only and ran with 5-coach Q sets. By the summer of 1941, the GW Aylesbury auto-train was withdrawn completely but the LNER auto continued its one trip to High Wycombe, and services over the branch were maintained at about two-thirds of their pre-war level. An Oxford-based railcar provided a return trip in the morning and another in the afternoon over the Oxford line and a return trip from Risborough to Thame previously covered by the Aylesbury auto. From late 1940, the trip to Thame was covered by the Watlington branch train, as mentioned in Volume 1 on page 143.

The Banbury auto was retained with three trips, one of which ran through to High Wycombe. Although suspended for a while, the 4.35 p.m. Paddington to Banbury was reinstated in late 1940, leaving at 4.38 p.m.

In contrast to curtailment of some passenger services, wartime requirements increased the burden on goods services and GW goods trains passing through Risborough increased to around twenty each way per day. The two Slough/Taplow–Oxford trains in each direction (61XX or 56XX) were now supple-

The Watlington branch auto-trailer, abandoned in the west bay on 27th December 1951. The Watlington brake van was often left at the entrance to Forest Products private siding, as seen here.
G. D. Parkes

No. 7441 and the Watlington branch auto-trailer in the west bay and the Watlington brake van on the back road, one evening in 1951. The hand lever-operated point on the right led into the Forest Products Laboratory. On lay-overs at Risborough, Watlington fireman Tony Benham and his driver would sometimes exchange a few words with the crews of trains held in the down platform or 'watch the runners speed through'. The Watlington drivers had done their share of firing on main line services before promotion, but young Tony watched the more prestigious workings with envy – "You'd feel twice the man with a Hall". Occasionally the Watlington engine was called upon between trips to bank to Saunderton, and once, when the engine of a troop train failed, the main line crew requisitioned the Watlington engine to take the train on to Paddington.
Lens of Sutton

mented by a vacuum 'C' and a fast 'F' class freight each way between London and Worcester, usually hauled by a 49XX or 68XX. In addition to the common types, 26XX and 72XX also appeared on some of the freight passing through Risborough at this time, whilst the Acton and Banbury pick-ups were rostered for 2301 and 2251 0-6-0s.

The LNER introduced twice-daily trains from Woodford & Hinton to West London (Southall) conveying coal, with return workings of empties from Hayes or West Ealing. These worked via Grendon Underwood and Ashendon Junctions, the Joint Line and Greenford loop, and were usually worked by O4s and B7s.

At the end of the war, there was no imme diate return to normality, but in 1946 the GWR and LNER made a determined attempt to bring a pre-war level of service back to their lines. The GW expresses increased to five for Birkenhead and three for Wolverhampton, with the 7.10 p.m. Paddington slip coach being reinstated. In the up direction, there were four from Birkenhead, one from Shrewsbury and three from Wolverhampton. The 6.45 a.m. Wolverhampton continued to call at Risborough.

These northern trains ran with between nine and thirteen coaches, but at peak times they were strengthened to fifteen. Whilst these trains continued to be mostly scheduled for work by 'Kings', 'Castles' were often substituted and the new 'Counties' were regularly used on the 9.0 a.m. and 9.10 a.m. from Paddington for a time.

A Cambrian Coast train was also reintroduced on Saturdays.

The number of through trains between Oxford and Paddington reverted to four each way, mostly worked by 49XXs, although the 11.26 a.m. and 2.40 p.m. from Oxford were both scheduled for Stafford

This upper quadrant down platform starting signal and route indicator, photographed on 13th June 1947, had replaced the GWR bracket signal featured on page 97 of Vol. 1, by 1935. The route indicator read to Oxford, down main or Aylesbury. By 1958 this signal had been replaced by a Western Region steel-posted lower quadrant, with a route indicator. The starting signal for the west bay was off this picture to the left, and features in the top picture opposite and perhaps more clearly in the background of the top picture on page 134. It was a twin-armed concrete-posted upper quadrant dating from about 1937. The top arm read to Watlington and Oxford and the lower arm to the down platform line. Again its GWR predecessor, a wooden-posted bracket, features on page 97 of Vol. 1. The picture on the top of the opposite page also features the water crane which stood between the down platform and down main lines. Internal correspondence for April 1906 reveals a proposal for the provision of water cranes for the bay lines: 'It would, of course, be more satisfactory to have facilities for watering the branch engines on the bay lines, but as we cannot induce our partners, the Great Central Company, to agree to the provision of the proposed cranes at joint cost, and the traffic officers have not made out a sufficiently strong case for expenditure on Great Western account solely, this part of the scheme had better stand over for the present.' The water crane illustrated on the opposite page remained the only supply at the north end of the station and was throughout various periods regularly used by the Watlington branch engine.

J. H. Russell

The down platform and west bay viewed from the compartment of an up train on a murky winter's day in the 1950s. The smaller building on that side provided (from left to right) Ladies room and lavatory, general waiting room, and at the far end gentlemen's lavatories. A whole variety of parcels were put off at Risborough from both up and down trains. Parcels for Watlington and Oxford were left on barrows alongside the down buildings for loading into the respective guard's compartments. Porter/relief guard George Howlett recalls the 7.57 empty stock to Watlington often conveyed parcels which had missed the last train the previous day and that the quantity for Brown Brothers and Searleys was "quite heavy".

Stephenson Locomotive Society

Road 'Castles'. There were now seven departures to and arrivals from Oxford, and three to and from Thame, one of which was worked by the reintroduced Aylesbury auto. Further to this, there were now seven through trains each way between Aylesbury and Maidenhead or Paddington, worked by 61XXs and Q sets, which were also utilised for three shorter return trips between Aylesbury and Risborough. The other Aylesbury branch services were covered by the Aylesbury auto which ran two return trips, and an LNER set which made three return trips.

Stations north of Risborough were again covered by the Aylesbury auto, which did two return trips to Banbury, and the Banbury car.

The LNER reinstated one up and three down expresses between Bradford or Manchester and Marylebone whilst 6-coach local sets were used for four return trips from Marylebone to Risborough or beyond, plus a late-night train on Wednesdays and Saturdays. The expresses were hauled mainly by V2s, which were increasingly replaced by new B1s, which in turn were eventually superseded by A3s. Local services were traditionally handled by A5 4-6-2Ts, but from 1948 these were replaced by L1 class 2-6-4Ts.

A list of trains passing through or calling at Risborough each weekday in the winter of 1946 is appended separately.

No. 9653 and Diagram U trailer W87 in the west bay on the afternoon of 2nd June 1952 together with AEC railcar W15 with tail lamp in place shortly after arrival from Oxford. The Oxford and Watlington trains shared the west bay at various times, which was very handy for the transfer of parcels between Oxford and Watlington. Porter/relief guard George Howlett recalls that because the railcar from Oxford ran into the bay hard on the heels of the 8.40 a.m. from Watlington, the branch engine was prevented from running round its trailer until the railcar left again. Diesel services from and to Oxford in October 1946 amounted to two return trips, with an intermediate journey to Thame. Following the alteration in services around 1950, this was increased to four (five on Saturdays) together with the return trip to Thame, amounting to half the passenger services over the line. Oxford auto-cars normally substituted for any diesel car failures.

G. A. Hookham

Extract from the Railway Observer for March 1952.
PRINCES RISBOROUGH – Like many junctions, this station has spasms of activity when trains converge from all sides, followed by periods of comparative calm. For example, between 3.25 and 3.42 p.m. trains arrive from Banbury, Marylebone, Watlington, Oxford and Aylesbury, and between 3.45 and 4.10 depart for the same destinations (except Watlington). One hectic operation during this period is the arrival of the Watlington train in the down bay at 3.36, followed by the Oxford railcar at 3.40. During those four minutes the Watlington engine (which is at the London end) has to run round its train, propel the single coach to the buffer stops, and then retreat to allow the Oxford railcar to enter the same platform. It is doubtful if this could ever be accomplished in four minutes. After these manoeuvres are completed the Watlington engine leaves with a short coal train; on 16th Feb. it was 2112 (81B).

STAFF AT PRINCES RISBOROUGH

For many years the station master at Risborough was Arthur Gozney who had a 'no-nonsense' attitude and was respected by all. He served there from around the time of the Great War until 1942, when he was succeeded by Samuel Rudd, who remained there until 1948, then by C. Day.

Gozney, who moved from Cleethorpes where he was chief clerk, is said to have been the first GC station master at Risborough. At first he lived in Station Road with his wife, two sons and three daughters, but the Joint Committee later provided him with a station master's house, the construction of which was authorised on 23rd July 1930 for £700. Gozney's eldest son George lived in or near London and Ralph was a clerk at Watford (Met & GC Rly) station. His eldest daughter Edith was a booking clerk at Risborough during the First World War. The second daughter Iris remained at home and looked after her mother who was an invalid (and later her father Arthur when he retired) whilst Esme, the youngest, married and later took a public house.

The following were among the staff at Risborough between 1928 and the late 1940s:

2 booking clerks	R. V. (Reg) Harding 1924-28 Frank Perry 1926-30 Hugh Harman 1928-41, then 46-8 G. R. John 1937-?
2 goods clerks	Francis Mead (son of parcels porter A. H. Mead) moved from High Wycombe Goods in the early 1920s when there was only one goods clerk at Risborough. However, the work was too much for one man and in 1929 he was provided with an assistant, Lewis Allen from Briton Ferry. In 1934 Allen moved on and was succeeded for a short time by H. R. V. (Gerry) Marks, from Paddington booking office, who travelled down from London each day. In 1937 Eric Nash transferred from Watlington and when he left to join the army, his place was taken by Mr. Lewis, then Mr. Jarvis. Eric Nash returned to his position after the war. Francis Mead remained at Risborough until about 1950 when he was promoted to the District Goods Superintendent's office at Reading.
2 foremen	2 shifts, 6.0 a.m. – 2.0 p.m., 2.0 p.m. – 10.0 p.m. (later 5.30 – 1.30, 1.30 – 10.30) with a 1 hour break on late turn. The foremen's office was under the up side of the station footbridge. For many years the two foremen were Bill Swatton and Frank Rutland. Bill was succeeded by Archibald George ('Pip') Turner, who retired in the early 1950s. Frank Rutland retired in 1944 and was replaced by Tom Gibbard. The foremen shunted during the afternoons up to the departure of the 4.15 p.m. goods to Aylesbury, the loco of which served as yard pilot. The last move before departure was a long shunt across the long crossover to deposit wagons for the various down goods to pick up.
6 porters	3 shifts, early, middle and late to cover station opening hours 6.45 a.m. to 10.30 p.m. (after the 9.0 p.m. Paddington–Aylesbury due at 10.15). Porters included E. W. Coleman (1924), S. Kelly (1924), S. Harwood (1928), M. A. Taylor (1936), J. Snook (1936), E. D. Bergmein (1947), E. G. Evans (1948), E. A. Smith (1948).
1 parcel porter	Arthur Henry (Bill) Mead
1 goods porter	Middle turn – William (Wally) Harvey.
1 ticket collector	Harry Jones transferred to Risborough from Marylebone, but when he returned in October 1934, the post was never filled.
3 number takers	3 shifts, 24 hr cover. Charles Swatton, Jack Leggett and Jack Squires. These men recorded the numbers of all wagons from and to destinations on the GWR. This applied to all trains running between Ashendon Jcn and Northolt Jcn, also those using the joint line between Risborough and Wycombe, e.g. on Oxford to Taplow goods, in both directions. This information was used to determine payment due to the GW/GC Joint Committee by the GWR. No similar records were made in respect of GC, later LNER, trains. Numbertaking ceased after the outbreak of war, Jack Leggett becoming a goods shunter, Jack Squires a signalman at Thame, whilst Charlie Swatton is believed to have become Foreman at Risborough in place of Pip Turner.
3 shunters	3 shifts, 24 hr cover. Sid Horwood, Frank Stevens and Bill ('Bomber') Wells. Horwood and Stevens were later succeeded by Walter Cherry and Jack Leggett respectively. Sid Horwood became a goods shunter at Oxford and Frank Stevens became a goods guard at Oxford. Percy Cox became a shunter at Risborough in 1946.
3 signalmen North box	3 shifts (continuous). Jack Walker, George Leggett and Fred White. Later Bill Mackie and Ben Howell.
3 signalmen South box	3 shifts (closed Sat. night/Sun. morning). Owen Gurney, Ted Copcutt, Arthur Crocker.
2 staff runners	Staff runners served at the North signal box 7.0 – 3.0, 3.0 – 11.0 for the coverage of single line staff exchanges and some platform work. They included Jack Rutland in 1937, and later Ted Coleman, Arthur Boddington, Bill Clark and Don Gray.
Relief signalmen	F. A. Rumble to 1937 (later District Inspector), T. L. Scrivens (from 1937), L. J. Howse, J. R. Saunders (1946).
3 C&W examiners	3 shifts, 24 hr cover. J. W. ('Jack') Grace, C. H. Harrison, W. P. Hughes, H. J. Choules. They were based in an old coach body near the water tower. The accommodation was shared with the pump attendant.
District lampman based at Risborough	W. G. H. (Bill) Hiscock.
2 pump attendants	When Hugh Harman started at Risborough in June 1928, the well was in the course of being deepened because of the increasing number of locos taking water. At that time one of the staff was Mr. Turner, father of 'Pip', the station foreman. These men were visited frequently by the Loco Superintendent from Neasden.
Permanent Way Dept. 1 ganger 1 sub ganger 6 lengthmen	Whilst the management of the joint line alternated between the parent companies every five years, the permanent way from Northolt Jcn to West Wycombe box remained under the GWR, and the rest of the line through to Ashenden Jcn was maintained by the LNER under Inspector James Reid who was directly responsible to Mr. Swindells, the District Engineer, Nottingham. In 1948 the P. W. Inspector was Jim Sirrell. Members of the PW gang included: C. Ridgley, ganger (later W. H. Reed, then H. Stevens) T. Walker, sub ganger F. Keen, underman H. Edwards, lengthman B. Clay, lengthman (retired Sept. 1938) A. Simmons, lengthman
S & T	Wally Mitchell.
Bricklayer	J. Lacey (retired 1936)
Bricklayer's mate	E. A. Emmett.

Following trials, the prototype Thompson 'L1' class 2–6–4T (No. 9000) appeared briefly at Neasden shed in 1947, but in February 1948 the first of the production engines was transferred in. Some two years later, over thirty of the engines were stationed there, taking over the outer suburban duties from the ageing ex-GC 'A5' 4–6–2Ts. This picture shows No. 67715 alongside the down platform at Risborough shortly after arrival with an early morning service from Marylebone in June 1948. At this time, the great majority of LNE (and ER) suburban services terminated at High Wycombe, with only five or so penetrating beyond to Risborough, Wotton or Brackley. In the mornings, the 5.55 a.m. Marylebone terminated at Risborough, whilst the 6.10 a.m. ran as far as Wotton, the station beyond Ashendon Junction on the ex-GC line. *H. K. Harman*

Marylebone terminating trains usually ran round outside the signal box, then propelled clear to run to the up platform. If this was not convenient, they ran round alongside the down platform, then propelled northwards to clear the crossovers to the up side or crossed at the London end and set back to the up platform. Dave Pinfold even recalled the train being drawn forward and set back over to the up platform before being run round there. In the late 1940s, milk churns were still transferred from the Oxford line to the Marylebone trains and this was done before they were shunted across to the up side for the return working. These four pictures, taken in the early 1950s, show a run-round sequence, the first with L1 tank No. 67776 signalled forward while the fireman had climbed onto the engine ready to take water. The second shows the empty stock being drawn out of the platform, the third, the engine at the opposite end of the stock rejoining the down platform line; and the last, the train being drawn into the up platform ready for the return journey to Marylebone. *H. J. Stretton Ward*

An unidentified 'Hall' running through the up platform line with an up goods during the early afternoon of a winter's day in 1948. Wyman's bookstall, seen beneath the canopy, was manned by Bill Copcutt from 6.0 a.m. to 6.0 p.m. His newspapers were sent by rail to Aylesbury, then ferried to Risborough by wholesaler Horace Marshall. Bill, who had moved to Risborough in 1918, sorted the papers for the nine boys he employed to deliver them around the town and out as far as Bledlow, Ilmer, Kimble and Saunderton. His only competition at Risborough was Hadock and Peachy. Bill also sold books, magazines, tobacco and confectionery, all of which arrived by rail during the day. In the evenings he sold papers by walking up and down alongside trains waiting in the platform. He tended to keep the shutters closed on the north end of the kiosk to protect it from the cold winds. Clerk Hugh Harman says Watlington crews crossed to the up side to visit the kiosk during the long lay-over waiting for the 9.10 a.m. from Paddington. Guard Tom Bowler "was a solid customer".

An earlier view of the up platform at Risborough, showing Collett '48XX' class 0–4–2T No. 4858 with the Banbury auto on 20th June 1939. Although allocated to Banbury, the 0–4–2Ts spent periods outstationed at Aylesbury shed (as did Banbury's '54XX' class auto tanks), where they worked the balancing auto duty to Banbury's own over the Bicester line. *Collection P. Winding*

Left: The bookstall features again in this mid-1950s view north along the up platform. Accommodation of the up side building was: gentlemen's lavatory at the far end, ladies waiting room and lavatory, and, this side of the bookstall, general waiting room, booking hall (through which passengers entered from the forecourt), booking office, station master's office, parcels office, and finally, at the south end of the building, the porters room which was used as a general mess by most of the staff, including guards. This picture also shows Doug Green, booking clerk from the early 1950s until the 1990s, Wilf Stevens, relief porter, and Brenda from Chinnor. *Right:* This later view, taken in the 1960s, of foreman Alan Strathdee giving the 'right away' to the guard of an up train, shows the south end of the main building and the steps leading up to the footbridge, giving access to the down platform. *Cty. Wilf Stevens*

TRAINS THROUGH RISBOROUGH – WINTER 1946

DOWN TRAINS – WEEKDAYS

					Arr.	*Pass*	*Dep.*	
F	GW	10/50 Park Royal	Worcester	Freight		12.12		Via Thame.
E	LNE	11/10 Neasden Jct	Woodford	Class A Freight	12.20		12.27	Calls to take water.
B	LNE	11/20 Marylebone		Passenger (WSO)	12.33			Terminating trains from Marylebone arrived in the down platform, ran round via the long crossover which was also used to move the train over to the up side.
C	GW	11/5 Paddington	Oxley Sdgs	Freight		12.42		
A	GW	12.8 Paddington	Cosford	Furlough Passenger (MO)		1.2		
E	GW	1.10 Old Oak Common	Tyseley	Freight (MX)	2.32		3.3	
F	GW	1.50 Park Royal	Oxford	Freight (MX)		3.12		Via Thame. In the 1950s, the 1.50 Park Royal (usually a 28XX) conveyed the occasional van of donkeys for Amersham. The train usually stopped in the down platform line, and detached the vehicle for subsequent movement across onto the Aylesbury branch, then backed into the loop spur.
E	LNE	2.25 Neasden Jct	Woodford	Class A Empties (MO)		3.48		
H	GW	2.35 Southall	Banbury	Empties	4.5		4.13	Calls to take water.
F	GW	3.0 Park Royal	Bordesley Jct	Freight (MX)	4.24		4.30	
H	GW	2.40 Hayes	Banbury	Pools		4.47		
E	LNE	3.50 Neasden Jct	Woodford	Class A Empties		5.13		
K	GW		Watlington	Freight			5.30	
E	GW	2.0 Paddington	Aylesbury	Freight	5.36		6.23	Left traffic for Risborough and Watlington in the down sidings at the south end of the station. By 1953 at least it rarely left anything for Oxford which was served by the 3.15 ex Slough. In the 1950s this train collected the occasional van of donkeys off the 1.50 Park Royal. The engine, an OOC 61XX, worked back with the 7.43 a.m. Aylesbury to Paddington via Maidenhead.
H	GW	4.35 Old Oak Common	Banbury	Freight		6.1		
K	LNE	2.45 Neasden Jct	Woodford	Class D Freight	7.2		7.17	According to George Howlett, the train stopped in the down platform while anything for Risborough was detached, run forward and propelled back along the line behind the platform to the down sidings at the south end where there might also be vehicles for collection. Exceptionally, the engine might use the long crossover to the up side, but this was unusual. Dave Pinfold remembers this train stopping alongside the down sidings.
B	LNE	5.55 Marylebone		Passenger	7.24			
B	LNE	6.10 Marylebone	Wotton	Passenger	7.37		7.41	
B	GW		Banbury	Auto			7.55	
B	GW		Watlington	Empty (Passenger when required)			7.57	West Bay.
F	GW	3.15 Slough	Oxford	Freight	8.12		10.0	Changes trainmen; via Thame.
B	GW		Oxford	Passenger			8.17	West Bay; via Thame.
B	LNE		Aylesbury	Passenger			8.25	East Bay.
H	GW	7.25 Old Oak Common	Oxley Sidings	Freight (MX)		8.59		
B	GW	7.35 Paddington	Oxford	Passenger	9.37		9.47	Via Thame.
B	LNE		Aylesbury	Passenger			9.50	East Bay.
A	GW	9.0 Paddington	Wolverhampton	Exp. Passenger (SX)		9.51		
A	GW	9.10 Paddington	Birkenhead	Exp. Passenger		10.5		
B	GW	9.58 High Wycombe	Banbury	Auto	10.16		10.20	
B	GW		Watlington	Passenger			10.22	West Bay
A	LNE	10.0 Marylebone	Bradford	Exp. Passenger		10.46		
A	GW	10.10 Paddington	Aberystwyth	Exp. Passenger (SO)		10.58		
E	LNE	9.40 Neasden Jct	Woodford	Class A Empties	11.8		11.21	Calls to take water.
B	GW	9.20 Paddington	Aylesbury	Passenger	11.13		11.17	
B	GW		Oxford	Diesel Car (SX) Pass (SO)			11.22	West Bay; via Thame.
H	GW	10.25 Taplow	Aylesbury	Freight (RR, SX)		11.37		
A	GW	11.10 Paddington	Birkenhead	Exp. Passenger		11.58		
B	LNE	12/0nn High Wycombe	Aylesbury	Passenger	12/17		12/18	
K	GW		Chinnor	Freight (SX)			12/20	
E	LNE	11.10 Neasden Jct	Woodford	Class A Frt & Eties (SX)		12/35		In 1953 the 'Woodford down' was regularly 'up to the limit' (i.e. maximum load). It stopped at Risborough to collect pools (i.e. empties) from the down sidings. [Austerity 2–8–0]
B	GW		Aylesbury	Passenger			12/37	East Bay.
B	GW		Watlington	Passenger (SO)			12/40	West Bay.
A	LNE	12/15 Marylebone	Manchester	Exp. Passenger		1/6		
H	GW	11.22 West Ealing	Woodford	Pools		1/26		

Continued on page 155

The forecourt elevation of the main station building on 24th July 1960.

Left: This 1930s snapshot of Jack Rutland shows the south end wall of the wooden building situated partly under the main span of the footbridge. It was used to store parcels and bicycles. *Right:* This view, taken c.1960, shows the replacement foreman's office erected next to the bicycle shed around 1960.

This late 1930s snap of a 'King' speeding through with an express on the up main, provides an earlier glimpse of the south end of the station buildings, footbridge and bicycle shed. The enclosed area beneath the footbridge steps provided accommodation for the foreman's office.

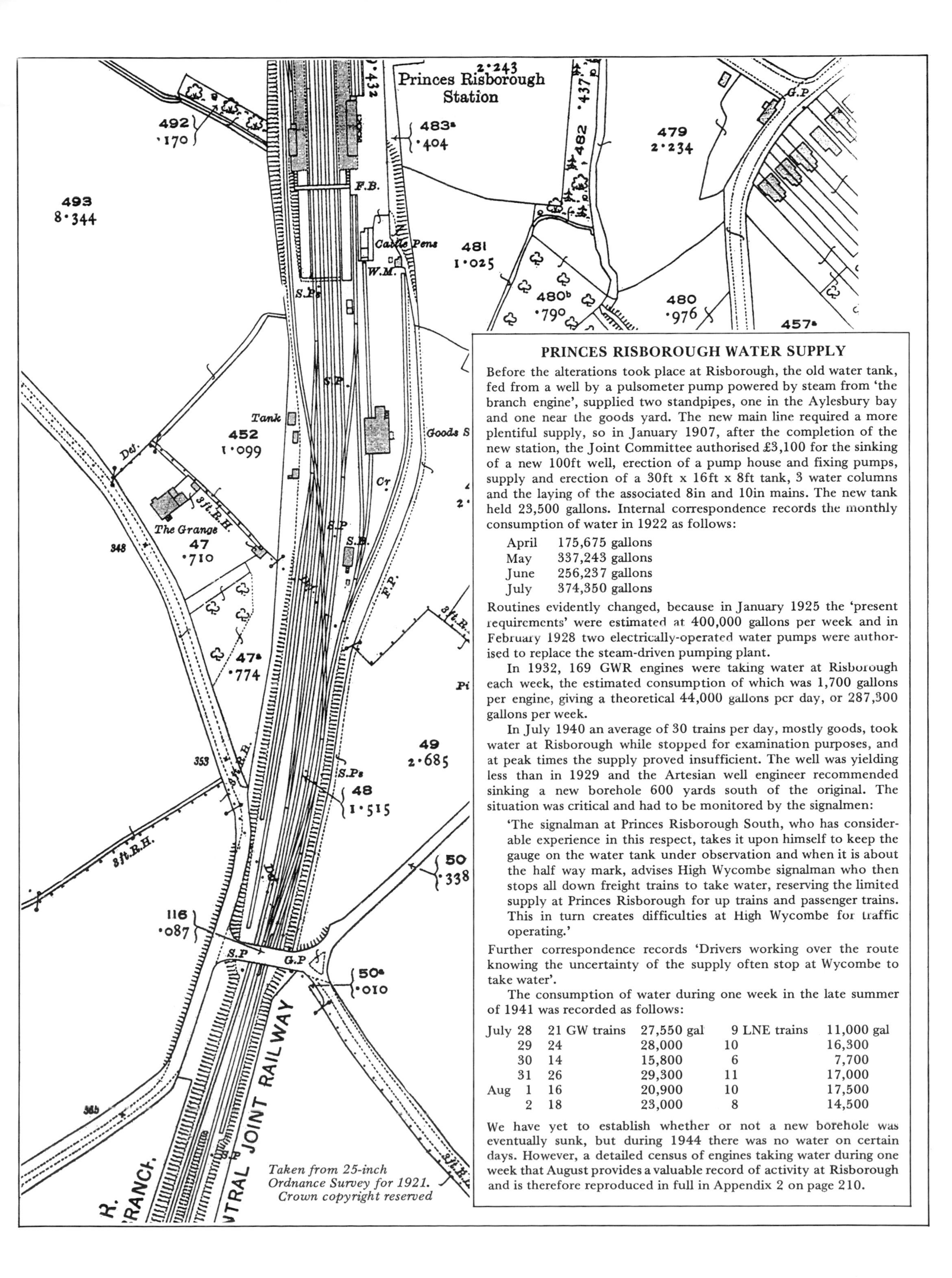

Taken from 25-inch Ordnance Survey for 1921.
Crown copyright reserved

PRINCES RISBOROUGH WATER SUPPLY

Before the alterations took place at Risborough, the old water tank, fed from a well by a pulsometer pump powered by steam from 'the branch engine', supplied two standpipes, one in the Aylesbury bay and one near the goods yard. The new main line required a more plentiful supply, so in January 1907, after the completion of the new station, the Joint Committee authorised £3,100 for the sinking of a new 100ft well, erection of a pump house and fixing pumps, supply and erection of a 30ft x 16ft x 8ft tank, 3 water columns and the laying of the associated 8in and 10in mains. The new tank held 23,500 gallons. Internal correspondence records the monthly consumption of water in 1922 as follows:

April	175,675 gallons
May	337,243 gallons
June	256,237 gallons
July	374,350 gallons

Routines evidently changed, because in January 1925 the 'present requirements' were estimated at 400,000 gallons per week and in February 1928 two electrically-operated water pumps were authorised to replace the steam-driven pumping plant.

In 1932, 169 GWR engines were taking water at Risborough each week, the estimated consumption of which was 1,700 gallons per engine, giving a theoretical 44,000 gallons per day, or 287,300 gallons per week.

In July 1940 an average of 30 trains per day, mostly goods, took water at Risborough while stopped for examination purposes, and at peak times the supply proved insufficient. The well was yielding less than in 1929 and the Artesian well engineer recommended sinking a new borehole 600 yards south of the original. The situation was critical and had to be monitored by the signalmen:

> 'The signalman at Princes Risborough South, who has considerable experience in this respect, takes it upon himself to keep the gauge on the water tank under observation and when it is about the half way mark, advises High Wycombe signalman who then stops all down freight trains to take water, reserving the limited supply at Princes Risborough for up trains and passenger trains. This in turn creates difficulties at High Wycombe for traffic operating.'

Further correspondence records 'Drivers working over the route knowing the uncertainty of the supply often stop at Wycombe to take water'.

The consumption of water during one week in the late summer of 1941 was recorded as follows:

July 28	21 GW trains	27,550 gal	9 LNE trains	11,000 gal
29	24	28,000	10	16,300
30	14	15,800	6	7,700
31	26	29,300	11	17,000
Aug 1	16	20,900	10	17,500
2	18	23,000	8	14,500

We have yet to establish whether or not a new borehole was eventually sunk, but during 1944 there was no water on certain days. However, a detailed census of engines taking water during one week that August provides a valuable record of activity at Risborough and is therefore reproduced in full in Appendix 2 on page 210.

Photographs of goods yards are never easy to find, but this panorama, looking south from the footbridge c.1960, provides a view of the back siding or coal road and even a glimpse of Risboro Furniture Co's factory and private siding behind it. The sleeper-built enclosure shown on a 1910 plan as a coal shed, between the dock siding and the up platform line, was used for station coal whilst the wooden shed further south, before the south signal box, may well have been the 21ft 6in x 7ft 6in cabin for goods train examiners authorised by the Joint Committee in 1918. The body of condemned horse-box No. 366, which was authorised to be sent to Risborough 'for use as accommodation for shunters' in October 1939, was situated just beyond the C&W cabin and the south signal box (see pagc 148). The 12 ton weighbridge situated by the yard entrance just off the left of this picture, was replaced by a larger 20 ton machine authorised in March 1944. The weighbridge office features in the top picture on page 169. Although there was only one water crane at the north end of the station, two were provided at the south, both visible here, between the up platform and up main lines. As detailed later, Risborough was an important water stop, the supply to the 22,500 gallon water tank on the right being hard pressed at times to cope (see page 145). The two south or down sidings to the right of the down platform line were used for Oxford and Watlington traffic, which was usually exchanged via the 'back line' leading off to the right, although the Watlington engine was often called upon to take traffic over to the up yard via the 'long crossover' in the centre of the picture. Arrangements varied but details of a minor incident on 14th October 1941 reveal that the Watlington engine and van, which had arrived on the down side about 4.0 a.m., was crossed to the up platform and thence into the dock siding through the crossover by the station coal pen to pick up traffic for Watlington and Aylesbury. This must have been left alongside the goods shed, because the vehicles were then propelled south, 'towards the long siding' (featured on page 157) to clear the points for the long crossover in order to return to the down side. However, procedures varied over the years according to requirements and staff. *B. Morgan*

Right: This photo of clerk Hugh Harman and the one of the articulated container lorry opposite are the best we have come across to show the 6 ton yard crane FM5022 which is not apparent in other photos. An estimate for its replacement with another (FM3016) from Slough (Old Yard) was made in July 1951 but a works order was not issued until March the following year when the old one was described as beyond repair.
Cty. Hugh Harman

The brick-built goods shed was a standard GWR design also used at Beaconsfield, dating from the 1899 renewal of the station when it replaced an earlier version featured on page 9 of Vol. 1. It housed the usual 30 cwt fixed hand crane which in 1948 was recorded as FM5018. The office at the north end, featured in the view opposite, was entered via the loading deck and was provided with the usual fireplace in the south-east corner, a table and a long desk or bench fixed across the full width of the north wall below the windows. The parcels van was a 3 ton Morris with an NVS chassis and a London Midland Region Drawing Office designed body.

S. J. Dickson

This photograph of driver Charlie Adby with a GWR Thornycroft 'Nippy' was taken by the yard crane, just south of the goods shed in 1947. Charlie had started on the railway in 1929 as a member of the Watlington permanent way gang. The Thornycroft had an ER4 engine and a TC wood-framed cab clad in masonite (tempered hardboard) with a painted canvas roof. Before this, unsuccessful trials had been made with a Scammell which was replaced by a Morris Leader. The Thornycroft is thought to have been replaced with a smaller vehicle as part of a goods concentration scheme at Wycombe.

Cty. Charlie Adby

This view of 'Princes Risborough South' signal box and the long crossover is believed to have been taken from the steps of the water tank around midday on 13th June 1947. It shows, behind the wagons on the left, the roofs of two structures, the first was probably the C & W examiners cabin and the second the grounded horse-box which served as a shunters cabin. The small corrugated iron hut to the right of the signal box was a lamp shed, whilst the corrugated iron building on the right-hand edge of the print covered the well and housed the water pumps. Watlington fireman Tony Benham recalls that in the late 1940s when goods were brought in from Watlington, the train ran straight through to the south end of the back road and the engine ran round via the down platform line. Shunting was supervised by Jack Leggett or Tom Gibbard (on opposite shifts) and Pip Turner, the foreman, but generally the Watlington engine was only used to split its own train and put the empties on one of the south sidings, in the foreground, and the loadeds in the other, with the occasional trip over to the up yard to leave vans of cement for Greenford. Most of the shunting was carried out by the Aylesbury pilot. Some of the traffic for Watlington and Oxford was put off on the up side and moved across afterwards, but whenever possible it was put on the down side. Coal for the cement works at Chinnor came from Woodford whilst merchants' coal arrived in the local goods from Banbury. Porter and relief guard George Howlett had known Risborough so congested waiting for clearance that traffic was held back at Chinnor where the yard and cement works were full to capacity.

J. H. Russell

'Bulldog' class 4–4–0 No. 3417 *Lord Mildmay of Flete* shunting on the down platform line c.1947/8 with shunters Jack Leggett and Percy Cox. The train may have been the 8.30 a.m. Banbury to Old Oak local freight, which spent about 30 minutes working at Risborough before moving on to High Wycombe at 12.40 p.m. In the war and postwar years, this service saw a variety of locos, including 'Halls', '43XXs', LNE and '2251' 0–6–0s and 'Earl' class 4–4–0s, though for very many years it had been the preserve of '2301s'. The engine, which was allocated to Wellington (Salop), was withdrawn in April 1948. *H. K. Harman*

LNER A5/1 No. 9800 leaving Risborough with what may have been the 5.25 Woodford to Neasden goods in April 1948. *H. K. Harman*

'61XX' class 2–6–2T No. 6164 of Slough shed leaving Risborough with what may have been the 8.30 a.m. Banbury to Old Oak goods in the early afternoon of Saturday, 21st May 1938. Old Oak and Banbury 0–6–0 locomotives normally alternated on this train, but the use of borrowed engines was not unknown. The other two locos in the right background were No. 6138 (from Oxford shed), which was probably working the 11.42 a.m. Oxford to Taplow (showing 'F' lamps) and had stopped on the up platform line for number taking and water (see overleaf), and LNE (ex-GC) 'J11' 0–6–0 No. 6047, which was probably on a late-running 5.35 a.m. Woodford to Neasden local goods. The pair of lines in the foreground served as headshunts so that the yard could be shunted without occupation of the running lines, the one further from the camera being known as the 'long siding'. *S. H. Freese*

A closer view of No. 6138 and J11 No. 6047 on the same occasion, with the fireman on top of the engine putting the leather bag into the far side tank ready to take water. Stopping a loose-coupled train in exactly the right spot so that the engine was in correct alignment with the arm of the water crane called for skill. Sometimes the slack couplings of the stationary train would allow a degree of fore or aft movement for any correction, whilst on other occasions drivers stopped a few yards short and the fireman uncoupled so that the engine could run forward unimpeded. While standing at the north or south ends of the station, the firemen of stationary goods trains were often sent to the signal box to collect hot water for a fresh can of tea. This picture also shows a numbertaker at work, as detailed on pages 132/133.

S. H. Freese

Taken on the same day, this picture shows Stafford Road 'Star' No. 4018 *Knight of the Grand Cross* passing through Risborough southbound with a Dunlop's Jubilee works outing, whilst No. 6138 and 'J11' No. 6047 are seen to the right. No. 4018 passed through Risborough with another excursion on the afternoon of 24th September that year with a Handsworth to Paddington train conveying 13 coaches of the 'Handsworth Unionists' party. *S. H. Freese*

No apologies for the inclusion of the fourth picture in this sequence, a close-up of J11 No. 6047 shunting the up yard. In the background it is just possible to see a 61XX alongside the up platform. This may have been the Aylesbury pilot which was booked to work at Risborough between 1.7 p.m. and 4.18 p.m. The signal in the foreground was the starter for the up platform line. According to Wally Mitchell, from at least 1937 until after the war, Wagon Repairs Ltd occupied an old carriage body which served as a workshop/messroom at this end of the back siding, apparently inside the vee of the goods yard sidings, but unfortunately it does not feature in these views. *S. H. Freese*

Another Stafford Road 'Star', No. 4060 *Princess Eugenie*, passing through Risborough with the 4.20 p.m. Wolverhampton to Paddington service on Saturday, 2nd September 1950. The first two coaches were extras, followed by six coaches from Wolverhampton, and at the rear, a through vehicle from Stratford-on-Avon (depart 4.40 p.m.), attached at Leamington Spa. Within a few weeks this engine was transferred to Bath Road, and was withdrawn from traffic two years later, in October 1952. The down loop serving the platform had diverged from the down main alongside the end of the shorter of the two down sidings on the left, but, because of the volume of traffic carried during the war, it was extended south of the bridge, as shown in the picture below. The work, costing £2,388 and financed by the government, was authorised on 10th March 1943. *J. F. Russell-Smith*

No. 6003 *King George IV* (from Old Oak) leaving Risborough one summer evening c.1948 with what was probably the 2.55 p.m. (Sundays) Birkenhead to Paddington service, due to call at 8.22 p.m. Apart from the 6.45 a.m. Wolverhampton to Paddington on weekdays, this was the only WR express scheduled to call at Risborough. The goods train in the background was held on the up main to allow the express to use the platform and depart ahead of it. *H. K. Harman*

E	LNE	12/20 Neasden Jct	Woodford	Class A Frt & Eties (SX)	1/35		1/43	Calls to take water.
B	GW	12/25 Paddington	Oxford	Passenger	1/47		1/52	Via Thame.
B	GW		Aylesbury	Passenger			1/52	East Bay.
B	GW		Watlington	Passenger			1/55	West Bay.
B	GW		Banbury	Auto			1/58	
J	GW	9.45 Acton	Banbury Jct	Freight (SO)	2/3		2/15	
J	GW	9.45 Acton	Banbury Jct	Freight (SX)	2/20		3/27	Occasionally put off wagons for Saunderton. These were set back over long crossover to goods yard.
B	GW	1/25 Paddington	Aylesbury	Passenger	2/44		2/46	
A	GW	1/58 Paddington	Wolverhampton	Exp. Passenger (RR)		2/54		
A	GW	2/10 Paddington	Birkenhead	Exp. Passenger		3/0		
B	GW	2/25 Paddington	Oxford	Passenger	3/40		3/46	Via Thame.
K	GW		Chinnor	Freight (SO)			3/55	
B	GW	3/5 Maidenhead	Aylesbury	Passenger	4/0		4/5	
B	GW		Banbury	Auto			4/10	West Bay.
B	GW		Thame	Passenger			4/12	West Bay; Watlington branch train.
E	GW	2/15 Acton	Tyseley	Freight	4/15		5/3	
E	LNE	3/0 Neasden Jct	Woodford	Class A Frt & Eties		4/25		
A	GW	4/10 Paddington	Birkenhead	Exp. Passenger		4/58		
B	GW	4/12 Maidenhead	Aylesbury	Passenger	5/9		5/12	
K	GW		Aylesbury	Freight			5/32	Train formed in down sidings – taken to Aylesbury (4.18 in 1950s) by returning pilot. Locos varied.
A	GW	4/32 Paddington	Banbury	Passenger	5/34		5/38	
B	GW		Thame	Diesel Car (SX) Pass (SO)			5/45	West Bay.
B	GW		Watlington	Passenger			5/48	West Bay.
B	LNE	4/35 Marylebone		Passenger (SX)	5/50			
A	GW	5/10 Paddington	Wolverhampton	Exp. Passenger (SX)		6/6		
B	LNE	4/45 Marylebone	Brackley	Passenger (SO)	6/13		6/18	
B	GW	5/23 Paddington	Aylesbury	Passenger	6/42		6/44	
B	GW		Oxford	Diesel Car (SX) Pass (SO)			6/45	Via Thame.
A	GW	6/10 Paddington	Birkenhead	Exp. Passenger		7/2		
A	LNE	6/15 Marylebone	Bradford	Exp. Passenger		7/11		
B	LNE	6/22 Marylebone	Brackley	Passenger (SX)	7/30		7/35	
B	GW	6/25 Paddington	Oxford	Passenger	7/42		7/52	Via Thame.
A	GW	7/10 Paddington	Wolverhampton	Passenger		7/58*		*Slip coach detached. One coach at home signal.
B	GW		Banbury	Auto			8/5*	*Slip coach conveyed.
B	GW		Watlington	Passenger			8/6	West Bay.
B	GW		Aylesbury	Passenger			8/8	East Bay.
B	GW		Thame	Auto			8/10	West Bay.
	LNE	6/40 Marylebone	Woodford	Class A Freight	8/21		8/28	Calls to take water.
B	GW	7/20 Paddington	Aylesbury	Passenger	8/37		8/40	
B	GW		Aylesbury	Auto			9/0	East Bay.
H	GW	5/50 Taplow	Oxford	Freight	9/7		9/30	Via Thame.
E	LNE	7/50 Neasden Jct	Woodford	Class A Freight		9/37		
C	GW	8/25 Slough	Oxford	Freight		9/48		Via Thame.
B	LNE	8/30 Marylebone	Brackley	Passenger (SX)	9/55		10/0	
B	GW		Aylesbury	Auto			10/2	East Bay.
E	LNE	8/55 Neasden Jct	Woodford	Class A Empties (SO)	10/8		10/15	Calls to take water
B	GW	9/0 Paddington	Aylesbury	Passenger	10/21		10/25	
K	GW		Watlington	Freight (RR)		10/45		
C	GW	9/10 Paddington	Birkenhead	Exp. Freight (SX)		11/5		
D	GW	9/55 Southall	Oxley Sidings	Freight		11/35		
J	LNE	8/55 Neasden Jct	Woodford	Class C Empties (SX)		11/54		

DOWN TRAINS – SUNDAYS

					Arr.	*Pass*	*Dep.*	
E	LNE	12.2 Neasden Jct	Woodford	Class A Empties		1.25		
F	GW	1.50 Park Royal	Oxford	Freight		3.12		Via Thame.
F	GW	1.50 Old Oak Common	Oxley Sidings	Freight	3.38		4.5	
E	LNE	2.30 Neasden Jct	Woodford	Class A Empties		3.53		
F	GW	3.0 Park Royal	Bordesley Jct	Freight		4.25		
E	LNE	4.0 Neasden Jct	Woodford	Class A Empties		5.23		
E	LNE	4.45 Neasden Jct	Woodford	Class A Empties		6.8		
B	LNE	5.23 Marylebone	Brackley	Passenger	6.39		6.41	
E	LNE	5.55 Neasden Jct	Woodford	Class A Empties		7.18		
B	GW		Aylesbury	Passenger			8.26	East Bay.
E	LNE	8.30 Neasden Jct	Woodford	Class A Empties		9.53		
H	GW	8.40 Portobello Sdgs	Banbury Jct	Empties	10.45		11.10	
E	LNE	9.35 Neasden Jct	Woodford	Class A Empties		10.58		
B	GW	9.40 Paddington	Oxford	Passenger	11.18		11.26	Via Thame.
B	GW		Aylesbury	Passenger			11.30	East Bay.
B	LNE	10.20 Marylebone		Passenger	11.44			
A	GW	11.10 Paddington	Birkenhead	Exp. Passenger		11.59		
B	LNE	11.20 Marylebone	Woodford	Passenger	12/44		12/46	
B	GW	1/15 Paddington	Aylesbury	Passenger	2/42		2/44	
B	GW	2/20 Paddington	Aylesbury	Passenger	4/15		4/18	
B	GW	4/20 Paddington	Oxford	Passenger	5/50		5/55	Via Thame.
B	GW		Aylesbury	Passenger			5/57	East Bay.
B	LNE	5/15 Marylebone	Brackley	Passenger	6/30		6/32	
A	GW	6/0 Paddington	Shrewsbury	Exp. Passenger		6/52		Relief to 6/10 Paddington.
A	GW	6/10 Paddington	Shrewsbury	Exp. Passenger		7/2		
B	GW		Aylesbury	Passenger			7/2	East Bay.
B	GW	7/2 Paddington		Passenger	8/28			
F	GW	8/0 Old Oak Common	Oxley Sidings	Freight	9/44		10/5	Calls to take water.
B	LNE	8/30 Marylebone	Wotton	Passenger		9/56		
A	GW	10/40 Paddington	Banbury	Furlough Passenger		11/37		
A	GW	11/5 Paddington	Shrewsbury	Furlough Passenger		12.0		

UP TRAINS — WEEKDAYS

					Arr.	Pass	Dep.	
F	GW	11/15 Oxford	Taplow	Freight (MX)	12.46		1.30	Via Thame. In 1953 ran as 11.20 p.m. Hinksey–Slough. Occasionally dropped off perishables and picked up Saunderton and West Wycombe traffic from behind South box. This train also served Wycombe North Yard.
C	GW	7/45 Birkenhead	Paddington	Exp. Freight (MX)		2.14		
F	GW	12.55 Banbury	Old Oak Common	Freight (MO)		2.26		
F	LNE	1.20 Woodford	Marylebone	Class B Freight (MO)	2.57		3.13	
C	GW	2.20 Banbury	Paddington	Freight (MX)		3.12		
C	GW	2.40 Banbury	Acton	Freight (MX)		3.31		
C	GW	3.5 Banbury	Old Oak Common	Freight (MX)		3.57		
E	LNE	2.50 Woodford	Neasden Jct	Class A Mineral	4.17		4.24	Calls to take water.
C	GW	8/20 Birkenhead	Paddington	Freight (MX)		4.37		
K	GW	4.20 Watlington		Freight	4.48			
E	LNE	4.15 Woodford	Neasden Jct	Class A Freight (SO)	5.42		5.48	Calls to take water.
E	LNE	1.5 Annesley	Marylebone	Class A Freight (MO)	6.0		6.7	Calls to take water.
E	GW	8/20 Cannock Road	Paddington	Freight (MX)	6.10		6.17	Calls to take water. Dave Pinfold recalls that in the 1950s this train refuged at North sidings to wait for the arrival of a relief crew from High Wycombe. The train was too long for one siding and had to be divided between the two.
H	GW	4.35 Banbury	Slough	Freight (MO)	6.13		6.23	Calls to take water.
B	GW	7.0 Aylesbury	Paddington	Passenger	7.17		7.18	
D	LNE		High Wycombe	Empty Coaches (SO)			7.38	To work 7.56 High Wycombe.
B	GW	7.25 Aylesbury		Auto	7.42			
B	GW	7.25 Watlington		Passenger	7.51			West Bay.
B	GW	6.0 Banbury		Passenger	8.0			West Bay. Via Thame.
B	GW	7.45 Aylesbury	Paddington	Passenger	8.2		8.6	
E	LNE	6.45 Woodford	Neasden Jct	Class A Mineral (SX)	8.12		8.22	Calls to take water.
B	LNE		Marylebone	Passenger (SX)			8.14	
G	LNE	8.3 Aylesbury		Empty Auto	8.18			
B	LNE	8.20 Wotton	Marylebone	Passenger	8.42		8.46	
B	GW	7.45 Banbury	High Wycombe	Auto	9.1		9.4	
B	GW	7.30 Oxford		Diesel Car (SX) Pass (SO)	9.8			West Bay. Via Thame.
B	LNE	8.48 Aylesbury		Passenger	9.8			East Bay.
B	GW	8.42 Watlington		Passenger	9.11			West Bay.
A	GW	6.45 Wolverhampton	Paddington	Exp. Passenger	9.15		9.18	
B	GW	8.22 Oxford	Paddington	Passenger	9.24		9.37	Via Thame. Conveyed two or three 6-wheel milk tanks on rear. The train set back into the south dock to detach. Vehicles later collected by: April 1946 – 8.50 Brackley (9.36 Risborough) to Marylebone. This turn was used to test engines ex Neasden, i.e. V2s. 1953 – 11.5 a.m. to Marylebone. In the 1950s, the 8.22 Oxford also conveyed the occasional van of perishables on the rear for Aylesbury. These were left in the up platform for collection by the Aylesbury auto.
A	GW	8.0 Birmingham	Paddington	Exp. Passenger (SX)		9.32		
H	GW	7.35 Banbury	Southall	Freight	9.58		10.6	Calls to take water.
K	LNE	5.25 Woodford	Neasden Jct	Class D Freight	10.20		10.37	By 1953 principally coal. Traffic for Saunderton, West Wycombe and High Wycombe North Yard put off at north sidings (goods yard limited capacity) for collection by 11.5 p.m. Hinksey. If room the train then ran through the south end of the station to drop off wagons for the Watlington branch, which were set back across to the down side. Coal for Chinnor came from Annesley Colliery.
A	GW	7.25 Shrewsbury	Paddington	Exp. Passenger		10.33		
B	GW	10.28 Aylesbury	Paddington	Passenger	10.46		10.50	
B	LNE	10.50 Aylesbury	High Wycombe	Passenger	11.10		11.11	
A	GW	6.30 Birkenhead	Paddington	Exp. Passenger		11.36		
J	GW	8.30 Banbury	Old Oak Common	Freight	11.25		11.40	Known as 'The Little Banbury' (usually 22XX). Coal and 'odds and ends' for Aylesbury put off at south yard. The crews of this and the 9.45 Acton to Banbury changed over en route. Dave Pinfold recalls in the 1950s "This was a nuisance when the milk was about – they were both held on the up main."
E	LNE	10.25 Woodford	Neasden Jct	Class A Mineral		11.55		
B	GW	11.30 Watlington		Passenger	11.56			West Bay.
B	GW	11.5 Banbury		Auto	12/15			
B	GW	12/0 Aylesbury		Passenger	12/17			East Bay.
B	GW	11.26 Oxford	Paddington	Passenger	12/25		12/31	Via Thame. Occasionally tail traffic left in the up platform for collection by pilot.
H	GW	9.40 Banbury	Old Oak Common	Coal	12/33		12/48	Test engine via up platform.
H	GW	11.40 Oxford	Taplow	Freight	1/3		1/50	Via Thame. Collected Maidenhead branch traffic left in north sidings by up Woodford.
K	GW	12/58 Aylesbury		Freight	1/19			Engine remained at Risborough as pilot, until working back with 5.32 p.m. goods to Aylesbury. By the 1950s the pilot engine came off shed at 8.50 a.m. and ran light to Risborough although it sometimes travelled double-heading on the 8.43 a.m. passenger train. At Risborough it went into the yard to sort all the wagons left by earlier trains, priority being given to placing shed traffic, then coal wagons along the back siding for local traders. Its work at Risborough included serving the private sidings of Risboro' Furniture and Forest Research. Up to 1948 the loco was a 61XX provided by the GWR but after nationalisation the Eastern Region provided an L1, and subsequently J15s, N5s and even Fairburn tanks.
K	GW	1/18 Chinnor		Freight (SX)	1/30			
B	GW	1/22 Aylesbury		Passenger	1/40			East Bay.
B	GW	1/15 Watlington		Passenger (SO)	1/41			West Bay.
A	GW	8.30 Birkenhead	Paddington	Passenger		1/47		
E	LNE	12/40 Woodford	Neasden Jct.	Class A Mineral	2/5		2/12	Calls to take water.
B	GW	2/22 Aylesbury	Paddington	Passenger	2/39		2/43	
H	GW	1/20 Banbury	Old Oak Common	Freight	2/52		3/20	
A	GW	9.30 Aberystwyth	Paddington	Exp. Passenger (SO)		3/15		
B	GW	2/5 Banbury		Auto	3/25			
B	GW	3/10 Watlington		Passenger	3/36			West Bay.
B	GW	3/20 Aylesbury		Passenger	3/37			East Bay.

With the South box down main home signal at caution, this picture shows Old Oak-based No. 6007 *King William III* making a steady approach to Risborough with a down express from Paddington to Wolverhampton one winter's day in 1953. This would have been in sharp contrast to the more usual approach of non-stop expresses which tore down the bank from Saunderton, passing through Risborough at anything up to 100 miles an hour. Because of the steepness of this bank, it was decided to avoid the climb towards Wycombe, and that instead of simply widening the formation of the Wycombe line between Risborough and Saunderton, it would be better to route the new up line over a new course to provide easier gradients for the new heavier expresses. This picture shows the up line diverging to the left to run over the improved 2 miles or so route which involved a deep cutting and an 88 yard tunnel before converging to run alongside the down line on the old route. The track in the right foreground was the 1943 revised entry to the down loop and platform line, whilst the wagons on the left provide some idea of the extent of the 'long siding' referred to previously.

J. F. Russell-Smith

B	GW	2/40 Oxford	Paddington	Passenger	3/38		3/42	Via Thame.
D	GW		High Wycombe	Empty Coaches			3/55	Ex 3/20 Aylesbury (may be run as passenger train)
E	LNE	2/30 Woodford	Neasden Jct	Class A Mineral	3/57		4/4	
H	GW	2/40 Banbury	Southall	Freight (RR)	4/12		5/17	
A	GW	12/5 Chester	Paddington	Exp. Passenger (RR, SO)		4/24		
A	GW	11.40 Birkenhead	Paddington	Exp. Passenger		4/53		
B	GW	4/45 Thame		Passenger	5/2			West Bay. Watlington branch train.
K	GW	4/55 Chinnor		Freight (SO)	5/5			
B	GW	4/48 Aylesbury	Maidenhead	Passenger	5/6		5/10	
B	GW	4/50 Oxford		Diesel Car (SX). Pass (SO)	5/41			West Bay; Via Thame.
E	LNE	4/15 Woodford	Neasden Jct	Class A Mineral	5/44		5/51	Calls to take water.
B	GW	4/40 Banbury		Auto	6/4			
A	GW	4/25 Wolverhampton	Paddington	Exp. Passenger (SX)		6/16		
B	GW	6/0 Aylesbury	Paddington	Passenger	6/17		6/20	
B	GW	6/15 Thame		Diesel Car (SX) Pass (SO)	6/32			West Bay.
B	LNE		Marylebone	Passenger			7/10	
B	GW	6/18 Banbury		Auto	7/28			
B	GW	7/20 Aylesbury		Passenger	7/38			East Bay.
B	GW	7/15 Watlington		Passenger	7/41			West Bay.
A	GW	2/35 Birkenhead	Paddington	Passenger		7/42		
B	GW	6/40 Oxford	Paddington	Passenger	7/50		8/2	Via Thame.
E	LNE	6/45 Woodford	Neasden Jct	Class A Mineral		8/12		
H	GW	6/45 Banbury	Greenford	Freight & Coal	8/33		9/15	Picked up cement traffic only which the pilot had left behind South box.
B	GW	8/35 Thame		Auto	8/50			
A	LNE	4/50 Bradford	Marylebone	Exp. Passenger		9/12		
B	GW	9/22 Aylesbury		Auto	9/39			
K	GW	8/50 Watlington		Freight (RR)	9/40			
B	LNE	8/50 Brackley	Marylebone	Passenger	9/42		9/49	
H	GW	8/30 Banbury	Southall	Freight (SX)		10/6		
E	GW	9/40 Aylesbury	Paddington	Freight	10/2		10/45	To Acton (SO). Called as required for perishables.
C	GW	3/35 Birkenhead	Park Royal	Meat (RR, SX)		10/35		
J	LNE	9/5 Woodford	Neasden Jct	Class C Mineral	11/24		11/58	Depart at 12.8 (SO). In 1953 ran as 9.5 p.m. Woodford–High Wycombe. Went into the up refuge and put off coal for Maidenhead branch. Also put off Watlington branch traffic which was backed across long crossover and left behind down platform for Watlington engine to collect.
H	GW	10/15 Banbury	North Acton	Freight	11/47		12.45	(MX)
C	GW	3/30 Worcester	Paddington	Freight (SX)		11/53		Via Thame.
F	GW	5/10 Worcester	Paddington	Freight (SO)		11/58		Via Thame.

UP TRAINS – SUNDAYS

					Arr.	*Pass*	*Dep.*	
H	GW	11/0 Banbury	Old Oak Common	Coal	12.52 (Sat)		1.2	Calls to take water.
F	GW	11/15 Oxford	Taplow	Freight	12.46 (Sat)		1.30	Via Thame.
E	LNE	12.25 Woodford	Neasden Jct	Class A Mineral	1.52		1.59	Calls to take water.
C	GW	8/10 Oxley	Paddington	Freight	2.8		2.15	Calls to take water.
E	LNE	2.15 Woodford	Neasden Jct	Class A Mineral	3.49		3.56	
E	GW	8/20 Birkenhead	Paddington	Freight		4.37		
E	LNE	3.55 Woodford	Neasden Jct	Class A Mineral	5.22		5.29	Calls to take water.
E	LNE	4.38 Woodford	Neasden Jct	Class A Mineral	6.5		6.12	Calls to take water.
E	GW	8/20 Cannock Road	Paddington	Freight	6.21		6.30	Calls to take water.
E	LNE	5.45 Woodford	Neasden Jct	Class A Mineral	7.12		7.19	Calls to take water.
E	LNE	6.20 Woodford	Neasden Jct	Class A Mineral	7.47		7.54	Calls to take water.
B	GW	7.56 Aylesbury		Passenger	8.14			East Bay.
B	GW	7.15 Oxford	Paddington	Passenger	8.16		8.24	Via Thame. Sometimes conveyed up to 4 milk tanks and occasionally box vans which were set back onto the up main for collection by the 8.5 Brackley to Marylebone.
B	LNE	8.5 Brackley	Marylebone	Passenger	8.57		9.5	
H	GW	7.35 Banbury	Southall	Freight		9.14		
E	LNE	8.20 Woodford	Neasden	Class A Mineral	9.47		9.54	Calls to take water.
B	GW	10.55 Aylesbury		Passenger	11.13			East Bay.
B	LNE		Marylebone	Passenger			12/30	
A	GW	8.5 Birkenhead	Paddington	Exp. Passenger		1/29		
B	GW	3/55 Aylesbury	Paddington	Passenger	4/13		4/15	
B	GW	5/20 Aylesbury		Passenger	5/38			East Bay.
B	GW	6/33 Aylesbury		Passenger	6/51			East Bay.
B	GW	5/55 Oxford	Paddington	Passenger	6/55		7/8	Via Thame.
A	GW	4/40 Wolverhampton	Paddington	Exp. Passenger		7/1		
A	LNE	4/45 Nottingham	Marylebone	Exp. Passenger		7/45		
A	GW	4/55 Shrewsbury	Paddington	Exp. Passenger		7/58		Relief to 2/55 Birkenhead.
B	GW	7/48 Aylesbury	Paddington	Passenger	8/6		8/8	
C	GW	1/40 Birkenhead	Park Royal	Meat (RR)	8/11		8/50	When conveying 40 wagons or less.
A	GW	2/55 Birkenhead	Paddington	Exp. Passenger	8/22		8/26	
B	GW		Paddington	Passenger			8/41	
B	LNE	8/23 Brackley	Marylebone	Passenger	9/13		9/19	
C	GW	3/10 Birkenhead	Park Royal	Meat (RR)		9/29		When load exceeds 40 wagons.
D	LNE	10/25 Wotton	High Wycombe	Empty Coaches		10/42		

'Star' class 4–6–0 No. 4051 *Princess Helena* of Worcester shed approaching the south end of Risborough with the 12.32 p.m. Paddington to Oxford local passenger in 1939. Despite its distinguished power, the train was a slow, having already called at all stations (but no halts) from Ealing, thirteen in all, with the prospect of another eight between Risborough and Oxford. *S. H. Freese*

'43XX' class No. 6366 of Oxford shed heading southwards with what may have been the 'F' lamp 11.42 a.m. Oxford to Taplow goods in 1939. This train called only at Thame over the branch, and, after Risborough, at High Wycombe and all yards to Cookham, then Taplow. Before the extension of the down loop/platform line, the South box home signals, illustrated on page 38 of Volume 1, were situated immediately south of the road bridge. The GW bracket signal was replaced by an LNER upper quadrant about 1936, the guy wires to which feature here. Whether it was this signal which was resited in 1943 or a new one is not known. *S. H. Freese*

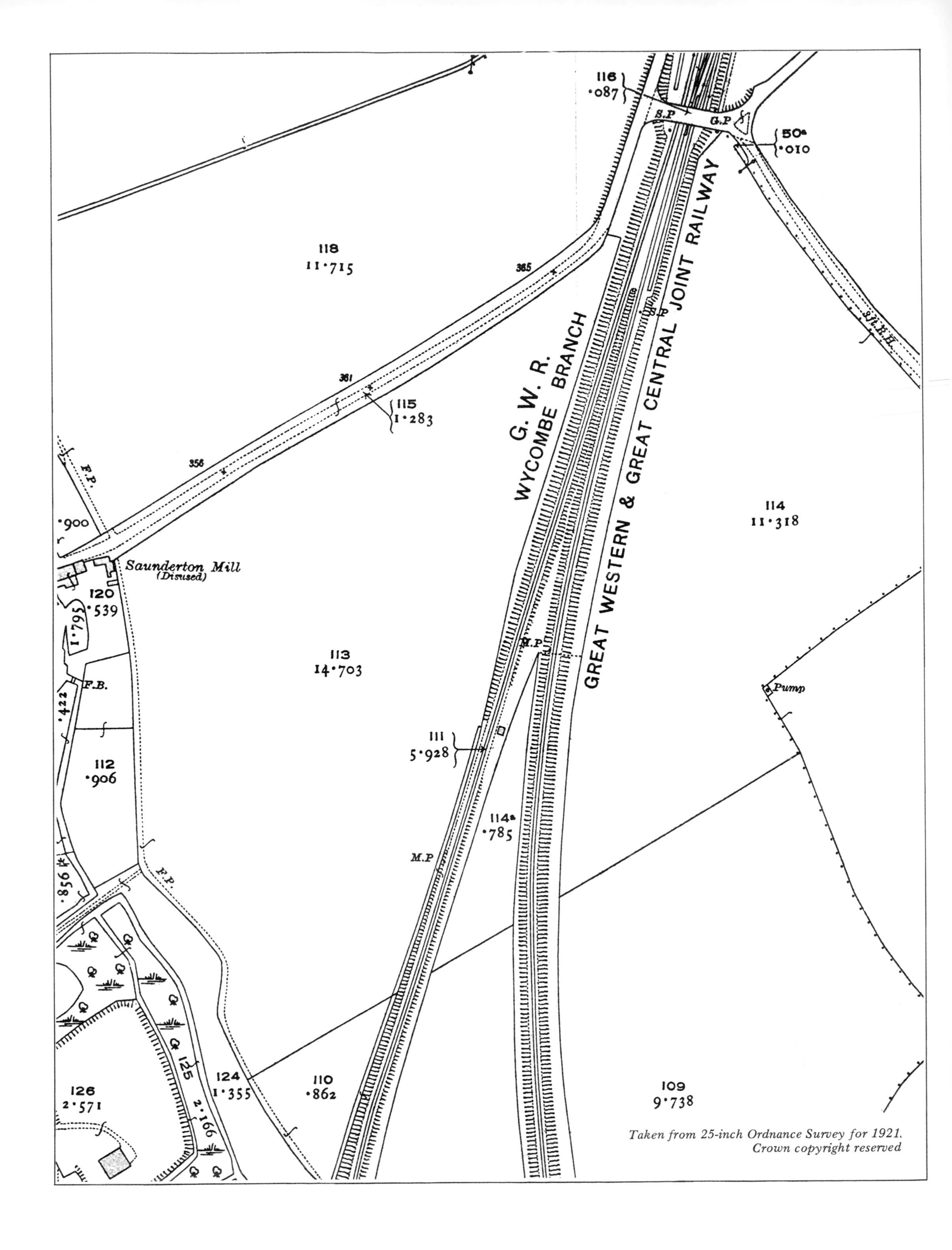

Taken from 25-inch Ordnance Survey for 1921. Crown copyright reserved

Stafford Road 'King' No. 6006 *King George I* climbing into the Chilterns about a mile to the south of Risborough with an up express, possibly the 9.5 a.m. Birkenhead, c.1938. At this point, the up and down lines were around 200 yards apart, and at considerably different levels. The deep cuttings were prone to blockage by snow or by slips in adverse weather conditions; in 1947, very heavy snow blocked the up line at this point, whilst remedial work on a slip during that year cost the companies £13,000. *H. K. Harman*

GOODS AND PARCELS TRAFFIC

PASSENGER-RATED TRAFFIC

During the 1920s and 30s, four farmers regularly sent a total of 12–18 churns of milk to London on the 8.18 a.m. Oxford to Paddington, which had two milk vans or 'siphons' on the rear. Besides miscellaneous parcels, other passenger-rated traffic included the odd bundle of newspapers during the day for Wyman's station bookstall, the main supplies for which arrived by road at about 6.30 a.m. There was also occasionally watercress from farmer Walter Goodchild of Longwick as well as fruit and vegetables from local growers. Early in the century, wicker hampers of locally-bred Aylesbury ducks were collected by Easts and sent by rail to Leadenhall market in London.

LIVESTOCK

Staff recall occasional consignments of horses and cattle for local farmers. These included horses for Desmond Molin, the local riding school and the hunt. Hugh Harman also recalled the occasional truckload of sheep from Kent for grazing and subsequent return.

SMALLS

Before the introduction of the Zonal system, smalls traffic (items weighing under 1 ton) for Risborough arrived each day in a station truck conveyed on the 2.0 a.m. Paddington to Aylesbury goods. The truck, normally a box van, was shunted into the goods shed where it was unloaded by the goods porter ready for Easts, the cartage agent. From about 1939, they used a Morrison electric truck for deliveries around the town, but items were often delivered by coal lorry.

Commercial stationers Cheverton & Laidler and Aston & Full sent out regular small consignments.

GENERAL TRAFFIC

Incoming traffic was largely coal, including supplies for Risborough Furniture (see page 170) and Forest Products Research Laboratory (see page 176), both of which also received timber.

Incoming agricultural traffic was largely fertilizers, with the occasional arrival of farm machinery. Will Anderson of Saunderton received regular supplies of cattle feed, some of which was apparently blue-dyed vegetables, which were unloaded along the back road.

Outgoing produce included hay and straw, not least from Allan G. Chilton of Parkmeadow, a London hay and straw merchant, and furniture tripped by road from the despatch department of Risborough Furniture for loading in the yard.

Austin Hoy of Lacey Green also despatched mining equipment (mainly coal-cutting chains) in open wagons.

CARTAGE AND COAL

The main cartage contractor who worked in conjunction with the railway was Risborough-based H. Hickman & Sons Ltd whose men had a reputation for hard work. They moved large quantities of flour which arrived by rail for local distribution. Bert Hickman started after the Great War and had two British Berna lorries with Swiss engines. Later the company used Studebaker, International, Leyland and AEC vehicles.

Under the Zonal scheme, Risborough became a sub-railhead of High Wycombe, smalls items thereafter being sent to Risborough by road. The first lorry based at Risborough for the new scheme was a 3 ton Morris Leader with a trailer, but this was replaced shortly afterwards by a 3 ton Morris Commercial. The Risborough driver was former Watlington branch lengthman Charlie Adby.

There was also a 6 ton Thornycroft with ER4 engine, but it is not known whether this was based at High Wycombe or Risborough.

TIMOTHY EAST LTD.

Timothy East was born in 1845, the son of Thomas East, saddler and harnessmaker at Monks Risborough with his own tannery. Timothy was apprenticed to James Cotter, fellmonger at Church Street, Risborough, whose premises he eventually acquired. As a fellmonger, he dealt in hides and skins and prepared them for the tanner. In 1868 Timothy began a partnership with Daniel Chowns, a coal merchant of Duke Street, Princes Risborough, renting some outbuildings at the Rose & Crown, Aylesbury.

In 1870 they moved into the Church Street premises formerly owned by James Cotter, eventually purchasing them from Joseph Loosley and John Eggleton in 1872. The partnership was dissolved in

1878, Chowns continuing with mineral water manufacture and farming, and Timothy East with coal and fellmongering at Church Street. Timothy was later joined by four of his sons, Rupert, Clement, Garnet and Basil, who became assistant managers.

On 3rd June 1903 he was appointed GW/GC Joint cartage agent for delivery and collection of goods and parcels in the town. The agency had previously been held by Matilda Ann Dover of the Railway Hotel,

Timothy East was prone to chest infections and followed the doctor's recommendation to grow a beard for protection. ***Cty. David East***

from April 1900, and Frederick Martin from September 1902.

Timothy East also handled salt and fertilizer and is said to have kept up to ten or twelve horses at one time for seven carts and three horse-drawn vans. Permits were issued during the Great War for five horse-drawn carts and two lorries, a Halford and a Martini. The horse-drawn carts were painted 'Parsons Green'.

Horses and carts were kept at Church Street where the premises were also shared with the Risborough Volunteer Fire Brigade, which rented a shed and, after the Second World War, a second building for use as a fire station and garage until a new fire station was built in 1960. Timothy's youngest son Basil used a pair of horses for longer runs and these were also used for the fire engine.

Like many small merchants, Easts had their own railway wagons purchased from, amongst others, the Midland Railway Carriage and Wagon Co. Ltd. of Birmingham. These were allocated odd numbers, painted brick red with black lettering, shaded white, but later the livery was changed to grey, with the lettering 'TIMOTHY EAST LTD.' signwritten diagonally across the side of the wagon in black lettering, shaded white, on a red ground between dark blue lines. Easts are said to have run a fleet of about twenty wagons, bringing coal mainly from Staffordshire and Warwickshire and anthracite from South Wales.

In 1913 the business became a limited company, Timothy East Ltd, and in 1915 they purchased their first motor lorry, a De Dion Bouton with gas lighting. This had been a French taxi, but Easts converted it into a truck.

Around this time their interests had widened to include wool merchanting, farming and builders supplies.

Timothy East died in 1916 and was succeeded by his sons Rupert and Clement as directors. Just before

ESTABLISHED. 1868.

Timothy East.

Coal, Coke, Salt, and Fertilizer

MERCHANT and AGENT.

Telegrams:- Timothy East, Princes Risborough.

Church St.
Princes
Risborough.
AND AT
Haddenham
(Bucks.)

Telephone:- No. 4, Princes Risborough.

FRESH WROUGHT COALS DIRECT FROM COLLIERY TO CONSUMER.

All descriptions of Cannock, Leicester, Derby, Wigan, and Welsh Coal for House, Steam, and Smiths' purposes; Foundry and Gas Coke, Agricultural, and other Salt, delivered to any Station per Truck Load at the lowest prices for Cash, month following delivery.

Goods and Parcels Carting Agent,

to the Great Western and Great Central Railways,

Joint Committee,

at PRINCES RISBOROUGH and HADDENHAM.

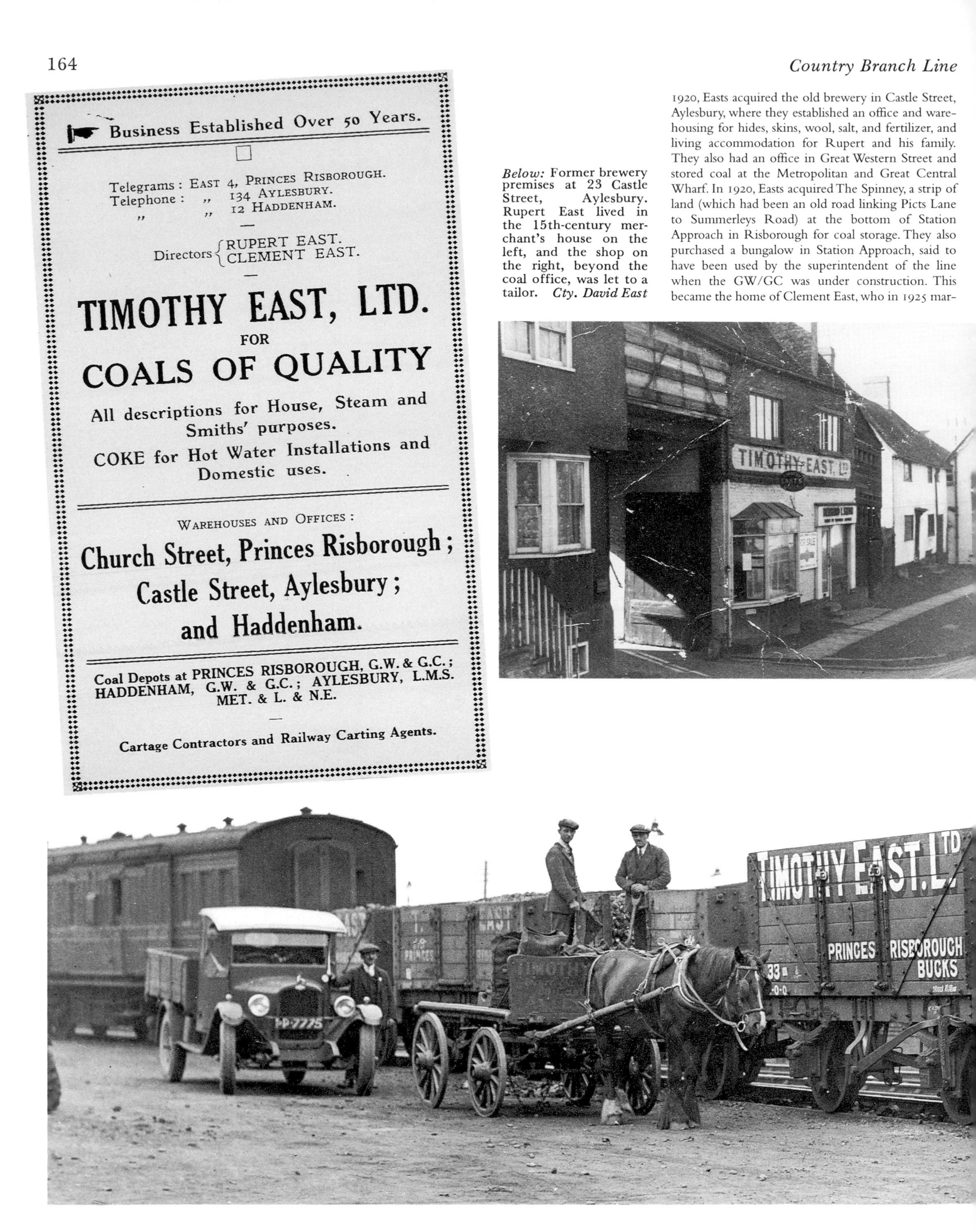

Business Established Over 50 Years.

Telegrams: EAST 4, PRINCES RISBOROUGH.
Telephone: " 134 AYLESBURY.
" " 12 HADDENHAM.

Directors { RUPERT EAST.
CLEMENT EAST.

TIMOTHY EAST, LTD.

FOR

COALS OF QUALITY

All descriptions for House, Steam and Smiths' purposes.

COKE for Hot Water Installations and Domestic uses.

WAREHOUSES AND OFFICES:

Church Street, Princes Risborough; Castle Street, Aylesbury; and Haddenham.

Coal Depots at PRINCES RISBOROUGH, G.W. & G.C.; HADDENHAM, G.W. & G.C.; AYLESBURY, L.M.S. MET. & L. & N.E.

Cartage Contractors and Railway Carting Agents.

1920, Easts acquired the old brewery in Castle Street, Aylesbury, where they established an office and warehousing for hides, skins, wool, salt, and fertilizer, and living accommodation for Rupert and his family. They also had an office in Great Western Street and stored coal at the Metropolitan and Great Central Wharf. In 1920, Easts acquired The Spinney, a strip of land (which had been an old road linking Picts Lane to Summerleys Road) at the bottom of Station Approach in Risborough for coal storage. They also purchased a bungalow in Station Approach, said to have been used by the superintendent of the line when the GW/GC was under construction. This became the home of Clement East, who in 1925 mar-

Below: Former brewery premises at 23 Castle Street, Aylesbury. Rupert East lived in the 15th-century merchant's house on the left, and the shop on the right, beyond the coal office, was let to a tailor. *Cty. David East*

ried Dorothy Britnell who worked at the station as a goods clerk.

Around this time, and certainly by 1922, Easts also established a branch at Haddenham, but the premises were sold in 1924, and customers were supplied from Risborough or Aylesbury.

By the early 1930s, horse drivers included Bill Tapping, Jack, Cyril and Gordon Avery, Fred Lockett and Fred Orchard, Easts apparently employing 8–10 men at Risborough. Lorries at various times had included a Lamboli, Martini, Halford, De Dion and British Berna. The 1930s began with Garners and Fords followed by Fordsons (BB and 7V), Dodges and Bedfords, and around 1936 they had a 25cwt Willeys Overland lorry. The fleet averaged three lorries and one horse dray at both depots then, although there were five lorries and one dray at Risborough for some time. Between the wars, lorries, drays and horse trolleys were all painted chocolate brown, as was a rather novel Morrison electric truck which, reminiscent of a milk float, had a 20–25 miles range. This was fitted with 'a dropside body with raves, side and front', and was lettered across its front 'Timothy East Ltd. Cartage agents. GW&GC Jt Rlys'. Although purchased for parcel delivery work around the town, after the agency was terminated, this vehicle was used for the coal round. The Aylesbury depot also had a similar vehicle for coal deliveries.

At Risborough, the agency lorry arrived at the goods shed around 8.30 a.m. to be loaded with 'smalls', then it was taken over to the parcels office to collect anything else for delivery on its rounds. Traffic varied but the agency routine usually included collections of stationery from Cheverton & Laidler and Aston & Full around the middle of the day. Another regular call was Messrs. Bloss, who sent out stool frames. Much of the traffic collected was taken straight into the goods yard and loaded into a row of box vans, usually left in the yard during the day with their doors open.

After lunch, the agency lorry served the town again and usually made Risboro' Furniture its last call. The factory often received boxes of springs and despatched assembled items of furniture. For a while, Easts apparently collected and delivered furniture containers using a Garner forward-control long-wheelbase flat lorry, but this was scrapped in the early 1940s, for lack of spares. In the mid-1930s they also had a shorter Garner which was used with a semi trailer for the delivery of steel water pipes for council road work. These arrived in Tube wagons from Staveley iron works whilst smaller feeder pipes came from Stanton iron works. They were unloaded using the yard crane, the larger ones being taken 12–14 at a time on a Garner lorry. Some were even collected from West Wycombe goods yard.

Easts seem to have had around three lorries at any one time for coal deliveries, which were generally within a 7–8 mile radius, including one customer at Christmas Common. For many years, however, horses and carts were used for deliveries as far as Speen. Supplies, said to have arrived in as many as 7 or 8 wagons at a time, often came from Baddesley, Bolsover and Hucknall collieries. As mentioned, Easts stored coal at The Spinney rather than renting wharfage at the railway, so it was either bagged straight off the wagon or shovelled onto the back of their lorries for transfer round to their premises, although in later years they also stored supplies in the centre of the goods yard. Before the end of the 1920s, domestic deliveries had been made using wicker baskets, but normally they used tarred hemp coal bags or tarred jute coke sacks.

Up to the 1960s, Easts supplied wagon loads of coal to Risboro' Furniture and every Monday made two deliveries to Risborough Gas Works, at first by horse and cart, and from the 1930s by lorry, often returning with coke. In later years, contractors were used to release East's lorries for domestic deliveries. Rupert and Clement East were directors of the Princes Risborough Gas Light & Coke Co. until it was taken over by the United Kingdom Gas Corporation about 1939.

Easts dealt in fertilizer at the Risborough and Aylesbury depots, apparently handling 6–8 tons per month. This arrived in bags in box vans from ICI and Fisons for sale to farms and market gardens. They also handled cattle cake, and salt which came in bags or

Easts' short wheelbase Garner and semi-trailer for conveying pipes, probably at Devil's Elbow at Speen.

The Aylesbury Morrison Electric. The Risborough vehicle was basically similar but it had no bumper bar and the lower edge of the front panel was rounded instead of being angular. The style of lettering was identical, but with 'GW & GC Jt Rlys' substituted for 'Aylesbury', and 'cartage agents' for 'coal coke'. The Risborough vehicle was converted from a milk float and replaced a Ford AA shortly before the outbreak of the Second World War.
Cty. David East

This beautifully posed view, taken in Aylesbury Met & GC goods yard in the early 1930s, shows Easts' Chevrolet and horse and dray alongside some of their own wagons.
Cty. David East

Unloading coal after a rough shunt in the dock road in the late 1940s. The figure on the left is unidentified but the two leaning over on the back of the 2-ton Fordson BB were Ted Thompson (driver/mechanic, a grandson of Timothy East) and Bill Rogers (his mate, also a driver). The figure standing in front of the rear wheel was Basil East but the other figure on the lorry is also unidentified. *Cty. David East*

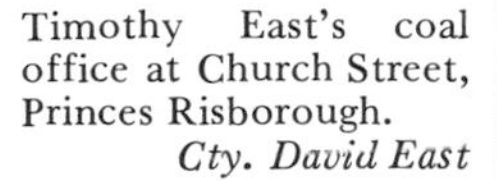

Timothy East's coal office at Church Street, Princes Risborough. *Cty. David East*

70 year old Bill Tapping with Robin in 1961 just before he retired. He was the last of the company's horse drivers, having served Easts for 35 years. *Cty. David East*

lumps (rock salt), all of which arrived in box vans and sheeted opens. This was purchased from the Stafford Salt and Alkali Co. (later absorbed by ICI) and was sold to C. Stevens & Sons Ltd, bacon curers, pork pie and sausage makers of Prestwood, near Great Missenden, and to local farmers who used it in building hay ricks. Salt was sprinkled layer by layer to sweeten hay which may have been made in damp weather conditions and otherwise have become musty. Although salt attracts moisture, it seemed to work. Farmers also gave rock salt to their animals to lick. This gave them minerals they needed, which they otherwise sought by licking iron fencing. Rock salt for 'animal licks' came in lumps, but when rock salt became restricted to use in treating roads in winter, iodised blocks were substituted. Other uses included domestic water softening and gardening, Horticultural salt was largely used on asparagus beds, but also for brassicas and beet, whilst heavy dressings acted as weed killer. Sliced runner beans were also stored in jars of salt.

The salt and fertilizer side of the business gradually gave way to the flourishing seed and horticultural business also developed by Clement at Risborough about 1952 and after Clement's death run by his younger son Paul.

In 1938 Easts had also opened a garden shop in Great Western Street, Aylesbury, moving to the market square in 1940 to trade as the County Seed Stores and Garden Shop (formerly W.E. Troup).

Rupert East died in 1941 and was succeeded by his son Harold, whilst Clement died in 1956 and was succeeded by his elder son David. In the postwar years the livery of Easts' coal lorries was changed to 'Brilliant Green'.

Eventually, the coal business was sold to Charles Franklin Ltd of Aylesbury (their headquarters were at Bedford), Timothy East Ltd. delivering their last sack of coal on 30th September 1964. Franklins retained the office in Great Western Street, Aylesbury, and later opened a shop in High Street, Risborough. Franklins eventually sold out to Charringtons.

(Left) Frank Redding, (centre) Fred Redding and (right) Will Tapping at Bridge Street, Great Kimble in the 1930s.
Cty. Sheila Harding

FRANK REDDING

Frank Redding, a coal and coke merchant based at Great Kimble from *c.*1931–1968, received his supplies at Risborough. His uncle, Harry Smith, had traded as a small wood merchant alongside the Plough public house at Cadsdean. When Frank took over the business, he purchased locally grown timber which he sold to the building trade and the scraps for firewood.

At first he used his uncle's horse and cart, additionally taking on removals and local deliveries, but before long he purchased another and for a short while also ran a pony and trap. When he married, he moved in to Beechwood, Bridge Street, Great Kimble, where he started a coal business, his wife Edith running the clerical side of things. The premises had a yard, garage and stables, so there was room to store supplies and keep the horses as well as a Chevrolet lorry which he bought in the mid-1930s. This must have made collecting supplies from Risborough a great deal easier. In later years he had 6-ton Bedfords, these and the Chevrolet being painted light grey with red lettering shaded black.

Redding purchased coal from factors Toomer Bros. of Reading, and Wallace, Spiers & Co. Ltd, and gen-

Frank Redding at Great Kimble with his horse, Tom.
Cty. Sheila Harding

FRANK REDDING,

Firewood Merchant,

GREAT KIMBLE, nr. PRINCES RISBORO',

BUCKS.

CHIPS	HARDWOOD
FAGGOTS	BEAN STICKS
BLOCKS	PEA STICKS

Fred Redding, Jack Redrup (on horse), Fred Redrup (partly hidden) and Frank Redding at their Bridge Street yard, Great Kimble.
Cty. Sheila Harding

erally received some 2–3 wagons a week. He also purchased coke from Risborough Gas Works. To assist him, he employed three regular men and casual labour when required, serving customers both in Risborough and the surrounding villages. In the 1930s he also carted road chippings for the local council.

Around 1950 he purchased from Jarvis what had once been Tom Oldfield's coal business. When Redding died in 1968, the business was taken over by Charles Franklin Ltd. of Aylesbury.

OLDFIELD & ABERCROMBIE

When Ernest Oldfield married into the Abercrombie family, his wife used her maiden name as a partner in the business, which seem to have been established in the early 1900s. They were based at Mill House, Saunderton, and collected their coal from Risborough station. They served their own area with a horse and cart.

After Ernest died on 10th December 1926, his wife continued to run the business with the assistance of Norman Mackie, who subsequently took over. Incidentally, Mill House was demolished in the late 1920s.

N.H. MACKIE

Norman Horace Mackie apparently based his coal business at a yard in Bledlow Road, Saunderton, but at some point he stored coal at his home, Upper East, Shootacre Lane, Risborough. He delivered around Risborough and as far out as Lacey Green using a Fordson lorry. He purchased supplies from Reading-based factors Toomers, Talbots and Thrushley, and, when unloading wagons in the goods yard, he apparently used a chain to hold the wagon door in a horizontal position instead of the more usual anti-regulation practice of wooden props.

In the early 1950s he was joined by his son Trevor, and during this period ran two 3-ton Ford Thames lorries, then a Commer Karrier, each of which were painted green with cream lettering shaded red and white.

Norman died in 1959 and in the early 1960s Trevor sold the business to Plumridge of Saunderton (one time Chinnor, see page 110).

TOM OLDFIELD

Not so much has been discovered about Tom Oldfield, Ernest Oldfield's brother (see above), who began with a horse and dray when based at 'Stanton', Station Road. He later acquired a Bedford lorry and moved to 'The Firs', Summerleys Road about 1934. He traded from the 1920s through to the 1940s using the horse and cart and the lorry, and is said to have sold out to Percy Green who, around 1959, sold to Jarvis, who in turn sold out to Frank Redding.

Frank Redding in the cab of his Chevrolet.
Cty. Sheila Harding

Frank Redding's Bedford.
Cty. Sheila Harding

Coal being unloaded directly on to one of the merchants' lorries alongside the back siding at Princes Risborough in the late 1940s. *H. K. Harman*

Tom Oldfield and his daughter Marianne, probably at 'The Firs', Summerleys Road, Risborough. *Cty. Margaret Bass*

RISBORO' FURNITURE LTD.

Risboro' Furniture began in October 1919 when a few workers from Goodearl Bros. in High Wycombe were stationed in the old British School building to assemble chair parts from the parent factory. William Goodearl had begun making chairs in 1870 and expanded the business with his sons, becoming renowned for Windsor chairs, cane-seat chairs and 7-piece upholstered suites, mostly for the London market.

With increasing demand for their products, Goodearls purchased land adjacent to Princes Risborough station in 1920 and 1924, establishing a modern sawmill on the 10-acre site which was also subsequently served by its own railway sidings under an agreement dated 21st January 1926. The sidings were used for the receipt of logs, some of which arrived from Brentford Docks, and regular supplies of coal for the boiler house. However, most products were collected from the despatch department by railway lorry and loaded onto wagons in the goods yard.

For a while the business became known as Goodearl Dean & Co, Albert and Percy Goodearl, who ran the Wycombe and Risborough factories respectively, having been joined by Ernest and Harold Dean. However, from 1924 the business became Risboro' Furniture Ltd. Their major products at this time were corduroy-covered, flock or spring-filled loose cushion, adjustable chairs.

The *Industrial World* for November 1931 carried such a delightful feature on the factory that we could not resist reproducing it in full:

> In that part of Buckinghamshire which includes High Wycombe and Princes Risborough, skill in the making of furniture, and particularly chairs, is traditional. It is a locality peopled by those who are not only themselves skilled in this branch of production, but who come of fathers who, before them, were often engaged in the same kind of work.
>
> In the neighbourhood mentioned there are establishments which not only supply furniture which goes to all parts of the British Isles, but those which manufacture for overseas markets as well. The area which, in the shadow of the Chilterns, is devoted to furniture production has done much to convince the world that in the realm of furniture manufacture as in so many others, the British product is capable of maintaining its position against those of all other nations.
>
> You may see this branch of manufacture carried out at its best at the Station Works at Princes Risborough, an establishment which is controlled by Messrs. Risboro' Furniture Ltd., and affiliated with Messrs. Goodearl Bros. Ltd. of High Wycombe. The former undertaking has achieved much in the comparatively short period in which it has been in

The Risboro' Furniture Co's factory, viewed from the station. From right to left, the various bays were in order of assembly: Machine shop, where partly processed timber was received from the mill and cut to the shapes required (a narrow gauge line ran to the back of the machine shop for handling supplies); Assemblers store, for components awaiting assembly; Making shop, where parts were assembled in the first stage of manufacture; Painting/polishing shop, where suitable finishes were given; Upholstery, some items (such as kitchen chairs, etc,) bypassed this shop, Despatch offices situated alongside Station Road. There was also a garage adjacent to the Despatch office where the company's fleet of road vehicles were maintained. The footpath at the front of the picture (which still exists at the time of writing), which ran along the back of the goods yard across Risboro' Furniture's private siding and on to Picts Lane, effectively marked the western boundary of the factory premises.

The old British School which was used for assembly of chairs from parts received from Goodearl's Wycombe factory.

The saw-mill, boiler-house and gantry. The low building to the right of the mill was the saw doctor's premises where the saws and other cutting appliances were sharpened. Although the gantry extended over both sidings, the left-hand one (which in this picture has logs stacked over it) was generally used to receive truckloads of coal for the boiler house. Coal usually arrived in 10-ton wagons and was unloaded by hand and stacked to the left of the siding (behind the logs on the left), then barrowed round to the boiler house as required. After the Second World War, wood offcuts and shavings were ground down by machine and used as fuel. The right-hand siding was primarily used for the receipt of logs which were offloaded by crane from open and bogie bolster wagons. Former railway staff recall occasions when up to twelve opens of timber arrived for the factory, six being put on each road. This view shows an abundance of logs, and on the right partly prepared timber stacked. In this process, known as 'sticking', wood was stacked with gaps in between enabling air to circulate throughout the whole pile. The sidings were rarely used for outwards loads as most finished products were collected from the adjacent factory and taken to the station by the railway delivery lorry. However, in the 1930s, chair parts were sent to other manufacturers, even as near as Amersham, by rail.

Shortly after the Second World War, the crane was extended into the timber stacking area shown in the foreground, to enable wood to be unloaded from lorries. The roadway shown was the only vehicular access to the mill and led to Picts Lane at the south-eastern end of the site. The chimney in the background belonged to the boiler house.

Looking out of the saw mill towards the railway. Timber stacked here was craned into the mill as required.

existence, and had its beginning when pupils from the furniture industry at High Wycombe were sent to Princes Risborough in 1920; they operated in a disused school there and eventually works were erected.

The firm has, since then, been gradually expanded and at the present time controls an exceedingly up-to-date and well-equipped factory, whilst another establishment of the most approved modern type has just been completed. This factory building is ideally adapted to its purpose; the north light roof principle has been applied and there is a large loading bay.

The company controls a very extensive timber yard and a sawmill, the last-mentioned being, we imagine, one of the best-equipped in the county. There is a large electric crane and an extensive gantry communicating with a large and up-to-date band sawing machine capable of sawing any class or size of timber. The power for driving the machinery is supplied by a very high-power steam engine. There are, too, extensive drying kilns and efficient bending retorts and plant.

Rapid and economical dispatch is secured as the result of the company having its own railway sidings. Risboro' Furniture Ltd. buys its own timber in the round and undertakes sawing and all the processes involved in chair making — bending, assembling, polishing, finishing, upholstering and so on. Fireside chairs, adjustable chairs, chair-beds and settees and folding chairs are also made and all the firm's products are characterised by an excellence of design, the use of thoroughly good materials and sound workmanship which ensures for them a ready sale not only throughout the home market, but also to some extent on the continent.

There are about 160 workers employed, most of them highly skilled in such work. Considering that this undertaking has only been in existence for a comparatively brief period, it is easily understood why its supplies should serve mainly the home market; but it requires little imagination, in view of present developments, to anticipate a large increase in the export business undertaken in the not-far-distant future.

About nine acres of land are occupied by the firm at Princes Risborough, the actual works cov-

Left: The saw mill, looking towards the station. The overhead crane ran the entire length of the mill and also spanned the outermost of the two sidings. The vertical band mill with its 6ft blade was supplemented by another but after the war they were both superseded by a fully automatic machine. Logs brought in by rail were picked up by the overhead crane and manouvred alongside the saw. Wood was moved around on narrow gauge lines with trolleys which ran the entire length of the mill. In the 1930s, four men worked in the mill and another in both the mill and adjacent timber yards. The man in the centre of the picture, alongside the saw, was Mr. J. Collins, one of the mill gang. *Right:* The saw doctor's shop where blades/saws and other tools were maintained. One man was employed here carrying out highly skilled work. The blade on the left was from the vertical band saw.

Timber being seasoned in the area of land bounded by Picts Lane.

The southern end of Risborough station on 13th March 1959, with Risboro' Furniture's timber yard in the foreground. *Hunting Aerofilms*

ering more than half of this area. Nowadays, the demand, so far as furniture is concerned, is for the quality product. At the same time, in days when purchasing power is necessarily limited more severely than usual, price considerations count for a great deal. Those in the furniture trade have, therefore, constantly to be seeking supplies of furniture which, whilst attaining a sound quality standard, is also moderately priced. This can certainly be said of the products of Risboro' Furniture Ltd.

The catalogue issued by the company should be in the hands of all trade buyers for it contains a brief description of a wide range of extremely attractive chairs, bed-chairs and settees, all of them marked by effective design and thoroughly sound workmanship and all available at prices which permit of their eventual display in the retail establishments at rates which represent extremely sound value.

The strongest and most compact of folding chairs, "Stakmore" Pat. No. 211626 is made here and also Portable Tip-up seating of protected design.

During the war the factory was requisitioned by the Ministry of Aircraft Production and used by Horden Richmond, from Haddenham airfield, for aircraft propeller blade production. Miles Aircraft from Reading also produced wooden parts there for a training plane, one of their employees, Gerald Hoar, recalling "I worked in Goodearls in the shop near the footpath to the railway station."

The sawmill produced a variety of items for government departments, including tent pegs and snowshoe soles, all of which were subject to rigorous inspection by a government official before being despatched by rail in box vans to the Bicester and Didcot Ordnance Depots.

After the war the factory was busy producing utility dining chairs and upholstered easy chairs, and in spite of the difficulties with timber rationing, their output expanded with a new range of furniture embodying diecast aluminium parts and sections, and laminated plastics. This led to a range of plastic-surfaced tables which in turn took the company into the market of kitchen units which, by 1947, were being sold under the name Whiteleaf.

The sidings saw little use after the war, and by 1958, when a new machine shop was built at Risborough for both factories, there was hardly any need for their retention. Consequently, the siding agreement was terminated in 1962.

French polishing in the painting shop.

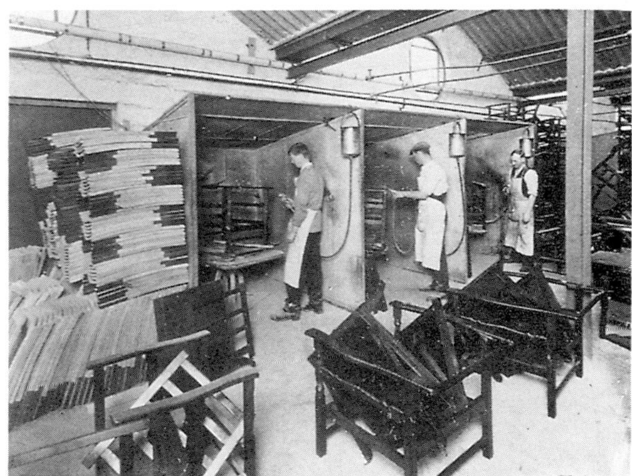

Spray booths in the painting/polishing shop.

The packing and despatch room.

This aerial view, looking south over Risborough station, shows Risboro' Furniture's extensive premises with the northlight factory building on the left and the saw mill and private siding adjacent to the goods yard. This photograph was taken on 13th March 1959. *Hunting Aerofilms*

H.M. OFFICE OF WORKS SIDING

The H.M. Office of Works Forest Products Research Laboratory was built alongside the railway at Risborough between 1926 and 1928. It was established to develop expertise on the properties, processing and utilisation of timber and wood-based panel products which included testing, seasoning and preservation trials.

The original buildings on the site were: timber mechanics laboratory, seasoning kilns, wood preservation plant, office accommodation, boiler house, stores, workshops, sawmill, an administration block housing offices, library, photography and physics departments. An entomology section with its stock of insect-infested timber was relegated to a sort of isolation unit, whilst ex-army huts from Farnborough provided temporary accommodation for a canteen, Office of Works staff, timber mechanics, seasoning assistants and a collection of exhibits.

The entrance off Summerleys Road led through rows of elms lining what had been the approach road to Horsenden Manor. However, the elms were considered dangerous and in the 1930s were cut down and replaced with a varied selection of ornamental trees.

The laboratory was served by a private siding provided under agreement with the Joint Committee on 21st October 1927. It was used for the delivery of logs for experimental evaluation and for deliveries of coal for the boiler house. A loop provided in and out roads, but in practice laboratory staff pinchbarred wagons along the gentle downgrade, typically bolster wagons for unloading by the hydraulic crane spanning the track, and coal wagons for unloading at the boiler house at the end of the siding. The empties were collected by a loco, usually the pilot from Aylesbury. Outward traffic was very rare.

During the war the laboratory provided working space for the research and experiments branch of the Air Raid Precaution Division of the Ministry of Home Security. Scientists seconded from universities and government departments worked on evolving a wooden version of the Morrison shelter. The laboratory's experiments in wood bending proved invaluable in aircraft construction and it undertook the testing of adhesives for the Ministry of Aircraft Production. It also became involved in the problems caused by the shortage of timber. The occupation of Norway by the Germans in the spring of 1940, followed by the collapse of France, meant that supplies from Europe were cut off and Britain was virtually dependent on North America and West Africa for imported timber.

The government had prepared emergency plans for the control of essential raw materials by the Ministry of Supply and the use of home-grown timber was encouraged. The laboratory became involved in this control and in the monitoring and inspection of new kilns, the modernisation of old ones and training.

It is not difficult to appreciate how the postwar timber industry has benefited from all this research.

By 1954 the laboratory was receiving fine-grain coal for the boiler house and the delivery of logs was almost entirely by road, but it was not until 1971 that the private siding agreement was terminated.

Scientific staff, G. E. Soame and L. S. Doman, inspecting plywood panels on the 'weathering site' where the long-term durability of adhesives was tested.

This aerial view towards the west, taken on 24th March 1961, shows the Forest Products Research Laboratory and private siding situated to the west of the GW/GC main line and inside the curve of the two single lines to Watlington and Oxford. The proposed engine shed for Princes Risborough (mentioned on page 55 of Vol. 1) would have been built on this site. This view also shows the Watlington branch diverging south-westwards (top right) away from the Oxford line and heading off across the fields towards Bledlow. *Hunting Aerofilms*

WILLIAM ELIJAH BENTON

Cty. Rev. Ralph Cartmill

Appendix 1

CHINNOR CEMENT AND LIME WORKS

According to the *Thame Gazette* for 17th December 1940, 'When County Councils were first established the Oxford Authority issued a pamphlet explaining that the rateable value of the county would remain at a low level because of the apparent absence of all manufacturing materials. Then came the exploring intellect of a new master of geological science whose experience was founded on worldwide travel and government research.' These words were part of an appreciation following the death of William Elijah Benton, a mining engineer who had founded what eventually became Chinnor Cement and Lime Company's impressive works.

It seems that when he left Birmingham University, Benton travelled to the Antipodes to broaden his experience. By the time he came to Chinnor, he already owned Brent Brick and Lime Works at Willesden and was living in Acton when he surveyed prospective sites for a new lime works. It is said that his first choice was land at Saunderton, alongside the railway to the south of Princes Risborough, and that he was apparently let down by the owner who called off the deal at the last moment. His second choice was at Chinnor, where Bill Seymour recalled the land concerned had been part of John North's farm (Seymour was working there as a farm hand). North's farm was divided between North's son and Harry Blake who had made money from mining in Australia. North's son continued farming in the village but Blake sold his part of the land near Chinnor Hill, and alongside the Watlington branch, to W.E. Benton on 19th June 1909. Blake then moved to Woodway farm, Aston Rowant.

The relationship, if any, between the two men is not clear, but if the story is true, it is an interesting coincidence that Benton should purchase the plot from a landowner who had been mining in Australia.

Although deeds show the sale of the land to Benton on 19th June 1909, the first sod is said to have been cut in 1908. Benton remained in Acton and lodged in Chinnor with a Mrs Copus who lived opposite The Crown public house. Presumably he must have spent much of his time at Chinnor throughout the establishment of the works, but he is otherwise recalled as visiting Chinnor on Tuesdays and Fridays, arriving on the 10.20 train and returning on the 3.20 p.m. In 1923 he had a new home built for him and his family on the south-east corner of the site, adjacent to the Icknield Way.

Benton needed good men to get his scheme off the ground and in that respect it was providential that in 1912 he should meet Joseph Digweed, an experienced navvy who was walking from his home in Bicester to Woodhay where he was helping to build a mansion. Times were hard, but he had stopped overnight at Chinnor and learned of work available at the new lime works.

Joseph had worked in various parts of the country on railways and other public works. These had included the construction of the Cheltenham to Honeybourne line and tunnel work on the Ashendon to Aynho line in 1910. However, more significantly, he had worked at the lime works at Burghclere in his younger days. It must have been of particular interest to Benton to have a man with practical experience of lime burning from another works.

Benton, who walked around with his hands behind his back and often repeated himself, said to Joseph, "Just the man I want; just the man I want! Come and look at my quarry."

Joseph was very confident and even criticised the methods of chalk extraction. Benton, who had a reputation for plain speaking himself, asked him when he could start, to which Joseph replied "Right away!" Benton then gave him £1 to move his family from Bicester to Crowell, This was a good move on Benton's part, for he not only secured a keen and enthusiastic worker who became a respected member of the community, but, as Digweek's five sons grew up, they also worked there. The youngest one, Jim, worked at the lime and cement works from 1928 to 1979 and kindly provided much of the information which follows.

THE ORIGINAL LIME WORKS

Chalk was dug by hand for the old lime works, the removal of the overburden, i.e. top and sub-soils, being known as 'uncallowing'. The top 12–20ft depth of chalk was generally softer and particularly suitable for cement, whilst anything below was harder and had a higher calcium content best suited for lime.

At the quarry face, the 'small chalk' was barred down from safe footholds, but the harder and more solid chalk below had to be blasted, then broken up with picks and a hammer wedge. The chalk was easily drilled using approximately 2in diameter drills ranging from 2ft to 8ft long. These were changed as the bore progressed, then the charge of gunpowder (originally in reels with a central hole for the fuse) was placed with a ramrod (grooved to clear the fuse) and tamped with drillings pushed in gently alongside the fuse.

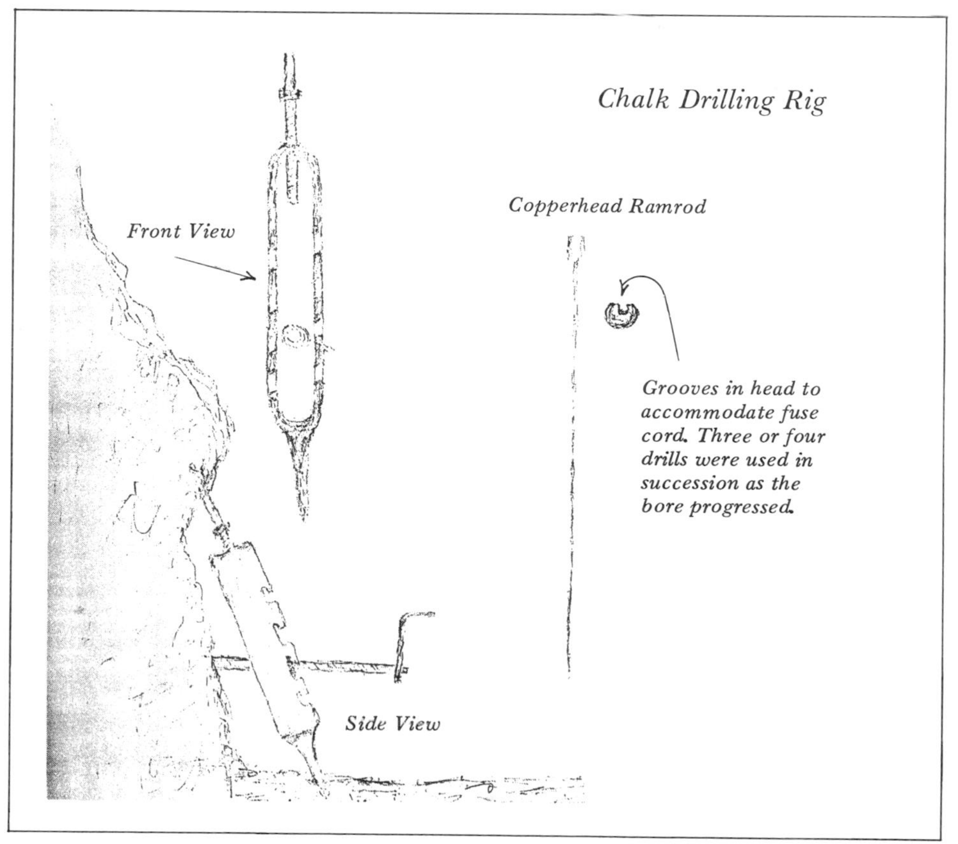

Sketches by Jim Digweed

Chalk was conveyed to the kilns in 6cwt iron tubs which ran on 2ft gauge rails and were hauled up the incline by a continuous overhead chain powered by a 15hp National gas engine housed in a building at the west end of the row of kilns. Travelling at ¾–1mph, the chain had 2½in links which engaged with 'V' slotted projections on the ends of the tubs. The tubs had to be fairly evenly spaced to avoid any long stretches of unsupported chain dragging on the ground and causing a braking effect. There were consequently usually between three and five tubs travelling in either direction.

At the pit bottom, the chain was returned around a 4ft 6in diameter horizontal chain wheel mounted on a 5ft high bollard. The chain was guided on and off the wheel by 2in diameter jockey wheels which lifted it, automatically disengaging the links from the empty tubs. On the return side, as the chain lowered from the jockey wheel, it engaged with the projecting 'V's on loaded tubs waiting to go to the kilns.

The tubs, handled by the men who had loaded them, were slewed into position on a heavy steel plate ("a flick of old engine oil made it easy") onto the rails, and engaged in one of the links of the chain for the slow haul up the steep gradient.

The men at the quarry communicated with the engine house for stopping or starting the chain by means of a pull wire connected to a bell. The tippers at the kiln could also communicate with the men at the pit by the same means.

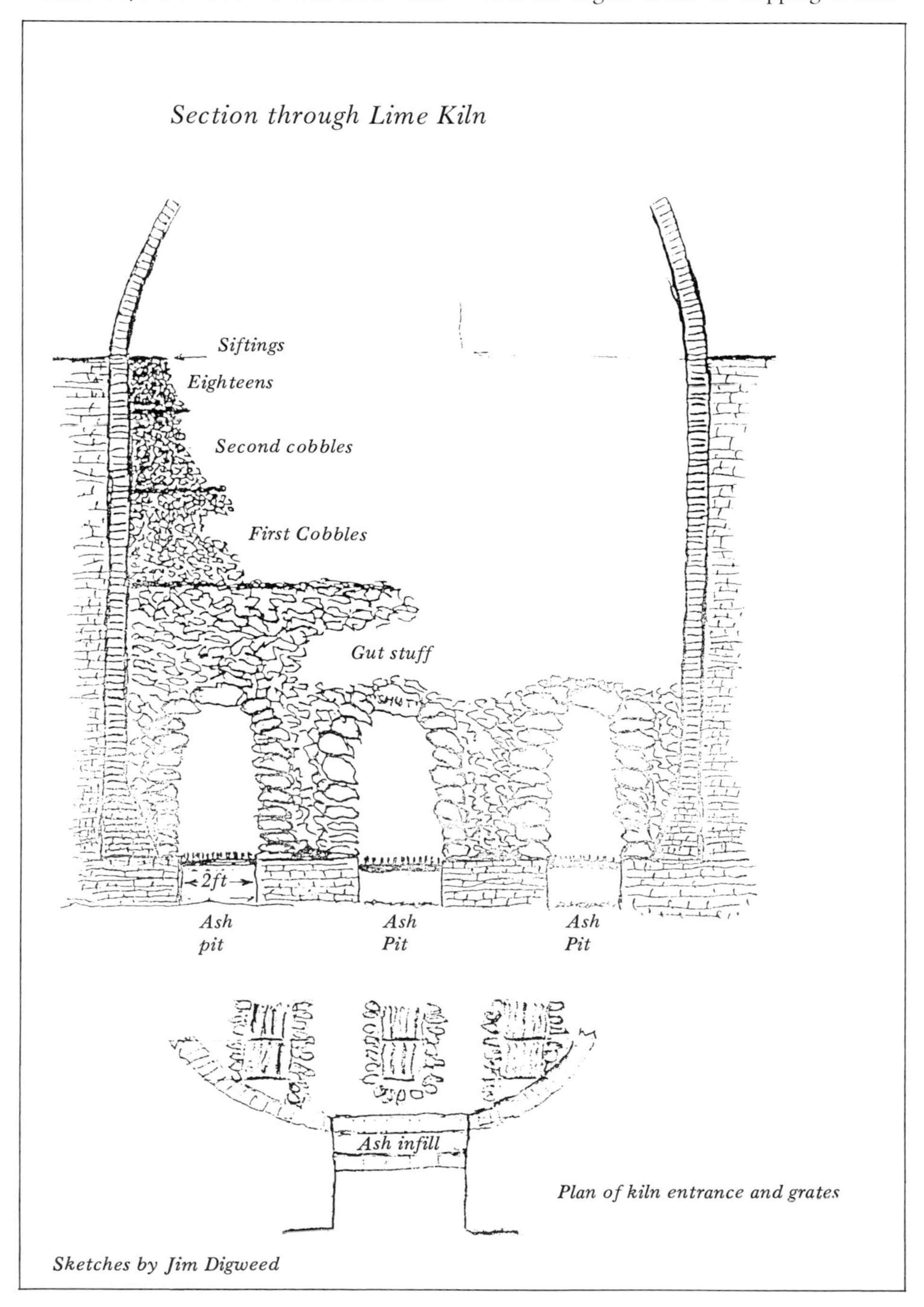

Plan of kiln entrance and grates

Sketches by Jim Digweed

LIME BURNING

Lime was made by burning chalk, the local deposits of which were known in the trade as 'Chiltern Greystone' or 'Greylime'. This process was carried out in brick-built 'flare' kilns, sometimes referred to as 'bottle' or 'beehive' kilns, fired by coal and coke.

Loading or 'setting' a charge was a skilled job which commenced with three parallel combustion chambers built like 2ft 6in wide tunnels over permanent ash pits which ran across the base of the kiln. Large hand-picked lumps of 'green' (wet) chalk were used for the sides of these chambers, which, built up in the manner of a dry-stone wall, curved inwards towards the top, where they were capped with large 'shut' pieces or 'keystones' which could weigh over a hundredweight.

Except for 5cwt of coke sprinkled on the kiln floor between the middle and outside grates and on the batter walls, all material was loaded into the kiln through a hatch about halfway up, and lowered to the base by means of 'chute poles'. This chute was assembled from three 'chute tins', curved or troughed metal sheets attached to long 7in × 4in deal poles something after the fashion of a First-Aid stretcher. A metal shovelling plate was laid at the base of the chute to protect the firebars and make it easier to shovel the chalk delivered down the chute.

It could take a day for the two men to build the three arches which were backfilled with rugby-ball-sized lumps of chalk, referred to as 'gut stuff'. When the arches had been completed, the chute was dismantled and pulled out of the kiln with the aid of a rope. The two outer arches or tunnels ran from the brick wall at the back of the kiln across to the firedoors, but the middle one was shorter and closed off with chalk walling just beyond the end of the fire grate, but short of the open hatch on the opposite side, through which the lime would be dug out, or drawn after burning. One of the 'archers' would work at the top hatch and continue to load the kiln whilst the other one would stay down below and build up the 'wicket' which sealed up the drawing hatchway. This crucial seal had to be airtight and this was achieved by a double wall consisting of a 9in inner skin of refractory bricks laid as headers, and a 4½in outside skin, built with Flettons, the 9in cavity between being filled with slack lime putty.

By the time the wicket was built, the other archer would have loaded most of the remaining 'gut stuff', which was tipped onto

The 'drawing' side of the original flare kilns, numbered 1 to 5 respectively, shown some time between 1923 and 1926 when the temporary water pipe, shown supported on posts, provided a supply used in the construction of W. E. Benton's house, 'Icknield Hatch'. By the time he took up residence, he had his own supply from a bore. Most of the materials for his home came in by rail and were unloaded on the top of the coal siding and transferred to the site on trolleys or tubs. This picture features one of the jockey wheels (right) which supported the haulage chain at the kilns, one of the 6cwt 2-wheeled lime loading barrows on the wharf, and two cross-braced trestles erected alongside the siding (the 'lime road') to support planks for a barrow run across the wagons, to dump slack lime on ground to the left. *Photos John H. Billston unless otherwise credited.*

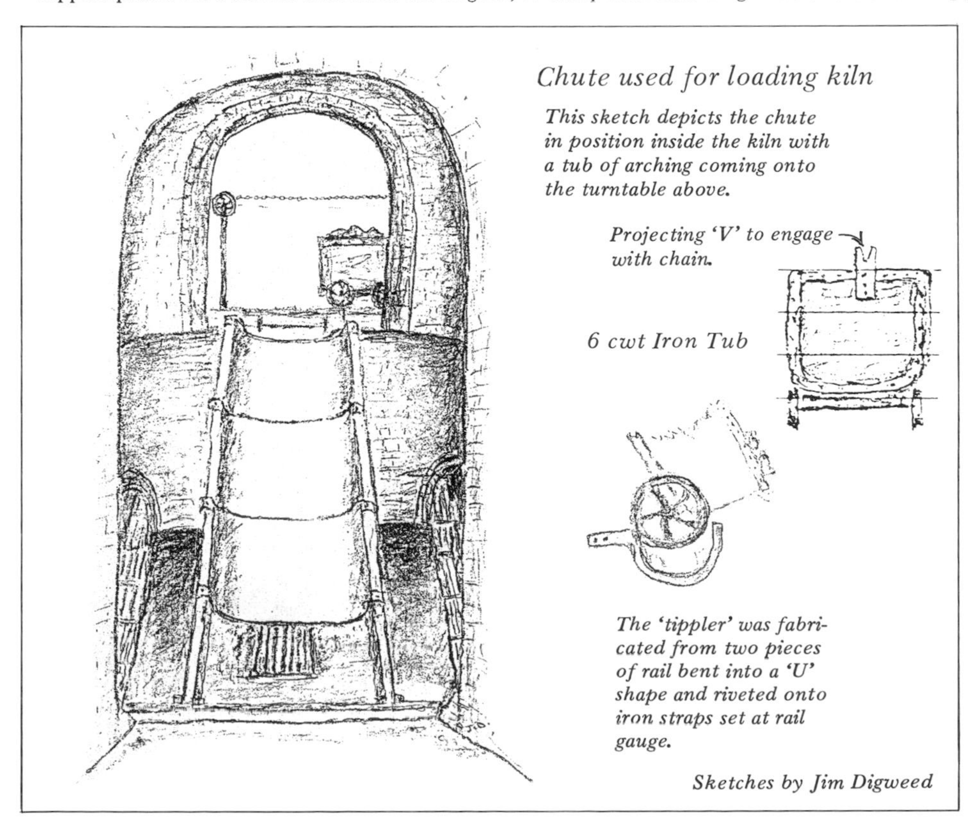

Chute used for loading kiln

This sketch depicts the chute in position inside the kiln with a tub of arching coming onto the turntable above.

The 'tippler' was fabricated from two pieces of rail bent into a 'U' shape and riveted onto iron straps set at rail gauge.

Sketches by Jim Digweed

a 6ft × 4ft metal shovelling plate and distributed into an even layer until it reached a depth of about 4ft above the arches. Both of the archers then added a layer of seven tubs of coke, again tipped onto a shovelling plate. Incidentally. the coke was delivered to them 'on the chain' by sending it down the empty road from the top coke stage to pit bottom, where it was slewed over and sent back along the up road.

The coke was topped with a layer of 'first cobbles', hand-picked chalk stone fork-loaded in the quarry, then a layer of six tubs of coke, followed by 'second cobbles' (shovel and fork-loaded), another layer of five tubs of coke covered with 'eighteens' (shovel-loaded), and finally two or three tubs of 'siftings' spread as a thin layer to 'blind' the charge, i.e. to restrict the air flow to prevent it all burning too quickly.

When the kiln was full to the top of the 'pan', the top hatchway was bricked up and closed off with a galvanised metal sheet as it was not so critical as the bottom one.

Firing the kilns was a skilled task from beginning to end, entirely dependent on the burner's experience. They were tended day and night. Each of the three combustion chambers had its own steel door but these were left off in the initial stages.

The 'firing' side of the flare kilns in the 1920s, showing the stockpiles of coke, coal and coke respectively along the wharf. The plank spanning the siding ('the coal and coke road') was used to barrow ashes to the tip on the right. The other ash tip at the far end of the kilns was cleared in 1936 to make space for the new Brockham kilns. The structure at the end of the kilns was the engine house, adjoining which, out of view at ground level, were the foreman's office and stores, blacksmith's shop and anthracite store.

The fire was started typically on a Monday, using brushwood brought down from the beech-covered slopes by Jim Plumridge and Harry Harding. A faggot of wood was lit using paraffin or old engine oil, then after half an hour about 1cwt of coal was added. The kiln had to be warmed through slowly otherwise the water in the chalk would boil too vigorously and keep popping, causing the arches to break up and collapse. When the bolster of coal was burning, it was extended along the grate with a short hoe, then more coal was added, and, when that was burning, it was spread until the fire was all across the grate, then a little more coal added, and after the coal fire had been burning for about an hour, a layer of coke was gradually sprinkled over the fire.

Coke was used for the 12–18 hours it took to dry the arches, during which time there would be a "lovely plume of steam" rising from the chimney. When the damp had gone, coal was used for about 14 hours, then, when the last trace of steam had gone, the cast iron doors were fitted and the kiln was fired gently until the arches 'crevassed'. Proper firing with coal then began until it reached 'primrose heat' which took about another six hours.

A dense plume of black smoke issued from the chimney until the fire was hot enough to burn all the gases. The hotter fire was maintained for 24 hours, during which time a charge of blasting powder was placed under the grate using a simple fused device known as a 'gun' to create an explosion to shake the firebars (and the rest of the kiln) to break up clinker and improve the draught passing through the bed of the fire. It also brought down the soot and improved the hot draught through the mass. The 'gun' was made from a 12in length of old 3in steel cart shaft, drilled with a 1in diameter hole to take the powder charge, which was plugged with wet chalk and fitted with a fuse. The cast-iron doors to each of the three chambers were red hot, so the fuse of the gun was lit by touching it against them. Then the gun was stowed in the aperture under the grate which was shaken hard by the explosion.

The gun was used prior to clearing the grate of clinker, which was usually done around 8 o'clock and 2 o'clock day and night. However, in practice, it was used as often as the burner found it necessary to keep the fire bright. This might average four or five times a day, but Jim Digweed remembers difficult conditions which led to its use no fewer than 108 times on one day! The sound of the explosions could be heard day and night throughout the neighbourhood as the sharp bangs echoed and re-echoed off the hillside, but there were no complaints — it was all part of life in and around Chinnor.

Incidentally, the gunpowder, 'Rockite' in peanut-sized nodules, was supplied by Curtis & Harvey of Faversham and arrived by rail in gunpowder trucks.

The charge was burned continuously for something like a total of 75 hours, during the last six of which a blue haze was emitted from the top of the kiln. After the last shovel of coal had been added, the kiln was left to 'soak' for another 10–12 hours.

During the burning, the charge in the kiln shrank about seven brick courses from the top of the kiln. The result was about 52 tons of lump or quick lime from some 90–100 tons of chalk fired by 11 tons of coal and 2½ tons of coke.

Although the kiln should have been allowed to 'soak' or cool down, this was overlooked when the demand was high. Opening the fire doors helped it to cool more quickly. 'Drawing' or 'digging out' a kiln was done with picks, poking bars and shovels. It was a hot dusty job, two men taking about two days to empty it, although a good man could load 18 tons of lime in one night by paraffin 'duck-lights'.

Thin steel plates were slid in position over the grates, partly to avoid the lime, or 'lump lime' as it was known, becoming mixed with the ash, and partly to make shovelling easier from the uneven brick floor. The lime was shovelled into a 6cwt 2-wheel barrow which ran on planks. It was sold at 21cwts to the ton so it took 14 barrows to load a railway wagon with 4 tons of lime, or 21 for a 6-ton load. There was no weighbridge.

Lime production was quite an efficient process with only about two per cent waste material. Known as 'slack lime', even this was used as a constituent of mortar for temporary buildings or as a soil dressing for local farmers or fruit growers with cherry orchards, mostly at Prestwood, near Wycombe. It was dumped in a spoil heap adjacent to the siding serving the kilns. Customers collected it themselves for 7s 6d a ton or cart load. Ashes and clinker from the fires were piled up on the 'ash bank' by the left-hand siding.

During cold winter months when there was the likelihood of frosts, there was not much demand for lime, but during the summer Benton burned three kilns a week between 6.0 a.m. on Monday morning and, hopefully, 6.0 p.m. on Saturday night, although when demand was particularly high, production continued through the weekends and increased production to seven kilns a fortnight, with "three kilns on at a time, one drying, one on hot fire and one burning off". The setting gang would also have to work extra time to keep up.

Before 1914, about 10–12 men were employed in lime production which gradually became more sophisticated, the original lump lime later being superseded by hydrated lime which, produced in a new generation of kilns, had better keeping qualities.

THE PRIVATE SIDING

Although the first sod of the lime works was turned in 1908, it is not clear when production started. The siding agreement with the GWR dated from 12th April 1910, Benton advancing £298 for the cost of the connection, 'to be refunded to him by a rebate of 5 per cent off his traffic payments half-yearly on 31st March and 30th September for seven years or until actual cost refunded whichever event shall first happen.' Benton constructed and maintained the sidings on his property. Great Western Traffic Committee minutes for 14th April 1910 also recommended 'Coupling up two existing dead-end sidings in the goods yard at Chinnor (at the Watlington end) with the Running line, to enable the practice of Tow Roping to be dispensed with'. The cost exclusive of 14½ perches of land required was estimated at £505. However, the work was evidently held in abeyance, Traffic Committee minutes for 10th October 1912 authorising expenditure of £530 for a slightly amended scheme, 'Lengthening siding and connecting it up with Running line, Metalling additional roadway, Provision of Goods Lock-up on Platform, Demolition of Goods shed', together with fencing and Signal Department alternations. It is possible that the private siding was first used for the delivery of bricks, perhaps from Benton's Brick and Lime Works, for the construction of the kilns. Alternatively, the kilns might already have been in existence and the siding first used for the receipt of coal and despatch of lime. We are unlikely to find out now.

Coal was delivered to the works by the GWR, whose engines were allowed inside the private siding only as far as a stop board near the end of the chaired track. Beyond, the track was lighter with flat-bottomed rails spiked to the sleepers.

There were two sidings both inclined towards the buffer stops so that wagons could be gravitated back into the outwards loop for collection. The siding on the left of the kilns was used to receive coal, loaded wagons being 'shoved hard' so that they would run up the gradient and could be braked alongside the storage bins situated between the track and the kiln. The right-hand siding was used for lime wagons which, as already mentioned, were loaded directly from the kilns.

During his time at the kilns, Jim Digweed remembers the contrast between the two Watlington branch drivers handling the loaded coal. One of them could always be relied upon to push the wagons just hard enough to reach the top of the gradient safely, whilst the other one was heavy-handed and wagons frequently crashed into each other, sometimes with the result that the buffers jumped and locked behind one another.

If the wagons were not left where they were needed, they could be hauled up the siding by a capstan-driven wire rope, powered by the stationary haulage engine.

Coke is believed to have come from the Gas Light & Coke Co. at Southall, whilst coal came from Old Pit Colliery, Nuneaton, often in the four wagons owned by Benton. These were painted red and bore the name 'Brent Brick and Lime Works Willesden, Prop. W.E. Benton' in white lettering shaded black. After the Great War they were lettered 'Willesden and Chinnor'. These vehicles each carried 9 ton 15 cwt and were numbered 14, 15, 16 and 17.

Empty lime wagons were ordered in advance from the Chinnor station master and, when loaded, were sheeted by the loaders and gravitated to the loop ready for collection. They were sent to various destinations including Benton's distribution depot at Greenford, where lime was sold for use in the construction of London's expanding housing.

THE FIRST CEMENT WORKS

After the Great War, Benton established a cement works just to the west of the lime kilns. The first cement was produced around 1919, but Joseph Digweed and his son Daniel had made test bores to try out the quality of the chalk for cement-making in 1912.

The new plant involved the building of a row of five-chamber kilns all connected via brick-built subsidiary flues to a main flue which discharged through a single 125ft high chimney erected by local builder Jack White. Three more kilns were added later.

These new kilns produced 'cement clinker' (for which the chalk was 'burned harder') from a slurry and were fired entirely using coke. They were used in continuous rotation by the burner Charlie Birkett who fired them during the daytime only, going back at night solely to adjust the damper. The kilns were built at right-angles to a new siding added in 1919 and, being at a lower level, were served by another elevated track leading off at 90 degrees from a wagon turntable and through the wash mill.

Depending on production, there could be 6–12 wagons on hand at the works, awaiting unloading. They were pushed to the end of the new siding (which was also inclined) and gravitated down to the wagon turntable when required. Here they were braked, turned through 90 degrees and pushed with the aid of a pinch bar onto the elevated track alongside the kilns, where they were gravitated into position on a gentle downgrade. The coke was shovelled into wicker baskets

The lime kilns and the construction of the first cement works before completion of the chamber kilns in 1919. Although the works could hardly have claimed to enhance the tranquil surroundings, it was nevertheless rather rustic in appearance, especially compared with its mighty successor. To modern eyes, it doesn't even look too incongruous alongside the neighbouring corn stooks.

Cty. Rugby Portland Cement

The '125ft chimney' for the new chamber kilns was actually 127ft high. It was built by Jack White, a particularly skilled local bricklayer. Prior to commissioning, Mr. Benton climbed to the top to inspect the work himself. Jim Digweed recalls that it was 'a marvellous piece of work'. The timber-built gantry extending from the flare kilns bore narrow gauge tubs of chalk from the quarry face. There were two tracks, the one nearer the camera being used to deliver full tubs and the other one for empties. The mound at the end of the gantry was an overproduction of chalk waiting to go into the wash mill.

Another view taken on the same occasion but showing the opposite side of the gantry and the junction of the standard gauge lime road and coal and coke road. The building in the right foreground was one of the workers' bungalows. The Digweed family lived here and Jim Digweed, who helped so much with this account, was born here. The building under construction behind was the mill house of the first cement works, the lower portion of which served as the engine house.

A contemporaneous view, showing the first of the chamber kilns under construction behind the mill house. The nearest entrance accommodated the coal siding which passed through the building to serve the kilns. Cement clinker drawn from the kilns was fed through a crusher located beneath the second entrance, then via a conveyor into the mill house where it was fed through a ball mill and a tube mill. The finished cement was stored in this end of the building whilst subsequent extensions provided accommodation for a sack store and, from about 1925, a canteen (see aerial photo on page 193).

A slightly later view, after clearance of most of the mound of surplus chalk (known as 'the money box') at the end of the gantry, showing the delivery chute into the new wash mill, and, in the background, more progress with the chamber kilns. The narrow gauge tubs were also used to ferry supplies of clay to the wash mill. The clay, which arrived by rail, was shovelled into the mixture to give the cement a more even texture but it was subsequently found that iron oxide was equally effective.

A closer view of the wash mill, taken from the end of the gantry, looking down the delivery chute. The mill, powered from the engine house through bevel gears, washed chalk which was elevated in continuously moving tubs housed alongside the inspection ladder. At the top of the elevator a trip device tipped the contents into a separator from which slurry was fed into an adjacent tank. Any slurry insufficiently crushed in the mill was returned in tubs to the mill where the process was repeated. The separator, also operated by the spindle which drove the mill, consisted of perforated metal sections attached to the spindle to form a circular plate. It was made in sections for ease of maintenance and formed a rotary screen for the collection of coarse material for direction back to the wash mill. The grids in the bottom left of the picture were "made up of old railway lines" and used to crush the chalk as it was being washed. The grids were moved around with the movement of the wash mill wheel.

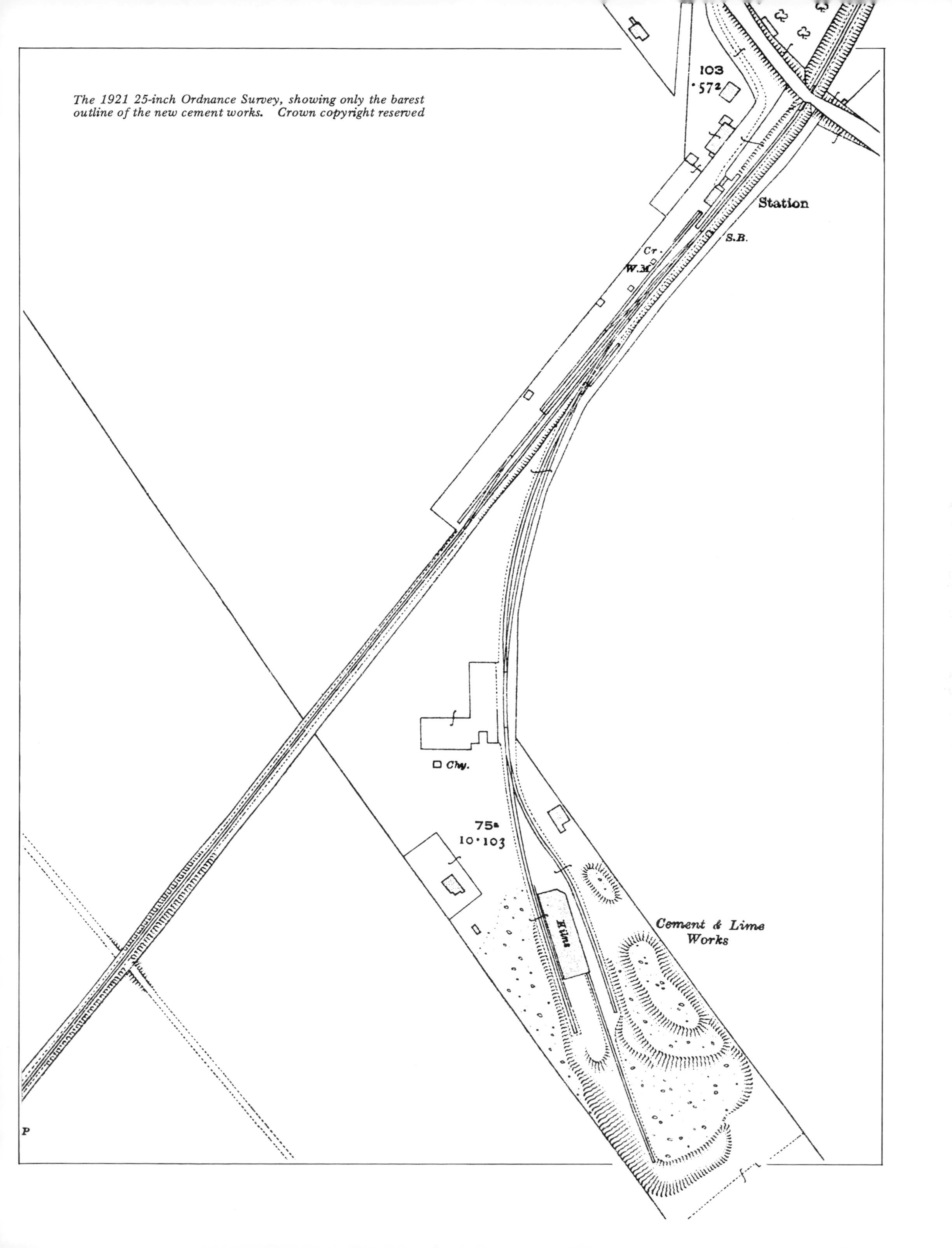

The 1921 25-inch Ordnance Survey, showing only the barest outline of the new cement works. Crown copyright reserved

These two views show the new chamber kilns and the overhead barrow runs used for taking coal from railway wagons (just visible on the left of the top picture) positioned along the elevated siding. It took about a week to burn a charge and allow it to cool ready for 'drawing' or emptying. Each charge produced about 33 tons of cement clinker. The lower view shows workers engaged in drawing one of the kilns; the man on the right was Bill Digweed. The bricks on the left were held for any repair work.

which were carried four at a time on a single-wheeled flat barrow over one of the sleeper-built barrow runs connecting the siding with each kiln. The empty wagons were hauled back by a capstan-worked wire rope.

The coke, again supplied by the Gas Light & Coke Co. from Southall, arrived in 7-plank wagons, painted grey with white lettering shaded black, which were often fitted with coke rails.

The area beneath the gantry and barrow runs was used for 'drawing' the kilns. A charge would take about a week to burn and cool, the 33 tons of cement clinker produced being left in the kiln until required.

In 1919 there were two 'clinker bumpers' who broke up the clinker, two barrow runners, two 'yellowboys', who picked out yellow clinker which had not been burnt properly, one miller (crushing clinker), one engine driver and mate, a wash mill gang of six, one burner and mate who set the kiln, two men (plus a part-timer who also worked in the canteen) in the cement stores, who bagged up with a shovel using scales set in the floor, and day workers who were employed unloading wagons, etc.

The office staff were accommodated in what had been a workers bungalow occupied by the lime-burner Digweed. This provided offices for W.E. Benton (managing director), Bertrand Ginger (chief clerk), Ron Woolford (typist and general office clerk); and John Billson (the chemist). The other workers bungalow housed the foreman Mr Adcock, and subsequently Harry Lichfield, the handyman. John Billson came from Jarrow in 1921 and remained at Chinnor until 1930. He covered as works manager while Norman Benton (W.E. Benton's son) was away in Canada. John's son, Peter, became works manager in 1971.

Chalk was still dug by hand at this time and conveyed up to the lime kilns by the continuous chain, but from there an extension of the 2ft gauge line diverged to run across a long gantry to the cement works, where newly acquired Jubilee tipplers delivered supplies directly to the wash mill. The new line was on a slightly falling gradient towards the works, loaded wagons being gravitated along it and braked by the member of staff accompanying it bearing down hard on one of the wheels with his shoe! The tipplers were pushed back along the gentle slope to the endless chain at the old kilns.

A new engine house for the cement works was built adjacent to the wash mill and alongside the standard gauge siding, where supplies of anthracite for the stationary engine were unloaded. The engine house bore a long overhead water tank.

Cement was loaded into sacks in the cement store by gangs of three, one holding the bag, one shovelling and a youth weighing, sackbarrowing and loading it into rail-

John Billson, the chemist, took over as works manager while W. E. Benton's son, Norman, was away in Canada. John started at Swan Cement (later British Portland Cement) at Jarrow as a laboratory tester and later chemist in charge. Following closure of the Jarrow works in 1921, he was re-employed elsewhere, but soon moved to Chinnor as chemist. He remained there until April 1930 when he went to Ketton Portland Cement as works manager.

Before the arrival of Ron Woolford, Bert Ginger, who lived in Lower Road, Chinnor, was the only clerk at the works. He is shown here in front of one of the workers' bungalows, which, since 1919/20, was used for the works offices.

The original 'flare kilns' viewed from the gantry serving the wash mill of the first cement works, which was behind the photographer. The mound on the right of this 1928 view was the 'slack lime' heap, waste material cleaned out after 'drawing'. This was sold mostly to farmers and fruit growers around Prestwood, High Wycombe. They could help themselves for 7s 6d a cart load. It was also used by builders in a mortar-pan together with good lime and sand. The old dilapidated shed on the right was Harry Litchfield's garage, his bungalow was just off the picture. The cone-shaped chimney of the No. 1 lime kiln was rebuilt in 1931 by Jack White. The wagons were awaiting loading with lime.

A group of workmen proudly displaying a sack from the new works. The man on the right was Les Bushnell who was in charge of the bag store and canteen.

way box vans from the platform adjacent to the store.

Some of the cement went to Benton's London depot, but much of it was sold locally and collected in lorries by W.W. Hall of Reading, Daltons of Wycombe, Hanson of Lane End, Rickards of Aylesbury, Thame Haulage Co., and Tillions of Marlow. Deliveries were also made for Benton by Hickman of Risborough and by Douglas Surrage, haulage contractor from Bledlow, who had a number of lorries. Certainly by 1931, when Surrage had teamed up with Chinnor haulage contractor Leonard Bushnell, their lorries were kept at the cement works in a garage behind the cement store.

The first cement works c.1929, and, to the right, its sophisticated replacement. The single-pitch-roofed extension at the near end of the old mill house in the left foreground housed the canteen and cement store, the main shell was the mill house, whilst the extension at the far end served as the engine house, which was equipped with two National gas engines. This view also shows the chamber kilns and the elevated siding serving them, whilst the original flare kilns feature above. The huge new rotary kiln of the new works was housed in the long curved-roof corrugated iron shed behind the twin storage silos. The structures behind the silos were the fitting shop (under construction) and mill house, whilst the structure around the base of the silos, and the shed to its right, served as the full bag store and empty bag store respectively. Chalk from the quarry in the background was routed via the new narrow gauge lines to the wash mill on the extreme right, whilst the slurry was fed to the rotary kiln via the three tall slurry tanks. *Cty. Rugby Portland Cement*

THE NEW CEMENT WORKS 'SECOND TO NONE'

The biggest expansion of the works took place in 1927 at a time of depression when most industrialists were loath to launch new ventures. In a determined effort to combat intense competition, Benton decided to erect an entirely new rotary-kiln cement works, one of the most up-to-date and technically advanced plants in the country.

The new works, producing Portland cement of the highest quality, was powered by electricity. To ensure regular supply, the electricity was brought in by two independent routes from Aylesbury Borough power station, 11 miles away, via Thame and Wendover. The 11,000 volt supply was transformed to 440 volts at the works. The plant was driven by 39 electric motors, and was, of course, electrically lit. It was not until *c.*1931 that electricity was available for Chinnor village.

The main feature of the new plant was a rotary kiln which went into production in September 1928. This was fired with pulverised coal (rather than coke) consumed at the rate of 5 tons per hour. The siding layout was greatly supplemented to serve the new plant and handle the larger quantities involved. An additional connection with the Watlington branch was also provided at the south end of the works where outgoing wagons were gravitated for collection from a new spur.

Coal supplies came from Judbud coal factors and were delivered in bottom-door wagons which discharged into a 'wet coal' hopper beneath the siding. From here it was lifted by a hopper elevator to a storage hopper which discharged into a tubular rotary coal drier, which in turn led to a ball mill where the coal was ground, then held in a dried coal hopper ready for use.

Judbud provided coal from Bolsover, Anersley and Ireland Collieries, but later, at some stage, coal factors Charington, Gardner and Lockett were used instead, and their supplies apparently arrived in 20-ton steel mineral wagons.

There was also mechanisation at the chalk face where a steam navvy was provided in 1928. By the early 1930s this was replaced by a Ruston diesel-driven excavator and later a Ransomes diesel electric excavator.

Jubilee tipplers were still in use to transport chalk from the quarry, but now on a

The new works developing alongside the old. 21st September 1927.

Looking towards Kingston Blount, with the ground alongside the Watlington branch being prepared for the new cement works early in May 1927. The farm crossing over the railway, used as part of a short-cut from Oakley village to the Icknield Way and the cement works, was later closed.

Looking in the opposite direction towards Chinnor station about the same time.

Taken during the construction of the new works, this photo shows a group of workmen in front of the worker's bungalow which had been converted for use as an office. The right-hand extension was built for use as a carpenter's shop and for the storage of metal barrels of oil and wooden barrels of grease. The men featured here were (from left to right): *Back row:* (?), Jack Witney, John Beecham, (?). *Front row:* Aubrey Ludlow, Vic Stroud, Dick Marriott, (?).

The components of the new rotary kiln arrived on low loader wagons and were unloaded with the aid of slings and ropes. The ordinary open wagons featured here brought in other materials. The 75ft chimney in front of the three slurry tanks was built to serve the rotary kiln, and the 'house' on top of the two storage silos contained a screw conveyor. The corrugated iron building alongside the silos was used for storing empty bags. At first, cement was bagged by men working in gangs of three, one holding the sack, one shovelling, and a youth weighing, barrowing and stacking on the wharf or loading into railway vans for the distribution depot at Greenford. The building on the extreme left was another of the workers' bungalows. It was occupied by Bob Walker and Harry Litchfield. February 1928.

Another view of the installation of the new rotary kiln, which, taken on the same occasion as the previous photo, also shows the new concrete bunker or set coal hopper beneath the rails for the discharge of coal from bottom-door wagons. When end-door wagons were used, they were shovelled out by hand into the bunker. From here coal was moved to the base of the vertical wet coal elevator, shown to the right of the open wagon, by rotating 'butterfly' blades. Wagons were gravitated through the siding by the cement works staff as required, and left in the siding (known as 'the hole') at the south end for collection.

A later view, taken on 5th May 1928, showing more progress, with the installation of the overhead coal bunker at the head of the coal elevator, and the framework for the structure which would enclose the gypsum and clinker hoppers. The gantry spanning the siding conveyed cement from the mill to the elevator serving the storage silos.

This picture shows the wash mill in the foreground and the three slurry tanks. The collar tank around the top of the left-hand tank held water for the wash mill and non-drinking water for the site. The gable end of the wash mill later bore the name 'Chinnor Cement & Lime Company Ltd'.

A companion view, showing the filled bag store at the base of the silos and the empty bag store in the foreground. The opposite end of the filled bag store incorporated a full width despatch dock long enough to load six lorries at a time. Rapid hardening cement was stored in a wooden compound within the empty bag store, the near end of which accommodated a fitting shop/store (on the left) and a time office (on the right) which became necessary when the business became a limited company. The small lean-to on this end was a temporary blacksmith shop serving the needs of the site for about two years.

An unidentified 2021 class 0–6–0PT with five wagons on the running line alongside the works while shunting Chinnor goods yard on 5th May 1928.

Fred Shirley, Ron Hopkins and Jack Holland at the quarry face with a pair of the 2ft gauge Jubilee skips, with Bert Seymour at the controls of the steam navvy. *Jim Digweed*

ropeway-hauled double track direct to the new works. At some stage the ropeway was replaced by a narrow gauge diesel hauling twelve wagon sets between the works and the quarry face four times an hour.

On arrival at the works, chalk was initially delivered directly into the wash mill where it was mixed with water and finely ground to form a slurry held in one of three slurry tanks. These acted as a kind of reservoir for the kilns. However, it was found that the wash mill could not cope with larger lumps of chalk, so a crushing plant was installed, chalk from the quarry thereafter being directed there instead. After passing through the roll crushers, it was carried on conveyor belts to the wash mill. Carefully measured quantities of iron oxide (at one time clay was used) were added at the wash mill from overhead storage bunkers, then, after leaving the wash mill, the slurry was pumped up to special screens, where the coarser particles which did not pass through were redirected through tube mills to be more finely ground before reaching the slurry tanks.

Inside each of the 600 ton slurry tanks, one of which bore a collar water tank for the wash mill, the slurry was mixed by vertical agitation using compressed air and blended to achieve the requisite calcium carbonate content.

The manufacture of high quality Portland cement to a consistent standard is an exacting science and the new works had an up-to-date laboratory to test the carbonate content of the slurry, the cement clinker, and the coal alumina silicate moisture every hour. 'A complete chemical analysis is carried out on

Driver Bert Seymour, fireman Bert Chown ('Gramp') on the first steam navvy, with, in the foreground, Cecil Webb ('Spider') and Laurence Munday. The rope tied to the roof support was pulled to release the door on the bottom of the bucket. *Jim Digweed*

the slurry from each tank before it is passed to the kiln, residues on coal and cement and setting times are made hourly, expansion tests are carried out during each eight hour shift and tensile tests daily.'

From the storage tanks, the slurry was fed to a mixing tank where it was agitated by a rotary arm and compressed air before being pumped to the rotary kiln via 'spoon' feeders which accurately regulated the supply.

The kiln, of British design and manufacture, was fired by pulverised coal which heated up the slurry as it travelled down the slowly rotating kiln towards the burning zone where the temperature reached about 2,700°F (1,400°C) and the slurry formed into clinker.

The rotary kiln was capable of turning out 1,000 tons of cement per week. The slowly rotating drum operated at a constant temperature of 2,700°F. The charge burner had to continually monitor the draught gauge, auto readings of the pyrometer, which affected the oxygen available, the speed of kiln rotation and slurry feed. It took about 1¾ hours to get a charge through.

When the new works was first put into operation, the small black pellets of clinker were apparently stored in the open on a concrete slab, but by 1931 they were sent through a cooler and conveyed to a large hopper in the mill house, a large covered store which also housed the rotary coal dryer, coal grinding mill, Portland cement grinding mill, and hoppers of dried and ground coal and gypsum, together with dust catchers and attendant plant. The store held 6,000 tons of cement clinker.

The final process was the grinding together of clinker and gypsum in large tube mills to form Portland cement. The resulting cement powder was conveyed by bucket elevator to a screw conveyor, through the kiln house and over a gantry spanning the rail tracks and via another screw elevator into one of the two large storage silos (four smaller ones were added later for individual customers) which between them could hold 5,000 tons of cement.

The cement flour was checked frequently by an 'eleutriator' — 'Unvarying high quality is the aim of these works regardless of expense of manufacture.'

Crushed gypsum rock, which was added to retard the setting rate of the cement, came in by rail in open wagons from Easthill, near Nottingham. It was a pinkish colour rock delivered in walnut-sized lumps. About three wagons a week were received at the works.

In 1934, another bold decision was made to install a calcinator, a then little-known piece of equipment, on the inlet end of the rotary kiln. The calcinator dried out the wet slurry to such an extent that it passed into the kiln in almost dry granules.

Cement from the silos was originally simply shovelled into bags stored under the silos, but by 1934 bags were automatically filled to the correct weight inside what was known as 'the bag store', where bagged cement was stored for at least a month to secure uniformity of colour and quality. The company claimed the product was 'second to none' and were at pains to maintain their claim.

Bagged cement was loaded away in railway box vans, again mainly for the Greenford distribution depot.

In the early 1930s, both lime and cement were in demand for the housing construction market which, as already mentioned, was expanding in London. Considerable quantities of lime went to Messrs A.A. King of Croydon who made mortar, and builders T.F. Nash, who received lime and cement for 5-star houses around Harrow and Greenford.

Much of the cement was sent out by road, lorries being loaded at the despatch dock where six vehicles could be dealt with at a time. As already mentioned, some of the

This 1920s group of cement works staff shows, from left to right: *Back row:* (?), Jack Witney, Jack Baldwin, Vic Stroud, 'Brother' Stone, Matthew ('Matty') Rogers, Clem Bass, Bert Ansant, George Witney, Joe Digweed, Dan Digweed. *Middle row:* Bill Collier, Charlie Seymour, (?), Alf Hopkins, Frank Collsol, Aubrey Chown, (?), (?), 'Pip' Witney. *Front row:* Frank Broom (gas engine driver), the miller, Harry Litchfield (with dog, called 'Binks'), Bob Walker (Harry Litchfield's father-in-law), John Billson (chemist), Captain Norman Benton, a 'clinker bumper', Charlie Birkett, Walt ('Pudgell') Gomm, Charlie Clare (chargehand of quarry), believed to be Dick Marriott. The boy sitting cross-legged has also not been identified.

A 1931 view showing the structure covering the new rotary kiln, the adjacent clinker shed behind (with the sloping roof), the coal elevator in the foreground and the chimney of the coal dryer. The smaller brick building with the single-pitch roof, alongside the track, housed the laboratory. When a second rotary kiln was installed alongside the original, the laboratory had to be partly accommodated in its corrugated iron covering, but, when a third kiln was installed in 1957, the laboratory was demolished. The building alongside the three slurry tanks was the electric pump house, and the substance in the pen in the foreground was gypsum.

works output was undertaken by Surrage and Bushnell whose lorries were garaged at the works. Cecil Bennet of Kingston carried out bulk deliveries using sheeted tipper lorries, but in 1928 Bentons bought their own 30 cwt Chevrolet lorry, and in the 1930s this was joined by a 6-ton Leyland Cub and then a Leyland Major with trailer. Incidentally, the works lorries all used the GWR weighbridge, as did McAlpine's lorries later at the outbreak of war when they collected supplies used in the construction of Chalgrove Airfield.

According to the 1934 report in the *Thame Gazette*, there were nearly one hundred employees at the plant, mainly from the district, but it had been necessary to 'import a number of skilled workers from other parts of the country' including Wales and the North East.

Whilst proclaiming the blessing of such a large workforce on Chinnor, the same report reminded readers of the friction caused by the dust nuisance, but pointing out that it was hoped 'when the new dust collecting plant is in operation, even this will be largely — if not altogether — abated'.

The new dust-collecting plant became necessary in addition to the existing dust-collecting chamber, at least partly because of the calcinator. The dust collected from various locations at the plant was delivered again to the kiln.

W.E. Benton must have been proud of the works and the way things had developed since the early days of the old lime kilns. In 1934 the new works was reported as having 'nearly doubled sales in the last 5 years'. However, sadly he was asthmatic and did not enjoy good health. During an illness in 1929 he even had a resident nurse for a few months to look after him.

His son, Norman Molyneaux, had been actively involved in the works, apart from an absence during the First World War and a 6-month spell lumbering in Ontario in 1922, but his older son, Walter, had gone away and did not become involved until 1929, and presumably then as a direct result of his father's illness.

W.E. Benton remained living at the family home on the edge of the site but he is not remembered visiting the works after his illness. He did, however, visit the bank in Thame every Friday in his chauffeur-driven Daimler, and was still chairman, so it is difficult to believe he did not remain involved at least to the extent of offering advice to his sons.

The works continued to improve and in 1936 the business was converted from a family one to a public one, Chinnor Cement and Lime Co. Ltd., with W.E. Benton as chairman and his son Norman as managing director. Pioneering continued in 1936 with the addition of a new type of dessicator kiln (No. 2) which doubled the productive capacity of the cement works; the joint daily output of the two kilns was 345 tons.

The following year, a new plant was installed for the production of hydrated lime, which was used for mortar and plaster. It was made by adding just enough water to 'kibbled' lime to slake it to a powder. The mixture was slaked and stirred for 20 minutes, then put through a cyclone separator to remove any ash, etc. It was packed into 56lb paper sacks and stored for seven days before being sold. The new batch plant (i.e. not continuous) was installed in the old mill house, the rest of the old cement works being

This aerial view, taken on 3rd August 1937, shows the works after the installation of a second rotary kiln the previous year. The 150ft chimney serving the No. 2 kiln was built by an Anglo-Danish company, and the small building at its base was the fan house. This picture shows how the laboratory was accommodated in the structure covering the second kiln. By this time the old chamber kilns on the left had been partly demolished and the elevated track serving them removed. The fresh-looking single-pitch roof against the first cement works enclosed a garage for Surridge and Bushnell's delivery lorries. The single-storey building alongside the road approach on the left, was an office block, the foundations for which were pegged out by Jim Digweed and Norman Benton one Saturday afternoon in 1929. This picture also provides a distant glimpse of the first two Brockham lime kilns immediately to the left of the old flare kilns. The second private siding connection to the cement works was authorised on 28th July 1927, the cost (recorded variously as £209 and £272) being borne by Bentons and refunded by a rebate of 5% on their traffic payments for a period of five years.
Cty. Rugby Portland Cement

gradually dismantled, and eventually a road was driven through the site.

In April 1937, the first pair of modern continuous-burning Brockham type shaft lime kilns came into production with the intention of superseding the original lime works. The new plant gave greater and more economical production, but, with summertime demands, the old No. 1 flare kiln was pressed into use again to supplement them on several occasions. It was last used in August 1938 shortly before Brockham kilns Nos. 3 and 4 were brought into use in September 1938 and March 1939 respectively.

W.E. Benton died in 1940, at the age of 85. His son Norman subsequently stepping in as chairman as well as managing director. Mrs W.E. Benton survived her husband, but only until 1945; then their son Walter died in 1947, around which time Norman retired to Hastings, bringing the era to an end. Even the Benton family home, Icknield Hatch, did not survive for long but was demolished in 1952–3 in the expansion of the quarry.

In 1949, in view of further developments, it was decided to form a holding or parent company, Chinnor Industries Ltd., with three subsidiary companies, Chinnor Cement & Lime Co. Ltd., Chinnor Transport Ltd., and Chinnor Properties Ltd. The transport company was formed to develop and operate a fleet of modern lorries to deliver most of the cement and lime, and eventually included large four-axle Fodens for bulk transport. The property company owned village and country properties including a hostel for employees at 'West End', part way up Chinnor Hill (pre-Great War) and another two alongside the Icknield Way.

In 1955 the works was reconstructed and expanded in a scheme to increase output by 85 per cent. The work included a new crushing plant, wash mill, iron oxide plant, and a third rotary kiln, new clinker grinding mill No. 3, two new 60ft high cement storage silos, wagon tippler, and new packing machinery in an annexe to the original packing house. A new 390ft × 80ft main stores building was also erected on the site previ-

Chinnor Cement and Lime Co's first lorry was a 30cwt Chevrolet driven by contractor Ernie Goldspink of Thame. Later, the main haulage contractors were Doug Surridge of Bledlow and Leonard Bushnell of Lower Road, Chinnor, who ran a number of Bedfords, but other hauliers included Hickmans of Risborough and Southern Roadways (both of which used steam lorries) and Surmans of Chinnor who used Commers. After the war, Bennetts of Kingston Blount also transported cement, but by the late 1940s the cement company had its own small fleet which later totalled more than forty lorries. This picture shows a Dodge in postwar livery of light grey with black lettering shaded white. Bags of cement were loaded into lorries with the bottom layer upright and the top layers flat, the rear ones progressively stepped away from the back for stability. *Cty. Joe Christie*

This Ruston Bucyrus diesel powered 'shovel' or 'navvy' was used at the chalk face in the postwar years, regularly driven by Daniel Digweed.

This aerial view, taken some time between 1952 and 1957, shows the addition of a replacement chimney to serve the first rotary kiln, rendering the original 75ft brick one redundant. The narrow gauge railway in the foreground delivered chalk from the quarry to the crusher, which was off the edge of the picture. From there, chalk was fed up the sloping covered conveyor to the separator, then up to the wash mill and into the bank of slurry tanks. The long building alongside the two kilns was a large covered store for clinker, slack coal and gypsum, whilst the one further along to the right was the mill house with its elevator to carry the cement over to the silos. According to the *Thame Gazette*, "The mill house contained a rotary coal dryer, coal grinding mill, cement grinding mill, and a rapid hardening grinding mill; also storage hoppers for 300 tons of raw coal, dried and ground coal hoppers, gypsum and clinker hoppers, together with dust catchers and attendant plant". The motors for the mill and coal hopper were inside the adjacent motor house (with the single-pitch roof), which also incorporated a fitting shop.

ously occupied by the clinker store, cement grinding plant, workshop, general stores and sub-station, all of which, with the exception of the sub-station, were demolished. The storage area, partitioned into sections, had space for approximately 9,000 tons of clinker, 2,500 tons of coal, 900 tons of gypsum, 250 tons of iron oxide, and was equipped with an overhead travelling crane.

In 1962 the plant became part of the Rugby Portland Cement Group and has continued to be modernised, including the replacement of the narrow gauge system with large dumper trucks, whilst scientists and engineers have continued to develop more advanced machinery and computerised control systems. However, could any subsequent achievement rival the spirit, enterprise, challenge and sheer enthusiasm that lay behind the establishment of the original lime works of the gifted W.E. Benton and his team?

At the time of writing, it is anticipated that the cement works at Chinnor will be closed at the end of 1999 and production concentrated at Rugby.

HANDLING THE CEMENT WORKS TRAFFIC

The delivery of coal, coke and gypsum, and despatch of lime and cement have already been mentioned within the description of the works, but, as the traffic fluctuated over the period under discussion, the staff's experience of rail traffic levels varies. George Harmsworth's son Eric recalls three vans of cement a day being sent to Greenford before the war, whereas relief guard George Howlett remembers a single van every Friday in the late 1940s or early 1950s. Bryan Bowler remembers cement being despatched to the GWR's concrete works at Taunton and, for a while during the war, sixteen vans each day to Charlton fibreboard works.

George Howlett also recalls a time during the late 1940s, when regular consignments were sent to one of the London docks for shipment to West Africa as part of a large contract for building work. This was probably the same exceptional traffic recalled by Eric Humphrey who could not remember the eventual destination, only that huge quantities of cement were sent to King George V Dock and Tilbury Docks for export during his time at Chinnor from 1947–51.

In the absence of official records, it is difficult to be any more precise, but he says 40-wagon trains of cement left Risborough, perhaps three times a week, timed to catch various ships. As the maximum loading between Chinnor and Risborough was eighteen loaded wagons, the branch engine had to run out from Risborough several times a day between trains to collect them. This probably explains the entry in the Summer 1947 timetable for an engine and van to Chinnor, as required, at 9.15 a.m., returning at 10.0 a.m., the timetable for the Winter of 1947 showing the return working back traffic.

Eric Humphrey, who had to order all the vans and keep on top of the paperwork, thought this went on for a long time, but as it is not so prominent in the memories of

This 1953 view of the cement works shows how it grew to dominate the landscape, the tiny Chinnor station featuring in the top left-hand quarter of the picture. As we have not come across any scale track plans which show the post-1921 arrangements at Chinnor, this photograph at least shows some of the private sidings. The Icknield Way can be seen in the top right running along the foot of Chinnor Hill and Bledlow Great Wood, whilst the chalk excavations were at the corner of No. 1 quarry. The land for the recreation ground immediately beyond the chalk excavations of No. 1 quarry was donated by Thomas Taylor. From 1914 to 1924 the ground lay derelict but was subsequently resurrected for use as a school playing field. The cement company's hostels along the Icknield Way are shown on page 116/117, but there was also 'West Down' near the junction of the Icknield Way and Hill Road (off the right-hand edge of the picture) and 'Roman Way' on the corner of Hill Road and Wykeham Rise (to the right of the bridge over the railway).

This 1950s view shows 9781 with the Chinnor goods. The cement workers finished at midday on Saturdays, many of them catching the train to High Wycombe to watch the football.
R. H. G. Simpson

others who worked there at the time, it may have been a more brief episode.

We have already described two variations of shunting the works and the yard, but there were many others according to the amount of traffic, the circumstances in the cement works sidings and the goods yard, and the individual guard. In Eric Humphrey's experience, a man either had what it took to plan a shunt, or he made hard work of it. The two Watlington branch guards were quite different in their approach, Eric admiring Reg Watkins who was very slick and managed to get the shunt finished in three-quarters of an hour, which he regarded as 'very good shunting'. He found Frank Hyde coped alright but took much longer.

Each of the four ground frames controlling access to the works and goods yard were locked by a key on the end of the train staff and this was another factor to be taken into account, both for the effort involved and the time taken in delivery and retrieval of the train staff for each lever frame. This was probably one of the reasons why, in Eric's time, the train was stopped short of the station and divided behind the coal for the works, which always seemed to be at the front of the train. The coal was then taken forward into the private sidings and run round on the loop on the approach to the lime kilns. If access down the side of the works to the outwards siding was blocked with vans awaiting or being loaded with cement, the loaded coal wagons were drawn out of the loop and propelled towards the coal drop where they were left. Engines were not allowed as far as the coal drop. The engine then returned to the rest of the train left on the running line. If, on the other hand, the line down the side of the works was clear, the engine ran through to the outwards siding, known as 'the hole', to collect the empty wagons and any vans of cement which had been gravitated there by the works staff using the gentle slope incorporated into the sidings of the new works.

After drawing these vehicles up through the works, they were coupled to the waiting loaded coal wagons, which were pulled back from the loop and propelled towards the coal drop, where they were left for the works staff. The outgoing traffic was left near the entrance gate and the engine returned to the rear portion of the train on the running line.

The rear vehicles, including the brake van, were then taken through the station and run round using the loop adjacent to the goods yard ready for sorting. The incoming traffic, mainly traders' coal, was exchanged for the empties, the return train being formed either on the loop or the running line, with the brake van at the south end ready for the return journey. Then the cement works empties were collected from just inside the top gate to the private siding where they had been left, or from the outwards sidings at the south end if, as discussed in the first instance, the engine could not get through because the down side of the works had been blocked.

When George Howlett was serving as a relief guard, he recalled that if the Chinnor goods was short enough to fit into the lime kilns approach loop inside the cement works, the whole train was taken in there and run round. It was then drawn back clear of the points leading to the new cement works, and the coal for the works was pushed towards the loop siding serving the coal drop where it was left. In George's experience, the right-hand line leading down the outside of the works was usually occupied by one or two vans awaiting loading with cement, so the empties had to be collected via the other connection at the south end of the works.

After the loaded coal had been placed, the rest of the train was drawn back out of the private siding and taken over to the goods yard, where incoming and outgoing vehicles were exchanged, the brake van was put on the running line and the empties 'on top of it'. When the work in the yard was finished, the empties and brake van were nudged towards Watlington and left to run down the gradient under the control of the guard, who brought them to a stand clear of the cement works ground frame at the southern entrance to the works. The engine then went inside to collect the coal empties and the occasional van of cement for Greenford and coupled it onto the rest of the train which was then drawn up alongside the works and left on the running line while the crew went into the canteen.

Although Princes Risborough might appear to have been a fair-sized station, it was not in fact overblessed with siding space, and soon became seriously congested when traffic levels were high. George Howlett remembers that the exchange sidings at the London end of the station were frequently full without the coal for Chinnor cement works. Consequently, this was sometimes left in one of the up sidings to the north of the station or on the back road behind the down platform ready for collection. There were even occasions in the late 1940s when they could find no room at Risborough to hold it, so it was stored in the loop at Chinnor. This prevented the engine of the Chinnor goods from running round its train, so instead, on arrival, the engine was put inside the southernmost entrance to the cement works, then the train was gravitated past it and down the bank on the falling gradient towards Kingston under the control of the guard's brake.

While inside the works, the engine collected the empties which were then put onto the back of the train and the whole lot hauled up through the station under the direction of the porter's hand signals until what had been the front vehicle (coal for the works) was clear of the top entrance to the private siding. The porter then changed the points and signalled the train back far enough into the cement company's premises for their coal to be left in position. The rest of the train was then pulled out onto the running line again and directed into the goods yard, where it was divided at the Watlington end of the brake van. The empties from the works, with the van in tow, were then taken back out of the yard and left on the running line while the engine collected the empties from the yard which, in the meantime, had been coupled onto the Watlington end of the new traffic. When the yard empties had been put with the rest of the train on the running line, the new traffic (mainly traders' coal) was returned to the yard.

If any of the wagons of coal being held in the loop pending acceptance at the works were required, they might be taken there before the yard traffic was placed, otherwise the train formed on the running line was ready for departure to Risborough.

All this traffic was very valuable to the railway and, as an important customer, the owners of the works were granted cheap season tickets by the GWR, the manager in particular regularly travelling to London. However, on a more local level, the day-to-day running of the operation depended on co operation and goodwill between the cement company and all the railway staff so it was just as well that they all got on together and helped each other. Mr Benton had showed his appreciation each Christmas by awarding the porters, guards and firemen ten shillings each, the drivers one pound, and the station master a goose. Furthermore, the railway staff were given a discount on any cement they wanted themselves.

By Mr Humphrey's time, the station master was given £5, and the guards and porters £3 each.

Appendix 2 – CENSUS OF WATER TAKEN AT RISBOROUGH

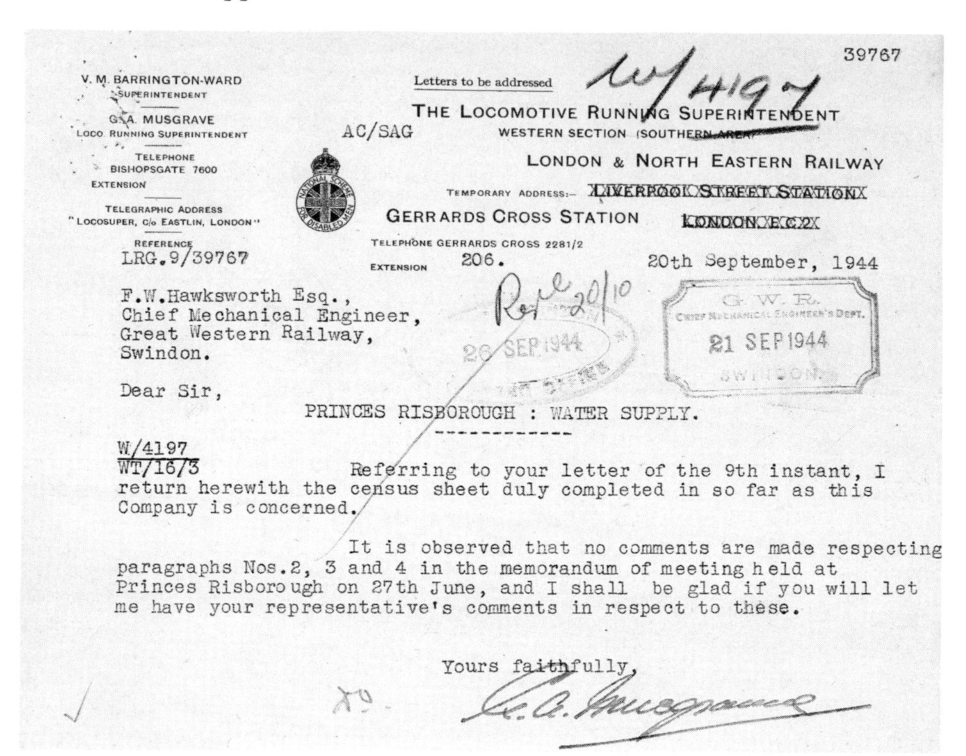

39767

W/4197

V. M. BARRINGTON-WARD
SUPERINTENDENT

G. A. MUSGRAVE
LOCO. RUNNING SUPERINTENDENT

TELEPHONE
BISHOPSGATE 7600
EXTENSION

TELEGRAPHIC ADDRESS
"LOCOSUPER, C/o EASTLIN, LONDON"

REFERENCE
LRG.9/39767

AC/SAG

Letters to be addressed
THE LOCOMOTIVE RUNNING SUPERINTENDENT
WESTERN SECTION (SOUTHERN AREA)
LONDON & NORTH EASTERN RAILWAY

TEMPORARY ADDRESS:- ~~LIVERPOOL STREET STATION~~
GERRARDS CROSS STATION ~~LONDON, E.C.2~~

TELEPHONE GERRARDS CROSS 2281/2
EXTENSION 206.

20th September, 1944

Recd 20/10

26 SEP 1944

G.W.R.
CHIEF MECHANICAL ENGINEER'S DEPT.
21 SEP 1944
SWINDON.

F.W.Hawksworth Esq.,
Chief Mechanical Engineer,
Great Western Railway,
Swindon.

Dear Sir,

PRINCES RISBOROUGH : WATER SUPPLY.

W/4197
WT/16/3

Referring to your letter of the 9th instant, I return herewith the census sheet duly completed in so far as this Company is concerned.

It is observed that no comments are made respecting paragraphs Nos.2, 3 and 4 in the memorandum of meeting held at Princes Risborough on 27th June, and I shall be glad if you will let me have your representative's comments in respect to these.

Yours faithfully,

G. A. Musgrave

The picture on page 99 of Volume 1 shows 6362 after arrival at Risborough with the 9.40 Banbury–Old Oak coal train one summer day in 1939. This picture, taken on the same occasion, shows the engine detached from its train and drawn forward to take water at the column situated between the up main and up loop lines near the south signal box. *S. H. Freese*

21/PF
R.55113

CENSUS OF WATER AT PRINCES RISBOROUGH COMMENCING 12 NOON SUNDAY 20/8/44 UNTIL 12 NOON SUNDAY 27/8/44

Engine No.		Time	Amount Taken Feet	Passenger or Goods	Estimated Water taken in gallons.
5783	G.W.	5/25	2	Passenger	750
4926	G.W.	6/0	2	Goods	2000
6158	G.W.	6/30	4	Goods	1400
1766	L.N.E.	6/45	2	Passenger	1000
3769	G.W.	5/30	2	Goods	750
			Monday 21/8/44		
7314	G.W.	5.10	4	Goods	3000
3769	G.W.	8-5	2	Passenger	750
1766	L.N.E.	8.25	1	Goods	500
2863	G.W.	8.30	1	Goods	1500
5007	L.N.E.	8.50	4	Passenger	2000
5407	G.W.	9.5	2	Passenger	750
1118	L.N.E.	9.55	3	Passenger	2100
3769	G.W.	10.15	2	Passenger	750
5238	L.N.E.	10.20	3	Goods	2000
5407	G.W.	10.25	1	Passenger	400
6124	G.W.	10.50	2½	Goods	800
5783	G.W.	11.10	1½	Light	550
3820	L.N.E.	11.45	2	Light	1100
3769	G.W.	12/0	2	Light	750
5783	G.W.	1/40	3	Goods	1000
7096	L.N.E.	2/40	2	Goods	1600
5404	G.W.	3/55	2	Passenger	750
2455	L.N.E.	5/15	2	Light	2100
5783	G.W.	5/25	2	Passenger	750
4926	G.W.	6/0	2	Goods	2000
6158	G.W.	6/30	4	Goods	1400
1766	L.N.E.	6/45	2	Passenger	1000
6865	G.W.	6/50	3	Goods	2500
5381	L.N.E.	7/10	2	Goods	1300
5404	G.W.	7/35	3	Passenger	1000
5783	G.W.	7/50	2	Passenger	750
369-96	L.N.E.	11/0	4	Goods	3000
6122	G.W.	11/30	4	Goods	1400
			Tuesday 22/8/44		
2143	G.W.	3.10	4	Goods	3500
5783	G.W.	6.0	2	Goods	750
2404	G.W.	5.15	3	Goods	2000
5783	G.W.	8.5	2	Passenger	750
5169	L.N.E.	8.10	2	Passenger	1000
1220	L.N.E.	8.25	3	Goods	2000
5373	L.N.E.	8.50	2	Passenger	1000
6299	L.N.E.	10.5	2½	Goods	2000
5783	G.W.	10.10	2	Passenger	750
5407	G.W.	10.30	1	Passenger	400
6132	G.W.	10.50	2	Goods	700
3851	G.W.	11.20	3	Goods	2500
5783	G.W.	12/15	2½	Goods	800
6120	G.W.	12/45	1	Goods	500
9310	G.W.	1/0	2	Goods	2000
5783	G.W.	1/30	1	Goods	400
1300	L.N.E.	2/0	3	Goods	2150
7078	L.N.E.	3/10	2	Goods	1500
5616	G.W.	3/25	2	Goods	700
5404	G.W.	3/30	2	Passenger	750
2883	G.W.	4/10	1	Goods	1500
4708	G.W.	4/35	2	Goods	2000

2.

Engine No.		Time	Amount Taken. Feet	Passenger or Goods.	Estimated Water taken in gallons.
			Tuesday 22/8/44 (Contd)		
7076	L.N.E.	4/40	3	Goods	3000
5785	G.W.	5/5	3	Passenger	1000
5404	G.W.	5/55	2	Goods	750
3821	G.W.	6/35	1	Goods	1500
6008	G.W.	6/45	2	Light	2000
5373	L.N.E.	7/5	2	Passenger	1000
5006	L.N.E.	7/30	1	Passenger	500
5783	G.W.	7/45	3	Passenger	1000
			Wednesday 23/8/44		
4640	L.N.E.	12.5	4	Goods	3000
8437	L.M.S.	4.45	4	Goods	3000
5783	G.W.	6.15	3	Goods	1000
5283	L.N.E.	6.55	4	Goods	3000
5783	G.W.	8.5	2	Passenger	750
5411	L.N.E.	8.10	1½	Passenger	1300
5169	L.N.E.	8.45	1½	Passenger	750
5783	G.W.	9.55	2	Passenger	750
7099	L.N.E.	10.0	3	Goods	3500
5199	L.N.E.	10.15	1	Goods	500
5404	G.W.	10.30	1	Passenger	400
6166	G.W.	11.30	3	Goods	1200
5369	L.N.E.	11.55	2½	Light	1250
5783	G.W.	12/10	2	Goods	750
2899	G.W.	1/5	3	Goods	2500
6127	G.W.	1/15	1	Goods	500
3844	G.W.	1/35	4	Goods	3000
5783	G.W.	1/40	2	Passenger	750
3841	G.W.	2/45	3	Goods	2500
5407	G.W.	3/30	2	Goods	750
2353	G.W.	3/35	3	Goods	2750
6122	G.W.	4/5	2	Goods	700
6127	G.W.	4/20	2	Goods	700
7076	L.N.E.	4/25	4	Goods	3500
5783	G.W.	5/5	3	Passenger	1000
5374	L.N.E.	6/25	2	Passenger	1000
2116	G.W.	6/35	3	Goods	2750
5006	L.N.E.	7/35	2	passenger	1000
5783	G.W.	7/45	3	Passenger	1000
5407	G.W.	7/55	1½	Passenger	550
5783	G.W.	10/20	3	Goods	1000
7078	L.N.E.	10/45	4	Goods	4000
			Thursday 24/8/44		
5783	G.W.	8.5	2	Passenger	750
5452	L.N.E.	8.10	1½	Passenger	750
7075	L.N.E.	8.30	3½	Goods	3000
5373	L.N.E.	8.50	2½	Goods	1250
6054	L.N.E.	9.0	1	Goods	1300
5407	G.W.	9.20	1	Passenger	400
5783	G.W.	9.50	2	Passenger	750
5211	L.N.E.	10.0	1	Passenger	500
5407	G.W.	10.30	1	Passenger	400
4708	G.W.	10.55	3	Goods	2500
5930	G.W.	11.5	2	Goods	2000
6122	G.W.	11.45	3	Goods	1200
5783	G.W.	12/30	2	Goods	750
9305	G.W.	1/10	2	Goods	2000
6364	L.N.E.	1/50	2	Goods	1300
7077	L.N.E.	2/55	2	Goods	2000
5616	G.W.	2/35	2	Goods	700
5404	G.W.	3/35	2	Passenger	750
4617	G.W.	4/25	1	Goods	400
5986	L.N.E.	4/35	2	Goods	1300
5783	G.W.	5/20	3	Passenger	1000
4990	G.W.	5/45	2	Goods	2000

3.

Engine No.		Time.	Amount Taken. Feet.	Passenger or Goods	Estimated Water taken in gallons.
6168	G.W.	6/20	4	Goods	1400
5390	G.W.	6/35	1	Goods	1500
5371	L.N.E.	6/40	2	Passenger	500
9310	G.W.	6/45	2	Goods	2000
8700	L.N.E.	7/0	1	Goods	1000
5404	G.W.	7/35	1½	Passenger	550
5006	L.N.E.	7/40	1	Passenger	500
4617	G.W.	7/50	3	Passenger	1000
2422	G.W.	10/20 pm	4	Goods	3500 pm.
		No water after 10/20 Thursday until 4/45 Friday			
		Electricity failure of pump.			
		Friday 25/7/44			
4617	G.W.	6/10	3	Passenger	1000
5003	L.N.E.	6/20	2	Passenger	1000
5912	G.W.	6/45	2	Goods	2000
6142	G.W.	7/0	4	Goods	1400
2099	L.N.E.	7/10	3	Goods	2500
5006	L.N.E.	7/30	1	Passenger	500
5404	G.W.	7/45	1½	Passenger	550
4617	G.W.	7/50	3	Passenger	1000
5901	G.W.	10/5	4	Goods	3000
5616	G.W.	10/40	4	Goods	1400
		Saturday 26/8/44			
7096	L.N.E.	12.10	4	Goods	4000
4617	G.W.	8.5	2	Passenger	750
5003	L.N.E.	8.50	2½	Passenger	1250
4617	G.W.	10.10	2	Passenger	750
5407	G.W.	10.28	1	Passenger	400
6106	G.W.	10.52	2	Goods	700
4617	G.W.	12/25	2	Passenger	750
4617	G.W.	1/50	2	Passenger	750
5616	G.W.	2/30	2	Goods	700
7073	L.N.E.	3/15	3	Goods	3000
5404	G.W.	3/40	2	Passenger	750
4617	G.W.	3/55	3	Passenger	1000
5445	L.N.E.	4/15	3	Goods	2000
4617	G.W.	5/0	3	Passenger	1000
6120	G.W.	5/50	4	Goods	1400
7078	L.N.E.	6/10	3	Goods	3000
6138	G.W.	6/30	3	Passenger	1200
5374	L.N.E.	6/35	1	Passenger	500
7077	L.N.E.	6/45	3	Goods	3000
4960	G.W.	7/15	2	Goods	2000
5404	G.W.	7/45	2	Passenger	750
4617	G.W.	7/50	3	Passenger	1000
5616	G.W.	11/15	4	Goods	1400
		Sunday 27/8/44			
4617	G.W.	8.15	2	Passenger	750
4702	G.W.	8.30	2	Goods	2000
5374	L.N.E.	9.0	2	Passenger	1000
1664	G.W.	9.15	3	Goods	2750
2946	G.W.	10.0	2	Goods	2000
4964	G.W.	10.20	2	Goods	2000
7075	L.N.E.	10.40	2	Goods	2000
4617	G.W.	10.55	2	Goods	750
6393	G.W.	11.25	2	Goods	2000
4916	G.W.	11.50	2	Goods	2000

TOTALS. G.W.R 142,700
L.N.E. 91,800
L.M.S. 3,000
237,500

Appendix 3 – TRACK PLANS OF CHINNOR AND ASTON ROWANT

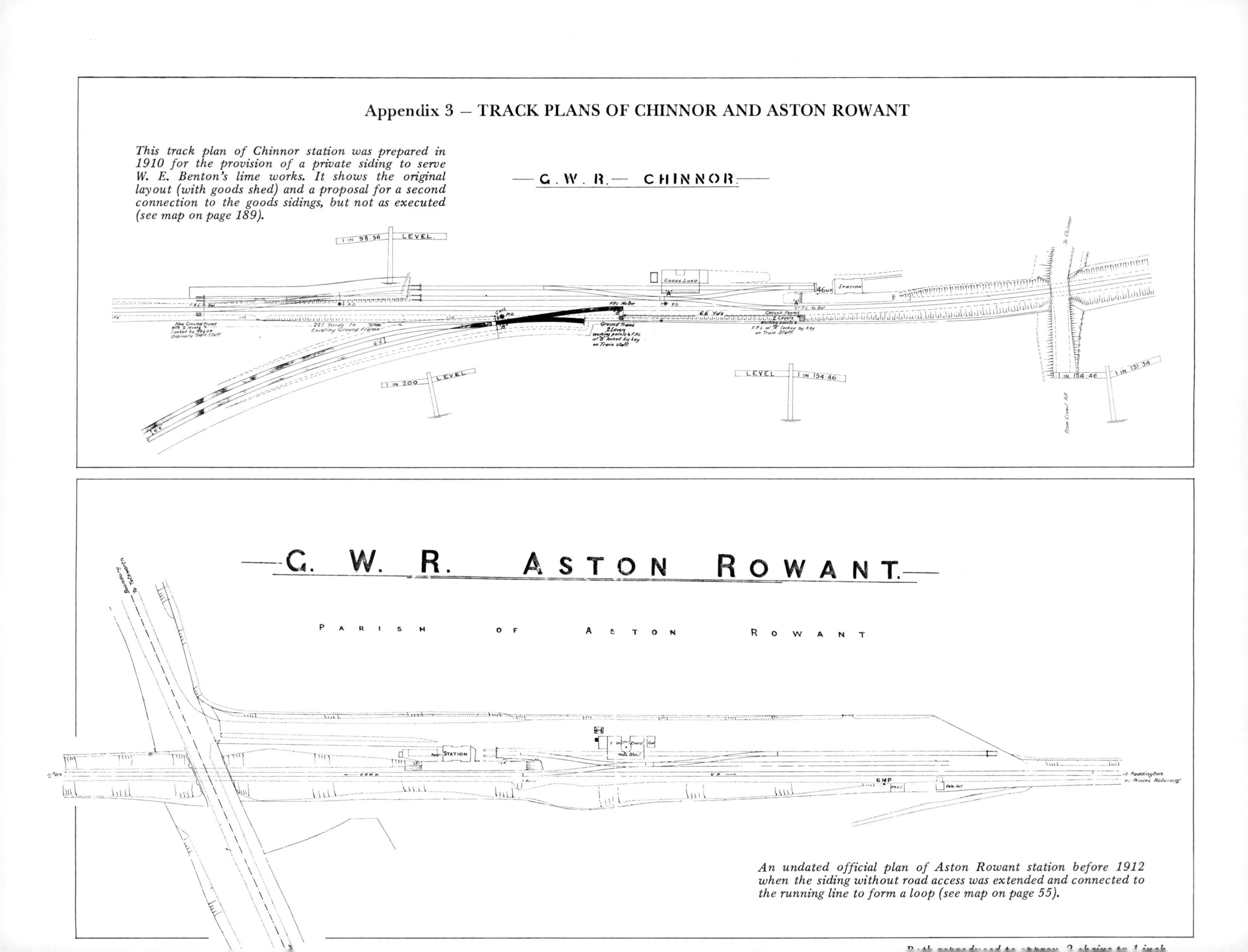

This track plan of Chinnor station was prepared in 1910 for the provision of a private siding to serve W. E. Benton's lime works. It shows the original layout (with goods shed) and a proposal for a second connection to the goods sidings, but not as executed (see map on page 189).

An undated official plan of Aston Rowant station before 1912 when the siding without road access was extended and connected to the running line to form a loop (see map on page 55).